ALL THE
PRESIDENT'S
WOMEN

ALL THE PRESIDENT'S
WOMEN

DONALD TRUMP AND THE MAKING OF A
PREDATOR

BARRY LEVINE AND **MONIQUE EL-FAIZY**

hachette
BOOKS

NEW YORK   BOSTON

Hachette Books
Hachette Book Group
1290 Avenue of the Americas
New York, NY 10104
hachettebookgroup.com
twitter.com/hachettebooks

First Edition: October 2019

Hachette Books is a division of Hachette Book Group, Inc.
The Hachette Books name and logo are trademarks of Hachette Book Group, Inc.

The publisher is not responsible for websites (or their content)
that are not owned by the publisher.

The Hachette Speakers Bureau provides a wide range of authors for speaking events.
To find out more, go to www.hachettespeakersbureau.com or call (866) 376-6591.

Print book interior design by Timothy Shaner, NightandDayDesign.biz

Library of Congress Cataloging-in-Publication Data has been applied for.

ISBNs: 978-0-316-49266-9 (hardcover), 978-0-316-49267-6 (ebook)

Printed in the United States of America

LSC-C

10 9 8 7 6 5 4 3 2 1

For my daughter.

—BL

For all the women who confront sexual harassment,
and for my husband and sons and the other men who get it.

—ME

CONTENTS

BUNGALOW 22

Note from Barry Levine

To find Donald Trump's favorite bungalow at the Beverly Hills Hotel, start by ascending the red-carpeted steps that lead inside the pink stucco landmark built in 1912. Once inside the grand lobby, walk past reception and continue toward the famed Polo Lounge, where decades ago Hollywood heavyweights like Douglas Fairbanks, Humphrey Bogart, and the Rat Pack once held court.

To the right of the lounge you'll see an exit door, which leads to a shady path. Tropical plants and citrus trees line the walkway as it takes you away from the hotel's main building. Nestled amid the lush greenery of the winding passage are the hotel's most famous accommodations—the bungalows. There are twenty-three in all, and the history of their occupants could fill many a gossip column: Elizabeth Taylor spent six of her eight wedding nights in Bungalow 5; Howard Hughes lived in Bungalow 4 on and off for thirty years; and John Lennon and Yoko Ono used Bungalow 11 as their hideout.

One day in March 2019, a hotel employee guides me to Bungalow 22, the only one of the private villas without a green and white marker. It has an octagonal ceiling, a terrace fireplace, Palm Springs mid-century furnishings, and a grand piano. In addition to being

Trump's preferred rendezvous locale, it's also rumored to have been Sinatra's favorite.

Hotel advertising describes the bungalow as a "wonderfully private and luxurious experience, steeped in ultimate glamour." It also teases, "If these walls could talk . . ."

No need.

From adult film star Stormy Daniels's exposé about her liaisons with the future president on *60 Minutes* to former Playboy playmate Karen McDougal's CNN interview to the details provided in the defamation lawsuit that ex-*Apprentice* contestant Summer Zervos filed against the president, we have a pretty good idea of their version of what went on inside the bungalows when Trump was staying there.

Stormy has said it was here that she watched *Shark Week* with Trump and ate swordfish. While their bungalow get-together was supposed to be about discussing her potential appearance on *The Apprentice,* she wrote in her book that Trump, feeling frisky, "started to trace his finger on my thigh."

Karen, meanwhile, remembered that their "first date"—around the time of his June 14 birthday in 2006—ended in a bungalow here with him offering to pay her after sex.

"Did he actually try to hand you money?" Anderson Cooper asked her in their CNN interview.

"He did. He did," McDougal responded. "And I said, I just had this look of . . . I don't even know how to describe the look on my face . . . must have been so sad because I had never been offered money like that."

It was also here that some of the events alleged in Summer's lawsuit against Trump took place. In her court papers, she claims a 2007 incident at a Beverly Hills Hotel bungalow began after Trump emerged from a bedroom and "immediately started kissing [her] open mouthed, pulling her towards him."

It went downhill from there with Summer claiming Trump "grabbed her shoulder, again kissing her very aggressively, and placed his hand on her breast" before she "pulled back and walked to another part of the room."

The documents describe his allegedly continuing advances and her continued attempts to rebuff him until "he paced around the room and seemed angry," adding: "He told her that he did not believe that she had ever known love or been in love."

————

Did he meet these women in Bungalow 22, or one of the others here? Accounts aren't clear, though Bungalow 22 was the site of a Trump casting call in 2008 for a short-lived MTV reality series called *The Girls of Hedsor Hall*, in which "a dozen young American women with unladylike traits would be shipped off to an English country house to learn social graces." According to the *Washington Post*, Trump "held court" as a series of possible contestants presented themselves. Trump allegedly suggested trying to find more attractive participants.

As I wandered the grounds of the Beverly Hills Hotel, I couldn't help but wonder about the influences in Donald Trump's life, including his long association with Hugh Hefner, the founder of *Playboy* magazine. Had the president's long history of affairs and boorish behavior just been an exaggeration of his lifelong attempt to fulfill his inner Hugh Hefner?

As a student at New York Military Academy, the all-boys boarding school in which he enrolled in 1959, young Donald was probably no different than others his age in wanting to emulate the hedonistic *Playboy* founder. Trump's five-year stint in the military academy began at age thirteen—six years after Hefner began publishing his men's magazine, which author Carrie Pitzulo wrote after his death, "defined an airbrushed and unattainable standard of feminine attraction and availability."

I can envision a teenage Trump and his bunkmates after lights out, passing around a dog-eared copy of *Playboy,* checking out that month's centerfold by flashlight and nodding off to Hef's philosophy of manhood and of breast-filled midnight dreams. Of Trump's times at the military academy, David Cay Johnston, one of his biographers, told me, "Donald has been living the year he was thirteen for the last sixty years."

It was clear Trump was channeling Hefner on the first night he was alone with Stormy Daniels at a hotel suite in Lake Tahoe. Stormy writes in her book, *Full Disclosure*, that "Trump came swooping in, wearing black silk pajamas and slippers. 'Hi there,' he said. Look at this motherfucker, I thought . . . 'Sorry to interrupt, Mr. Hefner. I'm looking for Mr. Trump . . . What are you doing? Go put some fucking clothes on.'"

One thing separates Trump from his would-be sexual idol, however. Like Trump, Hefner was accused over the years of various acts of sexual exploitation and abuse. But unlike Trump, the *Playboy* founder never faced a public reckoning like Trump did during the 2016 election. In the wake of the release of the "*Access Hollywood* tape" numerous women shared stories about Trump's alleged sexual misconduct.

At the time this book went to the printer, the president had publicly faced allegations from two dozen different women. In addition to placing those previously reported allegations into a narrative that attempts to show the arc of Donald Trump's relationship with women over his life, this book will reveal another forty-three allegations, bringing the total number to sixty-seven incidents of alleged inappropriate behavior, including twenty-six examples of unwanted sexual contact.

———

After what I had learned a year into the reporting of this book, I came here to the Beverly Hills Hotel to walk down that path to Bungalow 22—to try for a moment to walk in Donald Trump's footsteps and to contemplate why, again and again, he was willing to take such risks and to act with so little regard for women.

Numb from months of interviews and research covering the endless string of affairs, propositions, lies, accusations, and disparaging comments made against women by Trump, I nonetheless continued to wrestle with what Trump could possibly have been thinking. Looking at the elegant surroundings, I wondered if he ever imagined the trouble he would get himself into years later during his presidency because of his extramarital affairs with Stormy and Karen (the "hush money" mistresses, I call them).

As you will read in these pages, there are many places where Trump carried out his womanizing—places like Mar-a-Lago in Palm Beach, Trump Tower on Fifth Avenue, and the $100 million yacht he dubbed the *Trump Princess* as well as a string of exclusive nightclubs and private hotel suites. Of all these locations, however, the bungalows here, some costing as much as $17,000 a night, seemed to call out to him as a haven as he conducted his indiscretions early on in his third marriage.

Before bringing Stormy and Karen and Summer here, he even entertained the future Melania Trump on the premises. Then his girlfriend, there's a photo of Trump and Melania outside the Beverly Hills Hotel from February 2004. The occasion was the 14th Annual Night of 100 Stars Oscar Gala. In the picture, Trump stands between Melania and *Lolita* actress Dominique Swain.

In the evening of my visit to the Beverly Hills Hotel, I checked out its famed Polo Lounge. Of all people, Chris Harrison, the genial host of TV's popular reality dating show *The Bachelor,* was sitting across the room at a table of friends.

It suddenly hit me. I realized that, maybe, for Trump, the bungalows here were his own twisted version of *The Bachelor*'s "Fantasy Suite."

As I watched Harrison and his friends, in my mind I could hear him saying, as he often did on the show, "Should you choose to forgo your individual rooms . . ."

The tie-in to Hefner also began to make more sense.

After decades of beautiful women, Donald Trump—married or not—was still trying to live out his fantasies, no different than Hefner had done at his mansion, a mile down the road.

———

Decades before Stormy, Karen, and Summer and the bungalows at the Beverly Hills Hotel, and long before I ever thought about this book, I saw Donald Trump in person for the first time in Aspen. I was a young celebrity reporter based in Los Angeles. I had gone to the famed Colorado ski town over the 1988 Christmas holiday.

I probably wouldn't have even recognized him had he been wearing ski attire like everybody else at the base of the mountain. But no other guy was dressed in a white Oxford shirt and V-neck red sweater under a black wool overcoat.

"Mind if I snap a photo, Mr. Trump?" I asked.

Always happy to be noticed, the forty-two-year-old real estate developer and fledgling New York celebrity stared straight into the lens of my cheap camera. The picture taken, I wished him a happy New Year.

I didn't know it at the time, but while he was in Aspen with his family, he also had stashed his mistress nearby, *Vanity Fair* would later reveal.

His then wife, Ivana Trump, also had no idea at the time, and Trump and Marla Maples's affair would carry into the new year and through all of 1989 up until the Christmas holiday, when all the parties assembled again in Colorado. Unlike the previous year, Trump got noticed plenty on the ski mountain in December 1989. He, his wife, and mistress all ended up in the same restaurant on the side of the ski slope.

One person who witnessed the infamous confrontation was my old friend Bonnie Robinson, a Los Angeles reporter who regularly holidayed in Aspen. "I remember it was a beautiful day," she told me. "It's what we call in skiing a 'bluebird day' in Aspen—sun's out, no wind, so it's really warm."

All these years later, Bonnie could still recall the moment when Ivana and Marla locked eyes. "To put it mildly, it was very fucking tense," she said. "Donald became very uncomfortable. Words were shouted. People stopped eating their lunch."

Marla, after years of staying in the shadows, knew the inevitable confrontation had come and decided to stake her claim.

Marla told *Vanity Fair* writer Maureen Orth, "It suddenly became focused in my direction . . . I didn't want to scream." But according to onlookers, Marla did scream: "It's out, it's out! It's finally out!"

Another person who was there that day, like Robinson, was an old colleague of mine—Russell Turiak, an old-school paparazzi photographer. After Marla left Trump and Ivana, the couple skied down the side of the slope into an open area and continued their argument, as Turiak snapped photos. "When they stopped, I shot off a few frames," he said. As Turiak observed the pair, Ivana's look of "How dare you?" was met with a shrug by her husband.

Trump's apparent indifference that afternoon to his wife of more than a decade and the mother of his three children was striking, but a second incident on that trip really defined Trump for me. It actually occurred the following evening.

According to author Harry Hurt in his 1993 book *Lost Tycoon*, Trump and Ivana had gone out to dinner in Aspen that next day with a friend, a New York publicist.

Hurt wrote, "When the Trumps escort [the publicist] back to her room, Donald keeps asking about an attractive young woman who joined them at the table along with her date for the evening. 'Is her figure as good as it looks?' he wondered."

Hurt wrote that the publicist blushed "in embarrassment" and couldn't understand "how Donald could dare to talk that way in front of Ivana."

So, the memory no doubt still fresh in his mind of standing between his wife and mistress on the slopes, Donald Trump was already thinking past them—and about yet another woman.

———

The idea for this book came to me in the spring of 2018, as the Stormy "hush money" scandal was exploding in the "fake news" media, as Trump calls it. Amid the headlines about Trump's behavior with women in recent years, I wanted to go back decades earlier, and begin to try to connect the dots.

What else was there to know about Trump's behavior with women? What influenced Trump's views about the role of women in his life? And how would the nature of those relationships look if we cataloged them against a fuller narrative of Trump's life? Was Trump merely a boor and a philanderer—or was he a predator? My hope is that readers will find satisfactory answers to those questions in these pages.

In July 2019, I made multiple attempts to seek Trump's comment on the allegations contained in this book. Despite sending emails and FedEx requests to White House press staff, as well as placing phone calls to Press Secretary Stephanie Grisham and Hogan Gidley, neither Trump nor his representatives responded to our requests for comment by the given deadline. The closest we came to a comment was on July 9, 2019, when I managed to reach Gidley on his White House office number. Gidley claimed he had not seen my emailed request for comment, which I had sent nine days earlier to both his White House email and a personal email address he had been known to use. He seemed very eager to get me off the phone. He was polite but said: "I didn't see it, but I'm writing this down and I will look for it. I'm going into a meeting." He then hung up, and we heard nothing from the White House by the time the book's text was finalized.

I am proud of what I accomplished with the collaboration of three fellow journalists:

My coauthor, Monique El-Faizy, carefully and painstakingly wrote the narrative while I reported and chased down sources. A brilliant journalist and writer, she made me see the larger picture of why Trump's actions helped catalyze the #MeToo movement and helped revitalize women's activism.

Whitney Clegg joined our project after working for the CNN investigative unit and reporting on child abuse for NPR. She brought Trump's accusers into sharp focus through terrific and insightful reporting and I appreciated her challenging me every day to do better.

Finally, Lucy Osborne, whose work came to my attention through a BBC Panorama documentary she had produced on Trump and women, ended up unearthing important new disclosures for this book through her indefatigable reporting and spirit.

My extreme gratitude goes out to all.

WOMEN AND THE PRESIDENT'S BULLY PULPIT

Note from Monique El-Faizy

When I was first approached to be part of this project, my initial impulse was to turn it down. Immersing myself in accounts of Donald Trump's sexual misconduct was not something I was particularly interested in doing. I had read the headlines with the same dismayed disbelief that many women had but hadn't paid much attention to them beyond that. My natural inclination was to look at his policies, not his personal life.

But the prospect of working on this book spurred me to think more carefully about the way Trump has treated women in his life and to realize that the impact that, as president, his words and behavior have had resonates far beyond the encounters themselves. As president, Trump is supposed to personify the values of a nation that for many is still an exemplar of tolerance and equality. That anyone would speak about women in the objectifying terms that he does—let alone brag about being able to sexually assault them—is offensive. When it is a man who holds the most visible and powerful position in the world, it becomes something else entirely.

When the man with the largest bully pulpit in the world espouses the idea that women are objects that can be grabbed or kissed or insulted at whim, he is sending a signal to men everywhere that such attitudes and behavior are acceptable. And when we as citizens stop being shocked, we normalize it, not just for Trump but for all men. As unpleasant or as inconsequential as they may be, depending on one's perspective, we have an obligation to listen to the stories of the women who have accused Trump of sexual impropriety and to carefully consider them, not out of prurient interest or voyeuristic instinct, but because if we don't, we legitimize his behavior and tacitly endorse the denigration of women.

Of course, policy is important, but policies are a reflection of the society they spring out of. We cannot let even the slightest hint of sexism or misogyny go unchallenged if we have any hope of creating a world that values women and men equally. Since we cannot confront what we cannot see, revealing and carefully considering these alleged incidents of sexual misconduct is essential.

All too often, women who come forward with stories about harassment, assault, and verbal, emotional, and physical abuse are shunted aside, brushed off, dismissed, or disbelieved. As a result, women keep their experiences to themselves far more frequently than they make them public. And when they do report them, the repercussions are often so unpleasant that they regret having done so. Victims get revictimized.

It is essential, then, that those who came forward with allegations against Trump are given the fair hearing they are so often denied—especially given the efforts made by Trump and other powerful people to discredit them. Having carefully considered all the evidence we found, we believe the stories of the women whom we included in this book.

I also had a more personal reason for deciding that it was important to give greater scrutiny to Trump's behavior. I am the mother of two boys. Not only do I deeply care about the attitudes they have toward women and the example that prominent men set for them, but I have spent their lifetimes trying to impress upon them the importance of standing up and calling out what is wrong, even when doing so is uncomfortable, because not to do so is to be complicit. I knew if I wanted them to absorb that lesson, I would have to live it myself.

Writing this book has made me rethink many of my own attitudes and assumptions. There is a fine line between salacious exposé and legitimate investigation. While Trump's presidency has rendered that boundary almost indiscernible, writing about him prompted me to reconsider the behavior of previous presidents and other men through the lens of the #MeToo movement. It is impossible not to see that there were many women who made accusations against powerful men over the past several decades who did not get a fair hearing. My coauthor, Barry Levine, helped me see the importance of listening carefully to each and every woman with a story to tell.

In these pages, we tried to amplify the voices of women who have been silenced, diminished, and dismissed, and to show why what they have to say about Donald Trump matters, not just for them, but for all of us. My hope is that in reading their stories and seeing the power in the collective action that they helped unleash by coming forward, women everywhere will feel emboldened to make their own voices heard.

ALL THE
PRESIDENT'S
WOMEN

INTRODUCTION

On January 21, 2017, the day after Donald J. Trump was inaugurated the forty-fifth president of the United States of America, hundreds of thousands of women wearing pink cat-eared "pussy hats" flooded the streets of Washington, D.C. They did so to champion a panoply of issues, but mainly to rally against the elevation to the presidency of a man who had advocated, on tape, sexual assault. The women in Washington were joined by millions of women in other U.S. cities and around the world. In D.C. alone, the gathering represented the largest single-day march in U.S. history.

The hats, an allusion to Trump's now-infamous boast on the so-called *Access Hollywood* tape that he could "grab 'em by the pussy," were symbols of the anger and fear that had prompted these women to climb onto buses, board trains, and pile into cars to make the trip to the nation's capital and to other march sites around the world. Many of the women who took to the streets that day were in a state of despair at Hillary Clinton's defeat by Trump. They had gone to the polls on November 8, 2016, believing that they were casting their ballots for the first female president of the United States. Instead, they wound up with a president who they felt had shown himself on many occasions to be a misogynist.

During his campaign, Trump had mocked and insulted numerous women, from his opponent Hillary Clinton to media figures

1

like Megyn Kelly. When the *Access Hollywood* tape emerged, Trump dismissed it as "locker-room talk," but then, one after the other, a wave of women came forward alleging that Trump had inappropriately touched them. He was elected anyway, leaving many stunned that such discourse and behavior had not been disqualifying. What did Trump's victory say about the state of women in America?

In this book, we seek to take a comprehensive look at the subject of Trump and women—his attitudes about them, his history with them, their views of him, and the impact of his presidency on them. Where did Trump's sexist sense of male supremacy come from? To answer that question, we trace Trump's transformation from a kid from Queens to high school "ladies' man" into a womanizing, model-chasing, porn-star-frequenting philanderer.

We look at his early days on the dating scene in college and as a young adult in New York, his emergence as a prominent businessman, then as a television personality, and, finally, as a politician. We examine the things he has said about women, the language he has used to describe them, and the insults with which he has tarred them.

We spoke with dozens of women who had encounters with Trump, some positive but more negative. We explore his dealings with women who worked for him and those who were in relationships with him. In these pages, we have compiled the stories of women who have already come forward publicly with an allegation of sexual misconduct by Trump and placed them in a narrative alongside many new allegations revealed for the first time in this book. By June 2019, news organizations had documented as many as twenty-four women who have accused Donald Trump of varying degrees of inappropriate behavior, including sexual harassment or sexual assault. Our investigation found at least sixty-seven separate accusations of inappropriate behavior, including twenty-six instances of unwanted sexual contact.

On the basis of that evidence, this book will show that Trump repeatedly and systematically engaged in aggressive sexual pursuit of women over the course of many decades. It will show that his behavior was neither random nor occasional nor casual. Our investigation found that Trump's sexual misconduct, particularly during the 1980s and 1990s, was far more frequent than has previously been reported publicly—though it was widely known about in certain circles during that time—and followed patterns. It will show that he was not simply sexist, nor misogynistic, nor even a harasser. The behavior he has admitted to—grabbing women by the "pussy"—and many of the credible accusations he denies, were they to be proven in a court of law, would qualify as crimes, some of them serious ones. The accounts of the women and men who encountered Trump documented in the book should dispel any doubt that the president is merely boorish. After considering all the evidence, one cannot but conclude that Donald Trump is, and has been for some time, a full-blown sexual predator. So what does this all mean for our nation? Multiple allegations of sexual assault against any man must be taken seriously; all the more so when that man holds a position of power.

Of course, not all women opposed Trump—without the backing of white women, 47 percent of whom voted for him, he wouldn't have been elected in the first place. Along with chronicling the accusations of sexual impropriety against Trump, we speak to the women who stand by him. While some polls suggest their support is eroding, the president still largely enjoys the backing of white, evangelical women. What is it they like about him and how do they continue to stand by him given his misdeeds? Why aren't they bothered by his unarguably sexist comments? This book looks not only at the women who abhor him but at those who adore him as well.

The divisions within the country on the issue of sexual conduct were never more evident than during the confirmation process of

Supreme Court Justice Brett Kavanaugh, who was accused of sexually assaulting a young woman when he was in high school. The proceedings not only laid bare the fault lines in American society, particularly among women, but also starkly highlighted the impact of having an accused sexual predator with chauvinistic views occupying the highest office in the land.

Many believe that the enduring #MeToo movement would not have taken wing in the way it has had women not been so angry about Trump's victory, so fearful about what it would mean for them, and so furious about his depiction and treatment of women. Progressive women may have been unable to keep Trump out of the White House, but they were going to be damned if they were going to continue to stand by while other men groped, demeaned, and assaulted them. One public predator was enough.

Trump's victory galvanized the political left and, even more so, women. It forced many Americans who supported the gains in minority and reproductive rights of previous decades to consider that those hard-won advances could be taken away and therefore couldn't be taken for granted. Groups of women who first came together to oppose Trump in the days after his election continue to meet on a regular basis throughout the country, writing postcards, making posters, placing phone calls—and running for office in record numbers. The 2018 midterm elections, which ushered a rush of women into public office, were but the first fruit of those efforts.

It's tough to imagine that Trump anticipated the impact his words and actions would have on American women. He is likely sincere when he claims he values them. His anachronistic view of gender roles appears to be so deeply held that he is unable to even conceive of an alternative perspective. "A misogynistic belief in sexual entitlement is a, and probably *the*, foundational element of his self-conception," Jonathan Chait wrote of the president in *New York*.

"Fame and riches are the means, and a limitless ability to access the body of any woman he desires is the end."

Many on the political right, especially those who support Trump's policies on issues such as immigration, health care, and abortion, have found it expedient to dismiss his sexism as unfortunate but inconsequential. It is not. It lies at the very basis of his power. And it matters.

Meryl Streep summed it up concisely when talking about Trump's "instinct to humiliate" during the 2017 Golden Globes. "When it's modeled by someone in a public platform, it filters down into everyone's life, because it gives permission for others to do the same," she said. "Disrespect invites disrespect, violence incites violence. When the powerful use their position to bully others, we all lose."

Part One

PUPIL

ONE

ACCESSORIES MAKE THE MAN

"My favorite part [of 'Pulp Fiction'] is when Sam has his gun out
in the diner and he tells the guy to tell his girlfriend to shut up.
Tell that bitch to be cool. Say: 'Bitch be cool.' I love those lines."
—Donald Trump, 2005, in Trump Nation: The Art of Being the Donald

The photograph looks benign enough upon first glance: A smiling young woman is standing next to a teenage boy, who is leaning back on the barrel of a cannon with one foot thrust forward. Her face is turned toward his; he looks straight at the camera. The picture, which comes from the 1964 yearbook of the New York Military Academy, is captioned "Ladies' Man: Trump."

The young lady in the picture, however, was not graduating senior Donald Trump's girlfriend. Nor was she a visiting friend. The woman in the picture is nineteen-year-old Fran D'Agati Dunn, a secretary who worked at the school at the time and was asked to step in for the photo. Nothing more than a prop. "I think we said 'hi' to each other and that's about it," she said years later. "I was just a body to have a picture taken."

Donald Trump's parents shipped him off to the all-male New York Military Academy (NYMA) when he was just thirteen. Before then he had been a rambunctious, troublemaking boy who preferred sports to girls. "It's truly not talked about how good an athlete he was," said Peter Brant, who was arguably Donald's best friend from the ages of five to thirteen and a classmate of his at the Kew-Forest school in Queens. "He's a really good baseball player and he was a really good soccer player."

The only meaningful contact with girls or women that Trump had before being cloistered in his single-sex boarding school was with his mother and sisters. When Trump was a toddler, his mother, Mary, pregnant with Robert, her third son and fifth child, went into the hospital to give birth. After her delivery, Mary suffered severe hemorrhaging, requiring her doctors to perform an emergency hysterectomy. She went on to develop a serious abdominal infection, which resulted in several more surgeries. For a time, it wasn't clear if she would live or die.

Mary's prolonged hospital stay came during a determinative time for Donald. Eighteen months to two and a half years is a critical period in development, because at that stage children are starting to distance themselves from their caregivers a little and going out into the world and trying new things, making a stable home base essential, explained Dr. Sue Kolod, a psychoanalyst and chair of the committee on public information at the American Psychoanalytic Association. "It's a time when separations are extremely important, but also the reunion is very important. . . . [If] you go out into the world and you turn around and your mother's not there, it's traumatic." Even later on, after she had recovered, Mary Trump seemed to have a distant relationship with her children, or at least with her sons. "We rarely saw Mrs. Trump," Lou Droesch, a childhood friend of Donald's elder brother, Freddy, told *Politico*. "But we did see a lot of the housekeeper." Playmates of the Trump children say that Mary rarely interacted with the kids in front of their friends and didn't talk much at family dinners.

The son of German immigrants, Trump's father, Fred, a real estate developer who amassed a fortune by building low-income housing in Brooklyn, primarily concerned himself with the boys of the family. "His father would be around and watch him play," Trump's childhood friend Mark Golding said. "His mom didn't interact that way." Mary was left to tend to the girls. "That's the way it was," said John Walter, a Trump cousin. "Guys were guys and girls were girls."

Both Trump parents hewed to clearly defined, traditional—even stereotypical—gender roles. "My father was the power and the bread-winner, and my mother was the perfect housewife," Trump wrote in his 1987 autobiography, *The Art of the Deal*. She "cooked and cleaned and darned socks and did charity work at the local hospital." She understood that her role was secondary in importance to that of her husband. "If something got interrupted because [my father] was going to inspect a housing site or something, she would handle that so beautifully," Donald has said. "She was an ideal woman."

If Mary instilled in Trump a belief that a good woman is a sub-missive one, she also endowed him with a love of glitz and glam-our. The former Mary Macleod had grown up on a small island in the Outer Hebrides, off the coast of Scotland. After immigrating to New York in 1930 as a young woman, Mary worked as a maid in the Manhattan mansion of Louise Whitefield Carnegie, widow of scion Andrew Carnegie, and once Mary had a house of her own she adopted those luxurious tastes in her own life to the degree her wealthy but far more frugal husband would allow, driving around in a Rolls-Royce while she collected quarters from the laundry rooms in the buildings her husband owned.

While Fred Trump may have been a physical presence in his sons' lives, he was emotionally distant from all his children. When the children were struggling with the information that their mother had suffered complications during Robert's delivery, Fred showed little capacity for comfort. "My father came home and told me she wasn't expected to live, but I should go to school and he'd call me if anything changed," Trump's sister Maryanne Trump Barry told Trump family biographer Gwenda Blair. "That's right—go to school as usual!"

Fred Trump's distance from his daughters may have been born out of a general unease around women. Despite his wife giving birth to five children, members of the household were forbidden from uttering the word *pregnant*. The Trump paterfamilias was remote, emotionally abusive, and ruled the household with a metaphorical iron fist and a literal wooden spoon, which he employed for paddlings when deemed necessary. "He was a tough, hard-driving guy who didn't traffic in emotions except perhaps anger," said Tony Schwartz, who ghostwrote *The Art of the Deal*.

That reliance on physical dominance rubbed off on Donald, who exhibited a violent streak from an early age, throwing rocks at the baby next door, pulling the pigtails of the girls in his class, throwing cake at birthday parties, and beating up kids in the neighborhood. As an adult, such belligerence became a point of pride for Trump. "Even in elementary school, I was a very assertive, aggressive kid. In the second grade I actually gave a teacher a black eye—I punched my music teacher because I didn't think he knew anything about music and I almost got expelled," Trump boasted, likely falsely, in *The Art of the Deal*.

"I think Trump was in rebellion from a very early age," Schwartz, the ghostwriter, said. "The character that he became was set almost in concrete. And his self-image, his self-definition, was built around the idea that he was one tough son of a bitch." Trump thinks that's what made him the creditable son in his father's eyes. "I used to fight back all the time," he told Marie Brenner in *New York* in 1980. "My father's one tough son of a gun. My father respected me because I stood up to him."

He may have been right. It was Fred who drilled into his son's head the vainglorious mantra "you are a killer, you are a king," and Fred who drove all his sons to be ruthless and combative. Donald was his most worthy pupil. "When somebody tries to push me around, when they're after my ass, I push back a hell of a lot harder than I was pushed in the first place," an adult Trump would tell *Playboy*. "If somebody tries to push me around, he's going to pay a price."

Fred and Mary's firstborn son, Freddy, proved to be less of a chip off the paternal block. As the eldest, it was expected that he would join the family real estate business and someday take over the reins. But Freddy was a sensitive kid who struggled to live up to his father's idea of what a son should be. After a conflict-filled stint working for his father, Freddy fled to Florida to fulfill his dream of being an airline pilot. He was happy there, but whenever he returned to New York his family would harangue him mercilessly, telling him he was wasting his life. Eventually, Freddie turned to the bottle, descending into alcoholism. He died of a massive heart attack at the age of forty-three. Donald has always blamed Freddy's death on his drinking and doesn't touch alcohol because of it.

But Trump apparently took away another lesson from his older brother's experience. "The way the game got played in that household was, if you did not win you lost," Schwartz said. "And losing was you got crushed. Losing was you didn't matter. Losing was you were nothing. Losing was you're his older brother, Fred, and you become an alcoholic and you die young."

———

Ethical standards prevent mental health professionals from diagnosing people they have never met, but journalist Peter Lovenheim, author of a book on attachment theory, is not bound by those same restrictions. Having spent years researching the subject, he has drawn the conclusion, as outlined in a story in *Politico* magazine, that Trump developed what is known as an avoidant attachment style. People develop their attachment styles in early childhood, and when a child doesn't get the parental (or caregiver) attention necessary to develop healthy emotional connections, that child can develop attachment anxiety. The result can be a person who craves intimacy but has difficulty trusting people. Alternatively, someone might develop attachment avoidance, leading them to be generally distrustful of others and to eschew closeness. People with attachment avoidance tend to have unstable relationships and be overly self-reliant.

In explaining his assessment, Lovenheim pointed to Trump's dearth of close friends. He also indicated Trump's compulsive need to be admired, noting that researchers have found that "overt narcissism or grandiose self-regard" is often associated with attachment avoidance. Trump's bragging about his sexual prowess and his history of unstable relationships could also be signs of an avoidant attachment style.

Trump doesn't just boast about himself; he also lionizes his parents. That, too, is characteristic of adults with avoidant attachment styles, according to Lovenheim. Most of Trump's praise is directed toward a specific parent. "The most important influence on me, growing up, was my father, Fred Trump," he wrote. His father had "drive and ambition," he was "a wonderful man, but . . . also very much a business guy and tough and strong as hell."

Trump is notably unforthcoming on the subject of his mother. "He doesn't really have anything to say about her, except she was great," said Justin Frank, author of *Trump on the Couch: Inside the*

Mind of the President. Even in the biographies written about the Trump family, there are few details about Mary and what she was like. "There is not a single story where you get some specificity about her," Sue Kolod said. "The thing that comes across most powerfully is the absence of this person."

When Trump does mention his mother, it is to laud her, albeit in fairly two-dimensional terms. But his true feelings about his parents may be hinted at in the placement of family photos in both his office in Trump Tower and in the Oval Office: a picture of his father was prominently displayed in each, while any image of his mother was absent—an omission later corrected in the White House.

Without a strong parent-child relationship, it is difficult to develop key emotional skills. "Children learn empathy or lack of empathy from their parents, from the way they are treated and the way they see their parents treat other people," Kolod said. '[Trump's] style of interacting with people and his way of treating people seems to be very much modeled on his father . . . If Mary Trump had been a more powerful presence, she might have been able to counteract that somewhat," Kolod said. "It doesn't sound like she was able to modify or temper the impact he had on him."

———

Trump may have been somewhat of a bully as a kid, but in the eyes of his friends, such as Peter Brant, there was no discernible explanation for his precipitous banishment to the New York Military Academy in the eighth grade. Before then, the two had engaged in schoolboy capers such as sneaking off into Manhattan to explore Times Square, buying hand buzzers and hot gum and, as time went on, switchblades—but for the most part they spent their time on benign hobbies like collecting baseball cards and playing sports. Brant can't remember Donald getting into any kind of trouble that would have warranted his exile to military school. The decision was "a very severe response to a kid who hadn't gotten arrested and wasn't involved in drinking and drugging," Trump biographer Michael D'Antonio said. "This was a profound rejection of Donald." And yet, Donald thrived at the NYMA. The lingua franca there was one that he was comfortable with: brutality. Theodore Dobias, a World War II vet and training officer in the school—who ended up being something of a mentor for Trump—would strike kids with an open hand if they didn't do what they were told. "If you stepped out of line Dobias smacked you and he smacked you hard," Trump wrote. Dobias used violence as his primary corrective tool. If a student had poor grades or disciplinary issues, Dobias would put him in a boxing ring and force him to fight. Sometimes Dobias would even step into the ring with a kid himself.

Trump loved that about Dobias. "This wasn't like school, where a teacher would say, 'Now, Donald that's not very nice to do,'" Trump told journalist and author Michael Gross. "This guy would go crazy. He would grab you and throw you out a window. This was a rough group. And I don't say it in a negative way. I thought they were great. This was before you had prohibitions on stuff. Today, he couldn't do that."

The violence at the NYMA didn't just come from the top. Hazing was an intrinsic part of life there and took every form from the mundane, such as requiring young cadets to run errands or throw themselves against the wall whenever an upperclassman walked by, to more grievous forms, such as putting a laundry bag over a boy's head, then shoving it in the toilet and flushing. "The worst I ever heard—and which Donald may have insinuated that he personally performed—involved the beds at the academy, which were a mattress on top of a metal frame with springs," Trump schoolmate Sandy McIntosh told us in an interview for this book. "The idea was that you would get a kid on the spring frame and wire it up to an electric socket, then plug it in to shock the kid. Donald laughed and told me one time it blew the fuse in the whole main barracks."

Trump excelled in many things at NYMA; intimidation was one of them. Once he was appointed captain and had attained a position of authority in the hierarchal institution, there was one punishment he particularly liked meting out on his classmates. It was called "the Chair." "You had to squat down and lean your back against a wall," McIntosh explained, saying he had heard about it from a friend at the school. "Your arms go out straight and on your arms they put an M-1 rifle, which weighed about nine pounds. You had to hold the rifle in that position, and if you moved at all—dropping the rifle would be the worst possible thing—you could get physically hit. This kid told me that Donald really enjoyed inflicting 'the Chair' on him."

Later, when Trump had his own children, he didn't spare them the same rough treatment. Scott Melker, a former classmate of Don Jr. at the University of Pennsylvania, posted on Facebook about an incident in which, when picking up his namesake to go to a baseball game, Trump struck his son so hard that he fell to the ground. "There were quite a few students standing around . . . trying to catch a glimpse of the famed real estate magnate," Melker wrote. "Don Jr. opened the door, wearing a Yankee jersey. Without saying a word, his father slapped him across the face, knocking him to the floor in front of all his classmates. He simply said, 'Put on a suit and meet me outside,' and closed the door."

————

As tough a taskmaster as he was for those under his command at the NYMA, Trump is equally remembered by classmates for his focus on being seen in the company of girls—pretty girls—as much as possible. The school didn't allow members of the opposite sex on campus except on Sundays and on special occasions, and they had to be escorted by a family member or another adult at all times, but Trump still managed to have a steady supply, particularly in his final year. The other boys noticed.

"Donald, within the rules and propriety of the academy, was able to have a supply of very attractive women come up to visit," former classmate George White told us. "I had the room on the same upper floor as his, so I could see with my own eyes. . . . The notable thing about the women was that they were always extremely well-dressed; they had every fashionable accoutrement."

"During his senior year, every couple of weeks when his parents would come up to visit him, they would have some young woman with them," echoed McIntosh. "They looked like models. None of the women my friends and I knew would ever dress like that. They looked like women you'd see in a magazine. I would often see Donald parading the women around the Quadrangle, sometimes arm in arm. But two weeks later it would be a different girl. . . . to me that was the beginning of Donald's 'brand.'"

How Donald managed to meet so many lovely young ladies while insulated in an all-boys school was a bit of a mystery to the other cadets. "It was my assumption that Donald's father, Fred, brought the girls with him to visit Donald," White said. "Where he got them from, I don't know." McIntosh had a similar take. "Either Donald was the most seductive man in the world, or his father set up the visits to make it look like he was," he told a French documentary crew. "I don't know whether he actually knew them or not."

In burnishing Trump's rakish reputation, Fred was making his son over in his own image. The elder Trump was so well known for his own extramarital activities on Florida's Gold Coast that he had earned the moniker "the King of Miami Beach."

His efforts seem to have paid off. "There was a rumor—just a rumor—making the rounds as to why Donald was named 'Ladies' Man' in his senior year: It was because he had 'gone farther' with a girl during one of his on-campus dates than any other cadet," White said. "Given what's now recognized as his public boasting, I wouldn't be surprised if it was Donald himself who had started the rumor!"

Trump wasn't universally perceived as a Lothario. Classmate Ernie Kirk said he sometimes went on chaperoned afternoon double dates with Donald and "he was very respectful." Others, though, noticed a tendency to denigrate women. White recalled a Saturday night dance, to which he took a date from the local area with whom he had been fixed up. "The girl showed up; she was not from the higher echelons, more like middle class. She had on a beautiful dress, but it was handmade," White told us. "To me, that was very sweet, like she had worked very hard on it."

Trump, though, noticed the difference between her and the fashion plates he regularly brought to campus. Once the cadets were back in the barracks, he began mocking White's date. "He called her a 'dog' and asked me how I could go with her. His derisive mockery of her just would not stop—and this was in public. He said it to ten different people and he made a huge issue out of it," White said. "This was just a sweet sixteen- or seventeen-year-old girl. Donald made a point of mocking that poor girl, calling her a 'dog' over and over again. Then he would do a dog bark—'woof woof woof!'"

His anachronistic parents may have shaped his views on the role of women in the home, but when it came to women as romantic interests, Trump had a singular role model: Hugh Hefner. "Our whole idea of what sex was and the proper way to deal with women came from *Playboy*," McIntosh told PBS's *Frontline*. What the boys took away from the magazine "obviously revolved around the objectifying of women. But that was all we had at that age. We didn't have any real people," McIntosh said.

Trump's understanding of women doesn't seem to have evolved much since then. "When I listen to Donald now speaking and read reports of what he said, the circumstances are of course 2016, but the time—the conversation, the way he's talking, the topics he talks about, seem to be 1964, because in our barracks, we talked the same way," McIntosh told *Frontline*. "I think that the things that we talked about at that time in 1964 really are very close to kind of the way he talks now about women and minorities and people of different religions. . . . When I hear him speak, I hear these echoes of the barracks life that we had and that we grew out of."

———

If Trump had long-term girlfriends who could attest to the way he treated women as a teenager or young adult, they have kept their accounts of dating the one-day president to themselves. Trump has claimed he lost his virginity when he was about fourteen years old. "It was a young woman who was really beautiful, she was the hot little girl in high school," he told radio host Howard Stern. "She was hot."

Aside from the nameless girls who visited him at the NYMA, one of the earliest public stories of Trump's dating life was relayed by actress Candice Bergen, who, like Trump, attended the University of Pennsylvania as an undergraduate in the 1960s. Bergen fit Trump's liking for women who made other men take notice of who was on his arm, having been crowned homecoming queen and named Miss University of Pennsylvania. Even better, she was famous—not yet for her career, which she still hadn't embarked upon, but because of her father, ventriloquist Edgar Bergen.

Trump set his sights on Bergen even before he transferred to the University of Pennsylvania from Fordham University, where he spent the first two years of his college. He called the eighteen-year-old in her dorm one day to ask her out. She agreed, she says, because she was bored. Trump showed up in a three-piece burgundy suit, burgundy patent leather boots, and a burgundy limousine. Bergen was unimpressed. She was home by 9 p.m. and says the date was "really a dud." Her impression of Trump? He was "a good-looking guy. And a douche," she told Andy Cohen in 2017 on *Watch What Happens Live*, wearing a blue sweatshirt with "Free Melania" stitched on it in white.

Bergen may not have been taken with Trump but, according to him, plenty of other young Ivy League women were. "I don't think anybody had more sex than I did," Trump told Michael Gross. "I didn't do drugs. I wasn't a drug guy. But there was a lot of sex. Sex was all over the fucking place. At Penn it was wild. And after I got out, it was even wilder."

———

Upon graduating from Penn in 1968, Trump returned to Queens and joined his father's business, but his sights were set on Manhattan. He got his first toehold on the slender island in 1971, when he rented a studio on Third Avenue and Seventy-Fifth Street, a "dark, dingy little apartment," in his description. Still, he was thrilled by it. "I was a kid from Queens who worked in Brooklyn, and suddenly I had an apartment on the Upper East Side," he wrote.

Trump's living situation may have been modest, but he had his mother's luxe taste and a desire to impress. He would often take dates to Peacock Alley, the showy bar in the lobby of the chic Waldorf-Astoria hotel. He didn't always succeed in wowing his dates, though. He took artist Lucy Klebanow out to dinner one night in the early 1970s. He picked her up in a white Cadillac convertible and drove her to the famous Peter Luger's steakhouse in Brooklyn. When the check came at the cash-only establishment, he didn't have enough to pay for dinner. So she did. He said he'd pay her back, but never did.

Trump already had his innate understanding of the power of public image, so one of the first things he did upon moving to Manhattan was try to join Le Club, a small private nightclub on East Fifty-Fifth Street that was frequented by models and the European jet set and was, in Trump's view, "the hottest club in the city." Its coterie of members included Continental blue bloods and "some of the most successful men and some of the most beautiful women in the city," Trump wrote. "It was the sort of place where you were likely to see a wealthy seventy-five-year-old guy walk in with three blondes from Sweden."

But Trump was an unknown and, just a few years out of college, an awfully young one at that. The first time he called to ask if he could join, he was laughed at. But he persisted. He kept calling until he persuaded someone to give him the phone number of the club's president. It took a few tries, but he convinced the president to meet him for a drink. The first time they met Trump got no joy, but during their second meeting Trump made a compelling argument. He got his membership—on one condition: He had to promise not to steal any of the members' wives, something the club president worried might happen "because I was young and good looking," Trump wrote and the *Washington Post* later reported.

That was the beginning of Trump's club life. He was out every night meeting women. "You had drugs, women, and booze all over the fuckin' place," Michael Gross quoted Trump as saying in his book *My Generation: Fifty Years of Sex, Drugs, Rock, Revolution, Glamour, Greed, Valor, Faith, and Silicon Chips.* Having sex became his "second business."

Trump seemed to be everywhere. His former NYMA classmate George White bumped into him at a Manhattan club one night around 1973, early in the evening when the place was still nearly empty. Trump was sitting at a table in a back room with several women. "From what I heard him saying, he was having a 'contest' to determine which of those women he was going to take home that night," White told us. Not having seen Trump since they graduated from high school, White approached him and said hello. Trump made a bit of small talk with him, then used White as a pawn in his gambit. "He grabbed one of the women by the shoulders, turned her in my direction, forcibly pushed her face next to mine, and said, 'Would you rather go home with me or with him?'" White said. "I just walked out."

———

The most consequential encounter that Trump had at Le Club took place in 1973 and was not with a pretty young lady but with a nefarious cerulean-eyed lawyer named Roy Cohn. Trump was then twenty-seven. Cohn was twenty years his senior and his reputation as a ruthless New York political fixer was well known. A sometime lawyer for the mob, Cohn had previously been Joseph McCarthy's right-hand man during the Second Red Scare witch hunts in the Senate. Cohn had been instrumental in securing a death sentence for Ethel and Julius Rosenberg in their espionage trial. He would come to have a profound impact on Trump's life.

One night, Trump was seated at the table next to Cohn's at Le Club and the two struck up a conversation. Trump took his characteristically provocative tack by telling Cohn that he disliked lawyers because they caved too easily and ran away from fights, always preferring to settle. Cohn sensed that the conversation wasn't merely academic, so asked Trump if he was referring to something specific.

At the time, the real estate company Trump was now running alongside his father was being sued by the Justice Department for refusing to rent to black tenants. Their lawyers were advising them to make a deal, but Trump wasn't so sure. He asked Cohn how he would handle the situation. "My view is tell them to go to hell and fight the thing in court and let them prove that you discriminated," Cohn told him. That gladiatorial bent appealed to Trump, and Cohn was soon on the family payroll. In a classic Cohn move that Trump has now internalized as his own, he counterattacked, filing a defamation lawsuit against the Justice Department and asking for $100 million in damages. The suit was thrown out, but the Trumps walked away with a settlement in which they admitted no guilt, and Donald learned a tactic he would rely on for the rest of his life.

Age aside, Cohn and Trump had a lot in common. They were both privileged boys from the outer boroughs (Cohn was raised in the Bronx) who had broken into Manhattan society but would never be fully accepted. They both liked to be seen around town with pretty women. They had both grown up in the shadows of successful, distant fathers. And, said David Marcus, whose father was Cohn's first cousin, they shared something more malignant: narcissism. "Roy was a confident narcissist," Marcus told us. "Trump is a sort of uncomfortable, feeling-unworthy narcissist."

Cohn and Trump became close friends and a regular fixture together on the New York places-to-be-seen circuit. Being with the powerful Cohn opened doors in Manhattan for Trump, who never quite shook off the whiff of Queens, and gave him access to important and useful people. For the famously closeted Cohn, who eventually died of AIDS, hanging around the tall, blond, still-handsome, ascendant Trump was its own reward.

"Donald is my best friend," Cohn told people. They became so close that Cohn sometimes refused to charge Trump for his legal services. Trump also called Cohn a friend, though in somewhat less effusive terms. "Tough as he was, Roy always had a lot of friends, and I'm not embarrassed to say I was one," Trump wrote. "He was a truly loyal guy—it was a matter of honor with him—and because he was always very smart, he was a great guy to have on your side."

That fidelity didn't always cut both ways. When an intimate friend of Cohn's was dying of AIDS, Cohn asked Trump to give him a room in one of his hotels. Trump put Cohn's friend up in the Barbizon-Plaza hotel—and sent Cohn the bill. On another occasion, Trump gave Cohn a pair of diamond cuff links in a Bulgari box to thank him for decades of favors. They turned out to be knockoffs.

Eventually Cohn got the measure of Trump. Near the end of his life, Cohn told a journalist "Donald pisses ice water." In the end, Cohn's purported "best friend" was not invited to speak or be a pallbearer at his funeral, although author Peter Manso, who once shared a house with Cohn in Provincetown, told us he saw Trump "weeping" at the service. "Now whether these were crocodile tears or real tears, I don't know," he said.

Marcus sees Cohn's image in Trump. "Anything you can say about him and his lack of morality, his lack of decency, his lack of character, you can say about Trump," he said. The late gossip columnist Liz Smith, who covered Trump from the early days of his arrival on the Manhattan scene, once said that Trump lost his moral compass when he got involved with Cohn.

Trump has continued to live by many of the doctrines in the Cohn Bible. Cohn, for example, believed that truth was "fungible and changeable," Marcus said; Trump shows indifference to facts. Cohn manipulated the press and cultivated gossip columnists; it's tough to find a celebrity reporter who worked in New York during the 1980s and 1990s who didn't receive a phone call from Trump, often posing as PR agent "John Barron" or "John Miller." (Cohn may have showed Trump the benefits of manipulating the media, but Trump was a natural ballyhoo man.) Cohn believed that ends justify means; during the McCarthy hearings he fabricated facts and lied about witnesses and documents. From Cohn, "Trump learned you don't have to play by the rules. You can bend the rules to your liking. You can ignore the rules. You can trample on people," Marcus said. Equally tellingly, "Roy was a big advocate of bullying and bribing and buying out people," he added.

Trump's tried-and-tested MO of never surrender, always hit back, and then claim victory comes straight out of the Cohn playbook as well. "You don't admit to wrongdoing. You go full blaze on the offensive and you go after whatever person or whatever government agency is accusing you of something," Marcus said in describing Cohn's worldview. "Ultimately, in Roy's world, you could settle, but you always had to make it look like you won. That was really important to Roy and is important to Trump. You have to declare yourself the winner."

Aside from his father, it was Cohn who served as Trump's biggest mentor in life and in business. Though the lawyer had his fans, there are few who would vouch for his character. "He was reprehensible," Marcus said. "He was amoral. He screwed people left and right. . . . He was really sleazy, really powerful, really connected and really didn't care about conventional rules and ethics." His onetime roommate Manso is of the same opinion. "Roy Cohn was the ultimate existential figure—the ultimate outlaw. No fucking rules except his own," he said. "Very simply, Roy Cohn was probably the purest sociopath I've ever known."

That is the man Trump has most relied on in his adult life. "Trump is not a man of judgment," Manso said. "Roy, on the other hand, offered Trump not only sanction for Trump's criminality, but a level of intelligence that Trump didn't possess naturally."

TWO

ALMOST ORDINARY

"For a man to be successful he needs support at home, just like my father had from my mother, not someone who is always griping and bitching."
— Donald Trump, 1997 in *The Art of the Comeback*

"You can have a thousand mistresses if you want, but you can't have just one. And whatever you do, you never, ever let yourself get caught."
—Fred Trump to Donald, 1990

By the mid-1970s, Donald Trump was approaching thirty and showing signs of being ready to settle down. He was still hitting the clubs with Roy Cohn, but his relationships with two women were growing more serious: Australian LPGA star Jan Stephenson and Czech ski champion Ivana Zelníčková.

Then–LPGA commissioner Ray Volpe arranged for Trump and Stephenson, who was five years Trump's junior, to have dinner together at the Plaza hotel (which Trump would later buy) in 1975. Both Trump and Stephenson were coming off big years. Stephenson had joined the LPGA tour in 1974 and was named Rookie of the Year. She was a talented, promising golfer, and she was beautiful and not afraid to use her sex appeal to plug both herself and her sport.

Widely considered golf's first sex symbol—an image encouraged by Volpe—she once appeared in a bathtub covered only by golf balls.

Trump, too, was on the rise professionally. He had just purchased the Commodore Hotel in Manhattan, which he would reopen as the Grand Hyatt in 1980, in a complicated deal that established him as a serious player on the New York real estate scene. They were both young, good looking, and on the cusp of huge careers. The up-and-coming golfer and the aspiring real estate mogul seemed the perfect match.

Trump was already an avid golfer, having picked up the sport in college. During their dinner, he told Stephenson he'd been watching her on the tour and had a promotional campaign he wanted to include her in. "We kind of started seeing each other," she explained in an interview with a golf website in 2018. "It was all business at first—Donald had asked me to represent one of his casinos—but then he took me to all these beautiful restaurants and we did the whole disco thing and the 70s retro. You couldn't ask for anyone else to spend time with."

Their relationship grew more serious, and the two would fly to meet one another whenever they could. He would watch her tournaments and she would meet him for dinner in New York. "Donald was good looking, charming, very accomplished and wealthy," Stephenson said. "He always had a lot of beautiful women who wanted to go out with him. He was not the Donald you see today."

One day, a chance encounter with one of those other beautiful women—another athlete—created some serious competition for Jan.

Ivana Zelníčková had been a competitive skier (though not an Olympian, as Trump was later fond of saying) before she moved to Canada and started modeling. In July 1976, the twenty-seven-year-old went to New York as part of a group of eight models from Canada to model in a fashion show promoting the Montreal Summer Olympics. When they arrived in Manhattan, the girls decided to check out the New York nightlife. "My friends *really* wanted to go out and see the swinging seventies singles scene," Ivana wrote in her 2017 autobiography, *Raising Trump*. She wasn't fully up for the outing, but she nonetheless donned a red minidress and high heels and headed with them to a flashy Upper East Side singles bar called Maxwell's Plum. Maxwell's Plum was a hot spot back then, a decadent, flamboyant establishment known for its Art Nouveau decor, its swinging singles, and its celebrity clientele. "At least one young woman is said to have paraded some months ago through the place stark naked and no one said a word," Craig Claiborne wrote in the *New York Times* in 1970.

The maître d' told Ivana and her friends there would be a wait for a table and directed them to the bar. Tired and hungry and worried about her early start the next day, Ivana was feeling none too pleased. All of a sudden, she felt a hand on her arm. She turned to find "a tall, smiling, blue-eyed handsome blond man," she wrote. "He said, 'I am so sorry to bother you. My name is Donald Trump and I noticed that you and your friends are waiting for a table. I know the manager and I can get you one fast.' . . . I turned back to my friends and said, 'I have good news and bad news. The good news is that we are going to have a table soon because of that man over there.'" Her friend asked what the bad news was. "He's going to sit with us."

Once seated, Donald had a burger, and Ivana had chicken paillard. As the women were finishing their dinners, Trump got up, stealthily paid the bill, and left. When the models exited the restaurant, a smiling Trump was waiting for them in the driver's seat of his limousine. He drove Ivana and her friends across town to the

Americana Hotel on Seventh Avenue, where they were staying, and said good night. The next day, a hundred roses arrived to her hotel room, accompanied by a note that said, "To Ivana, with affection. Donald." Moments after they were delivered, he called and invited her to lunch. She declined, citing a work obligation, so he took her to dinner at Le Club instead.

Sparks did not fly. "I listened to Donald and held up my end of the conversation but I didn't feel a special affinity for him," Ivana wrote in her account. He asked her to have dinner with him again the next day. When she said she couldn't because she was flying home that afternoon, he suggested lunch. "This guy didn't quit!" Ivana wrote. She met him at the '21' Club the following day and then flew back to Canada and to the man she lived with.

Donald continued to pursue her—as well as Stephenson. He had two glamorous women to choose from, both foreign and from places where the difference between Queens and Manhattan was meaningless. "He was seeing Ivana and I at the same time," Stephenson said. "He was really open about it."

He was also open about growing tired of golf being more important to her than he was. According to Stephenson, Trump gave her an ultimatum: either the career had to go or he would. "I'd given up so much to become a tour pro," she said. "My family had given up so much for me. . . . I just couldn't have that relationship right then. I wanted golf. I felt I would be letting everybody down if I gave it all up."

Never one to take no for an answer, Trump put on the full-court press. He called her in Atlanta, where she was due to play a Pro-Am tournament, and asked her to come to New York to have dinner with him. He promised to send a jet down to pick her up. She told him she couldn't do that the night before she had to compete, so eventually he agreed to fly to Atlanta and have dinner with her there.

"So I drove out to the plane and when the door came down, Donald didn't come out and the pilot told me to come up," she said. 'When I stepped in, the plane was full of red roses—it was beautiful. And there was one rose and an invitation sitting on a seat. I opened it and there was the name of a restaurant I'd never heard of. So I turned to the pilot and asked him where the restaurant is, and he said, 'It's in Paris.' I thought, well I can't do that, I've got a tournament to play tomorrow, so I said thanks but no thanks. I didn't hear from him for a while after that."

Luckily for Trump, Ivana Zelníčková was made of more traditional stuff. Even before she had met Trump, Zelníčková was on record saying that her career took a backseat to the man in her life. Modeling was "a job to me, not a career," she told the *Montreal Gazette* in 1975. "I have my social life, my husband, and my home." By husband Zelníčková meant live-in boyfriend George Syrovatka, whom she had dated as a teenager in Czechoslovakia. The two had rekindled their romance when she moved to Canada, though Syrovatka was proving slow to make things legal.

Trump, on the other hand, was willing to move quickly.

As he had with Stephenson, Trump pulled out all the romantic stops. After their first meeting, he called Ivana every other day and in October flew up unannounced for a fashion show she was walking in. "I happened to notice a tall blond man in the audience," Ivana wrote. "Our eyes met, and he smiled at me. Donald was at the show? He'd somehow found out about it and come to Montreal to surprise me." She looked for him after the show but he was nowhere to be found. "The strangeness of his appearance and subsequent disappearance started to have an effect on me," Ivana recalled. "I thought about him more and more. He wasn't in my heart yet, but I was starting to like him and felt intrigued by him."

That winter, Trump called her and invited her to go away with him for Christmas. "Beach or mountains?" he asked Zelníčková. She chose mountains, and told Syrovatka about Trump, with whom she hadn't yet shared a kiss or even spoken with face-to-face since their meeting in New York. Syrovatka, who had become more of a friend than a lover, gave her his blessing. Trump bought first-class plane tickets to Aspen and rented a glitzy chalet, replete with mirrored ceilings, chinchilla bed throws—and two bedrooms. Ivana decided the gentlemanly gesture was unnecessary. "After seeing the place, I made up my mind pretty quickly," she wrote. "I'd made a clear, conscious choice to be there with him. I could have said no to his dinner invitations, his constant phone calls, this trip—to everything—but I kept saying yes to all of it."

At the time, Trump was still unaware that modeling was not Ivana's primary skill. When they hit the slopes the next day, he skied carefully, and she flew past him. "I disappeared," Ivana told an interviewer. "Donald was so angry, he took off his skis, his ski boots, and walked up to the restaurant. . . . He went foot bare up to the restaurant and said, 'I'm not going to do this shit for anybody, including Ivana.' He could not take it that I could do something better than he did."

Already, Trump was showing his need to always have the upper hand, but neither he nor Zelníčková noted the dynamic that would eventually prove corrosive to their relationship. They were still caught up in the throes of a whirlwind romance and enjoying what Ivana later said had been the most romantic week of her life thus far.

Stephenson, on the other hand, was quickly becoming a memory. "[Ivana] was an accomplished skier at the time, and he said she was prepared to give up her career to be with him," Stephenson said. "I told him I couldn't do that. I think that was the reason it never worked out between us." The rose-filled airplane had been a test, and she had failed. "It was kind of a yes or no," she said. "He started getting really serious with Ivana after that." Trump's cooling on Stephenson was an early hint of what would become starkly apparent just a few years later: Trump would not tolerate playing second fiddle to a woman's career.

———

In Trumpland, facts are mere inconvenience. When Donald retells the story of his courtship of Ivana, Jan Stephenson isn't even a footnote. Even the account he gave in *The Art of the Deal* of how he met the hazel-eyed Slav veers from reality. In the book, he claims they met at the Summer Olympics in Montreal. "I'd dated a lot of different women by then, but I'd never gotten seriously involved with any of them," he wrote. "Ivana wasn't someone you dated casually. Ten months later, in April 1977, we were married."

He expanded on his first impression of Ivana in his 1990 book, *Trump: Surviving at the Top*. "From the start, Ivana was different from just about all of the other women I'd been spending my time with," Trump wrote. "Good looks had been my top—and sometimes, to be honest, my only—priority in my man-about-town days. Ivana was gorgeous, but she was also ambitious and intelligent. When I introduced her to friends and associates, I said, 'Believe me. This one's different.' Everyone knew what I meant, and I think everyone sensed that I found the combination of beauty and brains almost unbelievable."

Trump was evidently wowed enough during their time together in Aspen to forgive Ivana her one-upmanship on the slopes. By the end of their week together, he had decided she was the one. "On New Year's Eve he said to me over dinner, 'If you don't marry me you'll ruin your life,'" Ivana wrote in her book. At first she thought he was joking, but when she saw his face, she realized he was serious. At that point, Trump was far from being the love of Ivana's life; that had been a Czech songwriter named Jiri Staidl who died in a car crash in 1973, less than two years into their relationship. As for Trump? "We had chemistry, similar drives, but the truth was, we barely knew each other," she wrote.

Ivana turned to the pragmatism that had been an essential survival tool during her upbringing in communist Eastern Europe. While she had been seduced by the romantic week she had spent with Trump in their Aspen ski chalet, Ivana's deliberations about Trump took place in her head, not her heart. She was about to turn twenty-eight, and if she wanted to have children she'd have to get married soon, she calculated. And after all the rich men she had met in Montreal who turned her off with their "entitlement and superior attitude," Donald was a breath of fresh air. "He liked simple food and simple pleasures," she wrote of the man who would come to singularly symbolize the culture of excess.

She decided to take him up on his offer. "My life is saved," she told him. "I'll marry you."

Trump's family and friends like Roy Cohn had picked up on signs that Ivana was different from other women Trump had dated. Cohn said he knew it was serious when Donald started picking her up at the airport. And Fred Trump told *New York* that Donald "folded like an umbrella" when he met Ivana. That assessment might not have been entirely laudatory. Ivana and Fred—whom she later described as "a really brutal father"—had butted heads early on, when she joined the Trump family for a meal. "We went to Tavern on the Green for the brunch one Sunday and [Trump's] father ordered a steak," Ivana said. "So all the, you know, the sisters and brothers, they ordered a steak. And I said, 'Waiter, can I have a filet of sole?' And Fred looked up at the waitress and, 'No, she's going to have a steak.' I look up at the waiter, I said, 'No, Ivana is going to have a filet of sole'—because if I would let him just [roll] right over me, it would be all my life and I would not allow it."

Still, the preternaturally resolute Ivana did a fair bit of wavering between the amorous Aspen dinner and her wedding with Trump just four months later. When she returned to Canada, Syrovatka told her that if it was marriage she wanted, he would tie the knot with her. His offer gave her pause, but only for a short time. She said an emotional goodbye to the man who remains her closest friend and headed off with her bags and her poodle for New York. She was ready to become Mrs. Trump.

Syrovatka's competing proposal wasn't the last hurdle the couple faced, however. Donald and Ivana's eventual union came precariously close to not happening thanks to the prenup that Trump, at the behest of Cohn, presented Ivana with a month before the scheduled nuptials. Two rounds of negotiations ended in walkouts, but with the deadline of the scheduled ceremony looming, the two managed to come to an agreement.

Donald and Ivana were wed on April 9, 1977, at the Marble Collegiate Church on Fifth Avenue, where the Trump family had been listening to Norman Vincent Peale's sermons on the power of positive thinking for more than a decade. Newly arrived and still finding her feet in New York, Ivana left the wedding planning to Donald and his secretary. "He booked the church and the '21' Club for dinner afterward. He hired the florists and I went in to approve the arrangements. The only thing I took care of myself was the dress," she wrote. For that she turned to a designer friend in Canada, John Warren. In one of the few photos publicly available of the day,

Ivana is wearing a simple, scoop-necked tie-front frock with ruffled sleeves, no visible jewelry, and an elaborate floral headpiece and veil atop her stick-straight platinum locks.

It was a Trump wedding. About six hundred guests attended, of whom Ivana knew six: a few girlfriends from Montreal; Nikki Haskell, Ivana's new best friend from New York; her aunt; and her father, who was meeting Donald for the first time. Her mother couldn't make the trip—Ivana wrote that she wasn't feeling well, but other accounts suggest her parents couldn't afford two plane tickets.

Faced with pews filled with strangers and VIPs, including then-mayor Abe Beam, Ivana caught a momentary bout of cold feet. She felt alone and was anxious about speaking in front of all those people with her heavy accent. The late arrival of her bouquet added to her stress. "I was so freaked out with bottled-up nerves that I locked myself in the antechamber next to the chapel and cried," she wrote. Her father, who had always doted on his only daughter, gave her a pep talk that got her down the aisle. The reception, she wrote, was a blur.

The party ended at midnight and the next day the couple left for a short honeymoon in Acapulco. On the very last day of that year, December 31, 1977, Ivana gave birth to a son, Donald Junior.

———

In snapshots taken early in their marriage, Donald and Ivana look like any young couple in love. He's naturally bronzed and smiling, shirtless on a chaise longue. He's in a red tie and the plaid vest of his once-signature three-piece suit, bending over a newborn wrapped in a hospital blanket and wearing a plastic ID bracelet. He's wearing a white T-shirt, lying in a bed made up in red-checked sheets and holding a tiny infant, showing the glazed exhaustion seen on the faces of young parents everywhere. There's even a photo of Trump changing a diaper—despite his later insistence that that is woman's work and something he has never done. In this treasure trove of pictures, found in a suitcase purchased in a Palm Beach thrift shop and published by the *Daily Mail* in 2016, the couple look like happy, ordinary newlyweds.

What is most remarkable about these once-lost pictures from Trump's first marriage—knowing what would happen later in Trump's life—is that Ivana doesn't look like an accoutrement. Unsteady as she may have been going into the marriage, once Ivana said her vows she embraced her new role with gusto. As soon as the couple returned from their honeymoon, an already-pregnant Ivana attacked both the New York social scene and the job her husband gave her overseeing interior design during the transformation of the Commodore Hotel with determination and vigor. "It was a heady, happy, busy time," Ivana wrote. "To many people, starting a new job as a pregnant newlywed would be a lot. But I thrived in a high-activity atmosphere. Having so much to do, and so many responsibilities, was exhilarating."

She juggled it all seamlessly, making sure to maintain an aura of glamour and feminine mystique. When it came time to give birth to Don Jr., for example, she wasn't having any of that American husband-in-the-delivery-room nonsense. "I kicked Donald out of the room," she wrote. "Let him witness the birth? Never. My sex life would be finished after that."

Donald John Trump Jr. was born at 5:20 p.m. on New Year's Eve. Donald stayed with Ivana and the baby for a while, "talking about the things we'd do and what a fabulous, happy life he was going to have. We also talked a little business." At 8 p.m., Donald went home. At 10 p.m., the baby went to the nursery and Ivana donned a boa and mink over her nightgown and went to ring in the new year with a friend recovering from back surgery on another floor of the hospital. On January 2 she was back at work. Breast-feeding wasn't for her, either.

Having a Mrs. Trump opened up a world to Donald that had been inaccessible before. The roles of husband and father bestowed on him a respectability he didn't have when Roy Cohn was his plus one. And it slowed him down, at least for a while. "Which is proba-bly a good thing," Trump said. "It kept me out of trouble. If I hadn't got married, who knows what would have happened?" The wild nights at clubs weren't totally behind him—just a few weeks after their wedding, Ivana's pal Nikki Haskell brought the couple to the opening of Studio 54, where Donald would become a regular—but some of them at least were replaced by charity balls and dinners with John Cardinal O'Connor at St. Patrick's Cathedral.

The image-conscious Trump may not have proposed to Ivana because of how she softened the public's perception of him, but he certainly reaped the benefits. Tying the knot caused people to take him more seriously. "Donald was perceived as a brash young kid with a lot of nerve and boldness and little substance," said Louise Sunshine, who held a senior position in the Trump Organization from 1973 to 1985. After getting married, though, he was a family man, and that altered how people saw him. The change came just at the right time; in 1977 New Jersey legalized gambling and Trump was keen to open a casino in Atlantic City. He knew that being perceived as an upstanding citizen would help him win a gaming license.

As his family grew—Ivanka was born in 1981 and Eric in 1984—so did Trump's real estate holdings, and his notoriety. His name started to creep into the New York tabloids, largely because of legendary gossip columnist Liz Smith, who had been put on Don-ald and Ivana's scent by a mutual friend. "They were attractive and had three divine little children," Smith's friend told her, according to Smith's book, *Natural Blonde*. "Mrs. Trump—Ivana—is really a very sweet, dear person. I think she's getting a bad rap." That was enough to whet Smith's appetite. "I immediately decided I liked Ivana Trump from afar and was curious," she wrote. "Before long I met Mrs. Trump, and then I met her tall blond husband. I found them both refreshing, if a bit presumptuous and naive socially, and I began to note their comings and goings."

At the same time, the Trumps' movements were becoming increasingly noteworthy. Buildings and enterprises bearing the Trump name proliferated: Trump Tower in New York; Trump Plaza and Trump Castle in Atlantic City; and Trump's short-lived airline, the Trump Shuttle. The couple bought Mar-a-Lago and a massive yacht they dubbed the *Trump Princess*. Donald and Ivana were suddenly everywhere—in the gossip columns, on the covers of magazines, on television and in movies. They were bigger than life, straight out of the script of *Dallas*, the perfect media couple for an extravagant era. "Donald became bigger and bigger," Smith wrote. "He was the king of hyperbole and he had just the requisite touch of Elvis vulgarity to endear him to the common man."

———

All the while, Ivana was becoming more and more of an equal partner on the professional front. After first joining the family business as a vice president of interior design, in 1985 she was made president and CEO of the Trump Castle Hotel & Casino in Atlantic City, and later named president of the Plaza hotel. Soon she was getting her own magazine covers, without Donald by her side. "Donald calls me his twin as a woman," Ivana told *Vanity Fair* in 1998. "She saw herself as his helpmate," a friend of Ivana's told *New York*. "Donald was using the media to enhance his image. They decided she needed to be part of this."

It worked. Donald and Ivana were the golden couple of the 1980s, and the press couldn't get enough of them. They shared everything and they were on top of the world. "They really complemented each other, and it was so great to watch," said Nikki Haskell, a talk-show host and close friend of Ivana's. "They were the perfect couple." With Ivana, Donald had everything the boy from Queens could have dreamed of. What more could he want?

A lot—or a lot less, as the case may be.

In the beginning, Trump took great delight in the businesswoman-wife he had created and whose image he helped promote. Liz Smith wrote about an appearance Ivana made on WNBC, billed as a top executive in the Trump Organization. "Donald stood on the side beaming and nodding," Smith wrote. "He also offered her up to me as running everything at the Plaza Hotel."

Ivana wholeheartedly embraced the schizophrenic image of the perfect woman that was proffered by the 1980s. She was simultaneously feminine and strong, sexy and powerful; she raised kids and had a career, all the while holding on to the traditional view of the world that Donald demanded. "Surrounded as she is by the trappings and corruption of extraordinary money, and enmeshed as she now is in a business equated with sleazeballs and organized crime, Ivana Trump has somehow remained a woman of old-world East European values and sensibility," *Vanity Fair* extolled.

As successful as she became in her own right, Ivana was always very careful to make it known that Donald was in charge. She had learned the lesson of their first day skiing together in Aspen and wasn't going to make the mistake of racing past him again.

"I always stand by the man, never contradict Donald, even though I might think it's silly," she said. "I'm a very traditional European wife and I don't mind that Donald is the boss. I like it that way. I have to have a strong man, not someone I can just ride over.

This is my upbringing." Ivana's deference was sincere. "She was second in her life to him," friend and socialite Joan Schnitzer told *New York*. "She was an appendage. But she loved it."

Still, Ivana thought that her business acumen was part of what kept her husband around. "If Donald were married to a lady who didn't work and make certain contributions, he would be gone," she told *Time* in 1989.

She couldn't have been more wrong.

Trump, the man who had described his subservient mother as the ideal woman, grew to abhor the tough business side of his wife and came to see putting her to work as a mistake. "I think that was the single greatest cause of what happened to my marriage with Ivana," he said in a 1994 interview with Nancy Collins for *Primetime Live*. He hated coming home and hearing her shouting on the phone at someone at the casino who had upset her. "A softness disappeared . . . she became an executive, not a wife," he said. What he really wanted was someone to cater to his needs. "I don't want to sound too much like a chauvinist, but when I come home and dinner's not ready, I go through the roof," he said.

Trump made that revelation long after his split from Ivana, but the cracks in their union began to show long before its collapse. When one scratched the gilded exterior of Donald's glowing pride in Ivana, something very different surfaced. Even while praising her, he patronized her. When announcing her appointment as president of the Plaza hotel in early 1998, he told reporters: "My wife, Ivana, is a brilliant manager. I will pay her one dollar a year and all the dresses she can buy." The *New York Times* referred his comment as "Edwardian paternalism" and Ivana reportedly cried to her friends about Donald's humiliation of her. But it wasn't the first time and it wouldn't be the last. Early in their marriage, he reportedly told friends, "I would never buy Ivana any decent jewels or pictures. Why give her negotiable assets?" And on *Oprah* in 1988: "There's not a lot of disagreement because, ultimately, Ivana does exactly as I tell her to do."

"He's not a chauvinist, is he?" Oprah queried, holding a disbelieving hand to her cheek.

"Oh, he's the worst," Ivana replied, laughing.

Nor did Trump spare Ivana the weaponized comments about her appearance. She was showing too much cleavage, her breasts were too small, her dress was ugly, she was too skinny: he had a litany of complaints. When she tried to fix the flaws he saw in her with a trip to Steven Hoefflin, Michael Jackson's plastic surgeon in Santa Monica, he reportedly complained that he couldn't stand to touch her "plastic breasts."

"Donald began calling Ivana and screaming all the time: 'You don't know what you are doing!'" one of Ivana's assistants told longtime Trump chronicler Marie Brenner in *Vanity Fair*. "When Ivana would hang up the phone, I would say, 'How can you put up with this?' and Ivana would say, 'Because Donald is right.'"

And yet, she had done everything Donald had asked of her. He wanted a big family, so she gave him three children (and got a $250,000 cash bonus for each, according to a rumor reported in *Vanity Fair*). He suggested she work for the Trump Organization, so she jumped in with two feet and excelled. She helped grow his family and his fame. She became as much a force as was he, letting him mold her in his image and morphing into a big, bright, brash Trump of his creation.

In the end, Ivana's success was her downfall. She had become too famous. She was growing dangerously close to overshadowing Trump. "He put her there, but he couldn't stand it," Oscar de la Renta executive Boaz Mazor said in *New York*. "The student surpassed her master."

"I create stars," Trump told Collins. "I love creating stars, and to a certain extent I've done that with Ivana. . . . Unfortunately, after they're a star, the fun is over for me. It's like a creation process. It's almost like building a building."

Ivana had grown beyond his control. That, for Trump, was fatal.

"You don't stand between the sun king and the sun," journalist Michael Gross told us. "And she did."

Part Two

PREDATOR

THREE

GIRLS ON FILM

"The beauty of me is that I'm very rich."
—DONALD TRUMP, 2011, *GOOD MORNING AMERICA* INTERVIEW

By the early 1980s, Trump's empire, wealth, and fame were expanding. In 1983, Trump Tower opened, putting his brand on Manhattan's tony Fifth Avenue and sealing his reputation as a major player on the New York real estate scene. He opened his first Atlantic City property, Trump Plaza, in 1984, and in 1985 he purchased Mar-a-Lago in Palm Beach. He was quickly becoming a household name and a fixture in New York's tabloids, generating headlines for his flashy displays of wealth and acts of self-promotion. As he accumulated money and fame, Trump's network began to expand beyond the real estate industry. He used his newfound fame to gain access to the kind of women he liked: young models. Some were so young that you could hardly call them women at all.

Ivana was friendly with several designers and was a regular at fashion shows both in New York and in Europe, eventually hosting many fashion events at the Plaza hotel. Trump would often attend shows with her. NaKina Carr was working in New York for Oscar de la Renta and was backstage in the models' dressing room at one of his fashion shows when she heard Trump's name mentioned for the first time. She was getting ready when all of a sudden she heard someone shout, "Put your robes on, here he comes!"

At twenty-one, the Texas native was already on the older side for a runway model, who generally start working when they are in their teens, but she was new to New York and had no idea what was going on. "I didn't know what they were talking about . . . but suddenly everyone threw on their dressing robes," Carr said, speaking publicly about her memories of Trump for the first time in an interview for this book. Carr asked another girl what was wrong, and the girl pointed to a man across the room. "She said, 'He's the money man. He can do whatever he wants. . . . unless you're a gold digger, you avoid him at all costs.'"

Trump walked in like he owned the place, according to Carr's account, with a pregnant Ivana trailing behind him. "He threw his arms wide open and said, 'Okay now ladies, drop 'em,'" Carr said. "The one thing I'll always remember is the dejected look on Ivana's face in the dressing room. I thought, how horrible, that he would treat her in this way."

As Trump strode around the dressing room, much as he would boast of doing years later at the beauty pageants he would come to own, Carr concealed herself behind a pillar, incredulous that someone would be so crude. "The other girls were obviously afraid of him, like they knew he meant it and it wasn't a joke," she said. Given the nature of the modeling business, where bikini and lingerie shoots and quick changes at fashion shows are the norm, models are used to being seen when they are wearing very little. For models to be upset about being seen in their underwear, something has to be seriously amiss, Carr said. And Carr wasn't alone in feeling uncomfortable. "The girl next to me was clearly disturbed by it," she recalled.

That was the first time Carr encountered Trump, but it was far from the last. Carr said she and her model friends would see him out in Manhattan all the time in those days. "He was nearly always there, especially any party at [Studio] 54 or the Plaza, he was there. And he always had his sights set on very young women," she said. The soirees that Trump attended during that era were guaranteed to have two elements, according to Carr: young models and cocaine— lots of it. "It generally wasn't done in the open, but it was rampant. I don't think I knew anyone at the time who didn't do it. In the eight- ies it was akin to having a martini," Carr said. "At Studio 54 it was done openly on the tables. We would have these little bowls."

According to interviews conducted for this book with dozens of people in the modeling world who are familiar with his behavior, Trump had a reputation for never missing an opportunity to meet models. "Trump would be at every model party there ever was," David Webber, a fashion photographer who was working in New York at the time, told us. "He was a model hound. He was always chasing models. . . . He was a predator. Absolutely." And he could be intimidating. "You know, he's a big guy. He's six three, six four or something," Webber said. "Self-confident is one way to describe him. Or wolf is another. He was really aggressive." And many of the models were no match for him. "You know, you're talking sixteen-, seventeen-year-old girls here and they're starstruck and they're in New York for a month, twenty of them stuffed into a model's apart- ment. And then all of a sudden, someone's saying, 'Come on, let's go and have dinner with a famous man, you don't have to do any- thing,'" Webber said.

One night in the mid- to late-1990s Webber was out at Life, a trendy club on Bleecker Street in Greenwich Village where mod- eling agencies often held parties. Trump was there, and Webber noticed that a young girl couldn't get away from him. Webber didn't know the girl personally, but had seen her at a casting. He believes she could have been as young as fourteen, he said, and was probably not older than sixteen. "Our faces met across the room and she mouthed 'Help' at me," he said. "[Trump] had her pinned against a wall—not physically pinned, but he had surrounded her with his bigness, if you like. He had one hand on the wall to one side and she was against the wall." Webber moved in to aid her. "I went there and I stepped right in between them with my back to him and grabbed her and said, 'Oh, there you are, I've been looking for you everywhere.' And I dragged her off into the next room, and she was like, 'Thank you, thank you.'"

According to Webber, Trump seemed none too pleased by the interruption. Later, when Webber was leaving the club, the bouncers, whom he knew, told him that Trump had given them money to beat him up. "They were all laughing with me when I left. They were like, 'Guess what just happened? You're never going to believe it,'" he said. Webber's account bears a striking resemblance to Trump's alleged use of intimidation many years later with accuser Stormy Daniels.

To some close observers of the modeling world, Trump was a known type. "I would compare him to the spectrum of model fuckers," Michael Gross, the author of the bestselling book *Model*, told us. "The spectrum of model fuckers runs from guy with no money to wealthy guys. And they're collectors of baubles, they're trophy hunters. . . . To some extent, they can be described as predators because they're not actually going out and looking for *a woman*; they're going out collecting, using, and discarding models."

These model-idolizing men may or may not end up sleeping with the women they pursue, but that's not what it's really about for many of them. The models are status symbols. "A lot of these guys, they don't actually have sex with the girls. They just want to be with them to impress other men," Gross said.

NaKina Carr's experiences observing Trump seem to confirm this impression. "With some of the girls he pursued, it was an attention-getting thing. You know, 'Look at me. Look at the young girl I have on my arm.' I mean, everyone knew he was married, but it didn't matter to him. It was obvious," she told us.

There is reason to believe that Trump was after both physical encounters and the status boost. Famously germaphobic, Trump allegedly made sure models had a clean bill of health before he hooked up with them. Trump would sometimes call a friend at one of the agencies and ask him to send specific girls to see his doctor so he could make sure they didn't have any STDs, sources inside the modeling industry told us.

"We all have the clear impression that Donald was having sex with these girls, but it was more about the boast—my building is taller, my car is longer, my apartment is older, and my women are prettier and have bigger tits," Gross told us.

Trump's hands, the size of which would later become the subject of significant public curiosity, were infamous for other reasons back then, according to sources. "He was gropey. . . . he had his hands in the most inappropriate places, always," Carr said. "When he went in to kiss someone, the hand always went to either the hip or the butt. He was also really good when he did pictures or when he'd side-hug someone. He'd always get his hand on the boob. Every time." Stories about Trump and his hands circulated within the modeling community. At one modeling event, Trump allegedly went down a line of women feeling their bodies to guess their dress size. Backstage at a lingerie show, he is said to have moved his hands all over a model's breasts under the guise of inspecting the bra's fabric.

Another trademark Trump move was honed back in the early 1980s. "I saw this several times: When he met a girl, he'd immediately move in to kiss her, not shake her hand or say 'Hello, how are you?' He'd immediately put his mouth on her," Carr said. "I saw him many times go straight to the mouth, to kiss them on the mouth, and they would turn their cheek. But a lot of them didn't because they knew he was the moneyman and it was a way up."

Among modeling insiders, Trump had a reputation at the time for preferring the younger girls. "If you're over twenty-one you don't have to worry," Carr said she was told.

Cathleen, a Swedish model who asked us to withhold her last name, was represented by Trump friend John Casablancas's Elite agency. She was fifteen when she met the future president in the mid-1980s. "It was an agency dinner. We had them all the time, and he was there. I had no idea who he was," she told us. "He came in with two girls from the agency and sat down at the other end to me. One of them was a Polish model. She must have been sixteen, seventeen, definitely no older than eighteen. He was all over her. Kissing her on her lips and neck and touching her."

Cathleen said there were about four men at the dinner and about six models aged between fifteen and twenty—and that there was nothing unusual in that. "This happened every week," she said of the dinners with older men. "You just have to show up, but we would leave after an hour, say you had a casting the following day . . . if you had sense."

Samantha Panagrosso, a Paris-based model who worked in New York in 1989 and 1990, described what it was like to be a young model living away from one's parents during that era. "There's a lot of pressure, 'Go to this dinner, go to that dinner,'" she said. Panagrosso was one of the women who accused Hollywood mogul Harvey Weinstein of sexual misconduct and has been a vocal #MeToo activist. "I had those experiences. Very wealthy men were there, who owned football clubs, guys who were much older than me, much older than all the girls. This is part of the business."

Panagrosso said it's often difficult for models to stand up for themselves. "It's psychological manipulation because these men will put these women up against each other," she said. "It's like they are the prize to be won and these women will do everything to be selected by the men." The imbalance of power skews the dynamic. "The women are usually intimidated, and in their minds—Trump and Weinstein—they believe they have the permissions to do what they want," she said. "The women are afraid to say no. . . . When you have a predator, a guy with so much power . . . women caved in."

Elite model Barbara Pilling was not yet eighteen when her booker took her to a party a few days after her arrival in New York in the summer of 1989. Trump was also in attendance. Pilling didn't know who the real estate developer was, but she noticed him looking at her. "I was standing with my booker and could see him eyeing me up and watching me," she told us. Once he caught her gaze, Trump started talking to her. "I remember him saying, 'Oh, how old are you?' And I said seventeen, and he said, 'That's just great; you're not too old, not too young.'" As they were talking, a waitress carrying a tray laden with flutes of champagne walked past and Trump slapped her on the behind. Pilling was shocked by this behavior, but the server didn't seem to be. "It was like she had had it happen to her by him before or something," Pilling said. "They obviously knew each other. She kind of laughed, and then he said, 'Don't worry, whatever her name was, that's not your tip.'"

Pilling said Trump tried to make small talk with her for a while, but his gaze kept veering to her chest. He asked Pilling if she liked where she was living and said he knew great places she could stay if she didn't. Trump offered to show her the city and to take her to dinner. He told her she was gorgeous, like a dark-haired Marilyn

Monroe, and asked her if she would ever consider going blonde. "I was starting to feel uncomfortable," Pilling remembered. "It's not a nice feeling for a young girl to have an older man making advances on her." Another model standing nearby whispered to Pilling that Trump clearly liked her, and explained who he was. "I wasn't impressed by it. I mean, I was only seventeen."

Pilling eventually excused herself to go to the restroom, where yet another girl was talking about the developer. "She said he grabbed her ass and kept going for her and was all hands," Pilling said. Between that and her own conversation with him, Pilling was so disturbed that she left the party without saying goodbye to anyone.

But that wasn't the last Pilling would hear of Trump. About five years later, Pilling was living in an apartment in Manhattan's Tribeca neighborhood with a few other models. One of them was a young Russian girl named Nadia who had been introduced to Trump by a modeling agent. She was showing off a ring and charm bracelet to her housemates that she said Trump had bought for her. When Pilling told Nadia she thought her involvement with Trump was disgusting, Nadia told her to "fuck off."

———

According to Panagrosso, the model and #MeToo activist, young, aspiring models often see powerful, rich, older men as their vehicle to success—or at least to a life of opulence. "I met so many girls, from the Ukraine to Monaco; rich guys, those women, it's their ticket out of misery," she said.

When Australian Shayna Love was living in an Elite apartment in New York in 1991, models were sometimes encouraged by the agency to attend dinners that became occasions for "men to pick up girls," she recalled.

"You'd go to these things and look pretty, give the men attention," said Love, who was just sixteen at the time and part of Elite's 'New Faces" campaign. "We might as well have been called 'fresh meat.'"

"It was kind of like a feeding frenzy and the girls were there as consumables," a fashion industry insider told BBC's Panorama for the documentary *Trump: Is the President a Sex Pest?* According to the documentary team's reporting, Trump not only attended parties where there were lots of young models, but threw them as well. There was always plenty of cocaine and alcohol at the parties, the insider said, and men who could be the girls' fathers "two times over." The point of the parties was to "get laid," he said. "We do know that [Trump] was having sex with [the models] because the next day or days after we'd hear about it," the insider said. "He'd brag about it to his friends that he scored, maybe one or two girls at a time, which is what he loved to do."

While the BBC documentary on Trump and women found no conclusive evidence that Trump had sex with underage girls, it reported that Trump attended small social gatherings with models who were not yet adults. Model Shayna Love, in an interview with journalist Lucy Osborne, recalled a dinner with Trump. "This time it was a private area, a big table and lots of girls—I'd say around ten to fifteen of us, all between the ages of fourteen and eighteen," she said. "It was just us models, Trump, and John [Casablancas]. We were all underage, but we were offered drinks." Disgusted, Love said she went home early, but other girls stayed. She doesn't know what happened after she left.

Over the years, Trump's involvement with Elite Model Management founder John Casablancas, who is credited with creating the supermodel, grew. Elite was one of the world's best modeling agencies and the sponsor of the prominent Look of the Year competition. Due to Trump's friendship with Casablancas and frequent appearances at agency events, models at Elite speculated about what Trump's relationship to the company was. Rumors began circulating: he was on the board of directors, he was a partner, he provided funding. What is certain is that Trump hosted many of the events of Elite's Look of the Year (now called Elite Model Look) modeling contest at his New York properties and provided lodging for the contestants in both 1991 and 1992—the only time the event was held in the same city two years in a row.

The Look of the Year event drew up-and-coming models from all over the world to compete, and many top models have been contestants, including Cindy Crawford, Helena Christensen, and Giselle Bündchen. In addition to hosting the 1991 competition at the Plaza hotel, Trump also served as a judge that year.

"It's clear that Trump was very interested in these girls. Organizers of the event remember him going through the head shot books and picking out what girls he fancied, and hanging around a bit too much," said Osborne, the journalist who worked on the BBC documentary and also conducted exclusive interviews for this book. "One of the organizers told me that never before or after had a host been so involved."

Eli Nessa had just turned seventeen and was representing Norway in the 1991 Look of the Year competition. The models were being put up at the swanky Plaza hotel on Central Park South, which Trump owned and where the weeklong finale of the competition was held. Nessa roomed with Hedvig Molin, a Dane who went on to have a big career, and now-famous German-American actress Diane Kruger. In addition to the events for the competition, which included a swimsuit segment that felt "humiliating and stressful" to Nessa, the girls were expected to attend several nights of parties. "There were all these older men," she said. "It was so seedy." Nessa was accompanied by her agent, who offered her a sense of protection, but other girls were alone and vulnerable. "I remember this Italian girl, extremely naïve, fifteen or sixteen, who couldn't speak any English. She was easy prey. They were all around her," Nessa said. "We were a bunch of kids, just put there with all these older men. I remember the youngest one, I think she was twelve, from Japan."

One of the parties was on Trump's yacht. "It was massive, and coming from a modest country, it seemed very flashy to me," Nessa said. What really struck Nessa, though, was that many of the men in attendance were older and seemed to have no professional links to the modeling business. "There was this weird asymmetrical age. You saw them drooling over girls," she said. "It just didn't make sense . . . there were a lot of sports people and a lot of people who didn't have any knowledge of the industry."

Stacy Wilkes competed in the 1991 contest as a sixteen-year-old, representing the United States. She remembers Trump coming into their dressing area during the contest, more than once. "I would feel really uncomfortable, because every time we would change, it was like Trump would find a reason to come backstage to see all the teenagers," she told us. "When you're doing a runway show, they have to strip you down and change you. . . . There was no need for him to be back there." Trump never tried to justify his presence backstage but would just walk in and start making jokes. The girls didn't feel that they were free to complain. "We were afraid to say anything bad when he was around because we didn't want anything to hurt our chances of winning," Wilkes said. "We were all young teenagers."

Wilkes's roommate ended up spending the night with one of the celebrity judges, Wilkes said, and later won one of the prizes.

Models report similar things happening during the competition the following year. Shawna Lee was only fourteen when she was the entrant from Canada in the 1992 Look of the Year contest. She also attended an event on a yacht. This time the girls were asked to walk one by one down a staircase and dance in front of Trump and Casablancas, who were seated in chairs at the bottom. "It was a very small area and I could see them laughing and making fun of the girls," most of whom were fifteen and sixteen years old, she said in an interview for this book. "You know, these men were older than my father at the time, looking girls up and down and objectifying them. It was just kind of gross. I don't think doing that had anything to do with being a professional model."

Lee told us that Trump wandered around their dressing room, too, before the runway show. "I was thinking, what's that old guy doing back here," she said. "I was changing and looked up as he was looking and doing a slow stroll by, checking out the girls."

————

Dressing rooms weren't the only places where Trump barged in on women. In the early 1990s, a world-famous supermodel had flown to New York to attend a fashion event and was staying in a suite at the Plaza hotel. She was seeing another industry insider and they had gone back to her room. The two were in bed together when they heard the door open, according to the man, who gave an interview for this book requesting anonymity because both he and the supermodel still work in the industry and fear retribution. Thinking it was housekeeping, the pair sat up in bed and hollered that they didn't need anything. A few seconds later, the door to the bedroom opened. "It's Donald standing there," the man said in his interview. Trump had let himself in. The supermodel and her companion were stunned.

"I said, 'What the hell are you doing?'" the man said. "We're naked, so she pulled up the covers and we're freaked out. I couldn't believe it. He looks in the room and he took a good look at both of us and he slammed the door really hard, like in anger. And that really pissed me off, that he came in and slammed the door with this arrogant attitude."

The two threw clothes on and ran out after Trump, arriving just as his elevator was leaving. They grabbed the next elevator and rushed into the lobby. Trump was already in the middle of the crowd talking to people. "I was livid," the man said. "She's hysterical, crying. . . . And I went at him, and just as I was about to grab him, his bodyguard jumped between us and pushed me back. I was screaming at him, 'What the fuck are you doing, coming into my room?' It was a scene."

While the bodyguard was trying to push the man away, Trump approached. "I hate sloppy seconds," Trump said. "It was loud enough for her to hear," the man said. "Like, she's holding on to my arm and trying to pull me away, too, and she heard him . . . and she had the courage to say to him, 'You fucking bastard.' So we walk away. We got shoved back into the elevator," he recounted.

Later, back in their room, the supermodel revealed to her companion that Trump had gotten her phone number from her agent and had been calling her for weeks. She had repeatedly rebuffed him. "And then it dawned on us . . . that had I not been in the room it would have been a scene," the man said. "She wanted nothing to do with him."

———

According to other accounts from this era, Trump sometimes hunted as part of a pack. Heather Braden was also an Elite model and, in the late 1990s, was instructed to go to a party in a mansion on one of the islands off Miami Beach. Trump was going to be there, she was told. "It was clear I would be dropped or fired if I didn't attend," she told us in an interview for this book. Braden went with a couple of model friends. When they arrived, the first thing they saw was a table manned by two security guards. The girls were handed papers. "I presume they were NDAs for us to sign," Braden recalled. The girls ignored the papers and walked into a big room where there were about fifty models. In her mid-twenties, Braden was one of the oldest women there; the youngest looked to be about fifteen. Many of them were from Eastern Europe and didn't speak English, so Braden and her friends stuck to themselves.

Braden and her friends found the party odd. There was no DJ, no food, and no bartender—though there were drinks, Braden remembers. "It was very awkward from the beginning," she said years later over lunch at the Beverly Hills Hotel. "Fifty females in this room, no real hosts. Very unusual. And then down this large staircase, in front of all of us, there was Donald Trump and behind him there were three actors, forties, maybe fifties. I don't want to name them because they're all still around." The actors were famous, she said. "They came down the stairs and spread out like sharks among the girls," who had broken up into little clusters throughout the room. "Obviously, some of these younger girls were starstruck."

From a couch in the farthest corner of the room, Braden and her friends observed the four men in action. "Clearly, we were there for one reason. It was a numbers game: fifty girls, and of them, ten to twenty would be down to hang out with us in private. Ask enough and somebody will say yes," she said. "We were just pieces of meat."

Braden said she had been in the industry long enough to understand what was happening. At a typical fashion industry party, there would be a mix of people, men of different ages, male models, men in the business. Not here. Braden understood that this party had been set up specifically for Trump and the three actors. "This was just so blatantly obvious in terms of what their intentions were," she said. "This was not eye candy. Sometimes you're brought to these big parties like that, but this was different."

Braden and her friends watched as each man made his way through the knots of models. They started with the standard opening lines, asking the girls their names and where they were from. "Five minutes later—this is what they did to me: 'You want to come upstairs?' It was anything from, 'You want to see the rest of the house?' to 'Do you want to see the bedroom? The view?' Or 'Do you want to partake in party favors?' That was the terminology," Braden said. The men's ultimate aim was clear. "When you're a forty-, fifty-year-old man and you're asking a seventeen-year-old girl to come upstairs to party, there's only one goal," she said. "Sometimes there'd be a couple of girls that would go up together; other times there'd be one or two."

At the time, Braden looked at the girls who went upstairs with the men disparagingly. Now she sees it all differently. "They were more desperate than us because they were younger and they were controlled by the agents, who controlled their visas, who controlled their money. They had nothing to go back to," she said. "On top of it, I would see the girls return downstairs distraught-looking and disheveled."

Braden says Trump approached her at the party, and chuckled when she turned him down. Braden had been to parties at Mar-a-Lago and had seen him around New York, so she knew exactly what he was about. Trump rarely had a date with him when he attended parties, she said, except one night when she saw him at Manhattan hot spot Moomba in the late 1990s with a blonde woman she didn't recognize. "Trump was making out with the woman. She was half-naked. She was wearing a very, very tiny outfit," Braden said. "She could have been any age. She was very much into it."

Braden said that the younger models were likely easier quarry for Trump because they didn't know his reputation. Among the older girls, "he was just known as a pig, to be honest. No one ever liked him who I had ever met. Everyone just took advantage of him and the money he was willing to spend to be there."

When Braden heard about the *Access Hollywood* tape in 2016, she laughed in recognition. "I'm shocked there's not hundreds [of tapes]," she said. Trump's behavior was widely known about, but his power rendered people fearful to talk about it. "They'd have to be hundreds of victims," Braden said. "Everybody knows. I have lots of connections about him, everybody is terrified of him, have had their lives ruined, or are afraid they'll be sued by him."

And some women, Braden said, just don't want to dredge up the painful memories of being the victim of a predatory man.

There's another reason more women don't come forward, however, another open secret of the modeling industry. Many of the women took money to have sex with the men. "A lot of them, initially, you could call it the gold diggers who just don't name a price," Braden said. "I know plenty of girls who got, call them 'tips,' traveling in private jets, yachts. It was understood everything's paid for. A lot of it was, 'They're taking me shopping.' Instead of cash, taken on a shopping spree." But the 'tips' could come in the form of cash, too. "Oh, I got five, ten, twenty grand," Braden said some girls would boast.

And then there was what Braden called the "Black List" in New York. "It was rumored, but I know it's true," Braden said, explaining that for "many, many years" a private list of women who were willing to have sex for money circulated among wealthy men. "To get access to it [the men] had to spend thousands and thousands of dollars to get accepted, vetted," she said. The women on the list were up-and-coming actresses and models who were on the covers of magazines. "If you want a weekend with so-and-so, it would cost you X grand, ten grand, twenty grand," Braden said. "And this was a known list and it went on for many years."

It's unclear if Trump had access to the list.

Maureen Gallagher, a top model in the 1980s and 1990s, said the "dates" were standard in the industry. "That's part of the job description when you're a model. If you don't think you can get down with the get-downs, stay home," Gallagher told us in a rare interview. "They took us on those trips because they knew they'd get their bang for the buck. But I never did anything I didn't want to." Gallagher said that men involved were often famous, like the lead singers of bands. "I mean, think about it. It's like the person you always wanted to shtup. When you're younger, it doesn't seem like a big deal."

———

In addition to Elite agency founder John Casablancas, whose marriage famously ended after he had an affair with a sixteen-year-old Stephanie Seymour and who later married another one of his models when she was seventeen, Trump's social circle in the early 1990s included Jeffrey Epstein, a registered sex offender who allegedly ran a sex ring of underage girls. He pleaded guilty in 2008 to soliciting a minor and in July 2019 was charged with two federal counts of sex trafficking before being found dead in his prison cell in an apparent suicide in August. Trump was friends with him and once said of Epstein: "Terrific guy. He's a lot of fun to be with. It is even said that he likes beautiful women as much as I do, and many of them are on the younger side."

Long before his conviction, Epstein had been well known for his predilection for young girls and the many parties he threw at which minors were present. His private Boeing 727 jet, upon which Bill Clinton was a regular traveler, was nicknamed the "Lolita Express." Eventually, Trump had to bar Epstein from Mar-a-Lago because Epstein allegedly assaulted an underage girl at the club.

Heather Braden also went to parties at Epstein's house, and said the girls she saw at Epstein's parties were all in their teens, and some were as young as thirteen. And though Epstein was an extreme, he was far from an anomaly in this social scene of wealthy business-men. "All these men were out trying to lure [models], get with them. It was a predatory world in a predatory market where young girls were preyed upon by these rich men," Braden said. "Trump, these types of men, are predators, exploiters. They are essentially traf-fickers. They're essentially passing girls among each other. We were used as bargaining chips, for sure."

According to a lawsuit, which was later dropped, Trump, too, had a penchant for young girls. On April 26, 2016, a woman using the alias "Katie Johnson" filed a civil lawsuit in California against Trump alleging that he raped her in 1994 at a party in Epstein's Manhattan home when she was thirteen. She wasn't represented by a lawyer and the suit was dismissed because of technical filing errors, but a similar complaint was filed in a federal court in New York on June 20, 2016, this time by a lawyer. It was later withdrawn, but was refiled that September with additional details before being withdrawn again in November. Shortly before the case was with-drawn, Johnson had canceled a scheduled press conference. Her lawyers said she had received death threats and was too afraid to appear.

According to her allegations in the lawsuit, in June 1994, John-son had taken a bus to New York to try to break in to modeling. A woman she met took her several times to Epstein's mansion. Johnson encountered Trump at multiple parties there, the suit alleged. "Each of the parties had other minor females and a number of guests of Mr. Epstein. . . . I understood that both Mr. Trump and Mr. Epstein knew I was 13 years old," the legal complaint alleged. "Defendant Trump had sexual contact with me at four different parties in the summer of 1994. On the fourth and final sexual encounter with Defendant Trump, Defendant Trump tied me to a bed, exposed himself to me and then proceeded to forcibly rape me. During the course of this savage sexual attack, I loudly pleaded with Defendant Trump to stop but he did not. Defendant Trump responded to my pleas by violently striking me in the face with his open hand and screaming that he would do whatever he wanted." The suit also said that Trump threatened to hurt the girl and her family if she ever told anyone.

When the new suit was filed in 2016, the Trump campaign dismissed the allegations against him as "categorically false, frivolous, and sanctionable."

When in July 2019, Epstein was charged in federal court with sex trafficking, authorities raided his Manhattan mansion and found hundreds of photographs of nude and semi-nude girls, some of whom appeared to be minors.

Johnson's suit contained allegations against Epstein as well, including that he raped Johnson both vaginally and anally while hitting her in the head with a closed fist because he was angry that Trump had taken her virginity instead of him. Johnson's real name has never been revealed and neither Trump nor Epstein has been given the opportunity to confront this accuser in court. Through an intermediary, she declined to be interviewed for this book.

When the allegations surfaced during the 2016 presidential campaign, news organizations wrestled with how to report them. Investigative journalist John Connolly was a coauthor of *Filthy Rich*, a book about Epstein. He said he and fellow authors James Patterson and Tim Malloy decided to leave Johnson's lawsuit out of their book. "It didn't smell right," he told us.

The story was initially shopped around to journalists by known conspiracy theorists whose behavior could seem unstable and included making harassing phone calls to reporters and apparently sending text messages posing as Katie Johnson. To complicate matters, the concealed identity of the accuser made vetting her virtually impossible. In November 2016, less than a week before the election, Johnson was expected to appear at a press conference in the Los Angeles offices of celebrity attorney Lisa Bloom, but at the scheduled time only Bloom came out to address the gathered journalists, saying the woman had received "numerous threats," including death threats, and was too afraid to speak. Bloom said her firm's website had also been hacked and that the online hacker group Anonymous had claimed responsibility. The lawsuit was withdrawn a final time just days later and, as of the writing of this book, has not been refiled.

According to sources for this book, Johnson's aborted bid to go public with her allegations may have been prevented by a last-minute deal to buy her silence, but parties acting on Johnson's behalf are still pushing her story.

Sources showed us a confidential memo that was sent to Special Counsel Robert Mueller on June 30, 2017, asking him and Deputy Attorney General Rod Rosenstein to look into the Johnson allegations as part of his investigation. A condensed version of video testimony Johnson gave was sent to Mueller.

The memo, the existence of which has not been previously publicly disclosed, contains testimony from the cameraman who filmed the interview with Johnson. "In February 2016, I was hired to film an interview with Katie Johnson in San Diego," he wrote. "Now just to be very clear, I have no personal agenda, no beef with Mr. Trump, and no political affiliations whatsoever. I was simply there as a hired gun to do what I do. Film. As the interview went on, she gave more and more graphic detail about the alleged rape. I could tell she was very upset and genuinely disturbed. She was shaking and had to compose herself several times during the interview. . . . I do not believe she was acting. I believed she was telling the truth as she saw it . . . what I saw in Ms. Johnson's interview was very convincing."

The memo was sent to Mueller but there is no indication as to what action he took. It is unclear what steps were taken to investigate the allegations.

We interviewed a person in the legal community—a Republican—who spoke with Johnson as part of her lawsuit and found her "credible." A second source who spoke to Johnson said that during their conversation she had trouble remembering details, though the source added that that is not uncommon among victims of sexual abuse. The source also reported getting strange telephone calls in which the caller would breathe down the line or simply hang up during the period the source was in touch with Johnson. While there is no evidence that the two events are connected, the calls stopped once the source ceased having contact with Johnson.

———

Eventually Trump found an easier way to surround himself with models than chasing them at bars and parties: He started his own modeling agency. "There was a certain point at which personal predilection became a business for him," Michael Gross said. "So he's hanging around models, he's hanging around model agents, he has a relationship with John Casablancas, and then he gets into the modeling business."

Beautiful young women were one more thing that Trump could put his name on, and starting the agency gave him a legitimate business reason to be out with young girls all the time. Trump Model Management launched in 1999, the same year Trump divorced Marla Maples. When Leonardo DiCaprio—another man with a taste for girls who walk the runway—heard about Trump's new venture, he approvingly dubbed it "one-stop date shopping."

Gross said that the agency was indeed a date farm, "but for yourself as well as your friends, which goes back to the transactional aspect," he said. "[Trump] is selling condos to rich guys, he knows what appeals to rich guys. It's no different than a box of Cuban cigars."

Trump Model Management went on to be a modestly successful if never particularly powerful boutique agency, and operated until just after Trump's election to the presidency in 2016. Famous models who reportedly were represented by the agency include Carol Alt, Paris Hilton, Yasmin Le Bon, Ali MacGraw, Isabella Rossellini, and Kara Young, who dated Trump for two years before he married Melania.

Now Trump had the girls coming to him and, as his father had done for him, he brought them to his sons. Ksenia Maximova said she worked for Trump Model Management in 2003 and 2004, and again a few years later. In 2004, when the Russian-British model was eighteen, her agent summoned her to a meeting in Trump Tower. "He said, 'Oh, we're just going to meet the owner of the agency,'" she said, speaking publicly for the first time about the encounter. "And then he told me to get all dressed up, properly, because I was quite tomboyish, so he did tell me to put a nice dress on and some high heels and stuff."

Maximova complied, and she and her agent rode the elevators up to Trump's offices. The developer was at his desk with Don Jr., then twenty-six, standing behind him, although they weren't introduced so Maximova didn't know Don Jr. was Trump's son. She settled on a chair, and Trump and her agent began talking. "I was just kind of sitting there," she said. Trump asked her a few little questions but for the most part didn't address her. Don Jr. was generally silent, too. "It was all really awkward because it was like, 'Let the grown-ups do the talking,' kind of thing," she said. "It was just like I didn't matter and he didn't matter. I just thought he was some aide or something." Maximova was made to feel so inconsequential that she began wondering why she had been brought there in the first place. "I didn't really get introduced much. It was more like just to actually show me, visually. It wasn't like anyone was interested in my personality or anything like that, so I was like, 'What's the point in this?'"

She asked her agent as much when they were back in the elevator on their way down to the street. "We've heard that [Trump's son] is maybe looking for a girlfriend now," Maximova's agent told her. "That's when I got really angry and told him off and asked him to never, ever, please, do this kind of thing again, especially without my consent." Maximova found the whole encounter disgusting.

Model Barbara Pilling, who went on to start her own agency in Canada, Edge Models, said there were many people in the business who wouldn't have anything to do with the Trump agency—some of them out of protectiveness and some of them for other reasons. Some of the Trump girls didn't have work visas, Pilling said, and many of the foreign girls were too young to be working legally in the United States. "You're not allowed to have a working visa unless you're a certain age, and there were so many that didn't," she said.

The Trump modeling agency closed in 2017, a few months after Trump's inauguration. During the campaign, models and staff members had started leaving the agency, many of them over Trump's divisive politics. Two days before the election, model Maggie Rizer announced her departure on Instagram. "As a woman, a mother, an American and a human being, I cannot wake up Wednesday morning being the least bit related to the Trump brand," she wrote. Shortly after his inauguration, fashion industry insiders started an unofficial boycott of Trump models, the *Guardian* reported.

FOUR

HEAD HUNTING

"I just start kissing them. It's like a magnet. Just kiss. I don't even wait.
And when you're a star, they let you do it. You can do anything. . . .
Grab 'em by the pussy. You can do anything."
—DONALD TRUMP, 2005, THE *ACCESS HOLLYWOOD* TAPE

Young girls were not the only targets of Trump's attention in the decades he spent climbing New York's social and real estate hierarchies

Back in the late 1970s, Jessica Leeds was one of the few women who flew alone for business. She had taken her seat in economy on a Braniff Airways flight from Dallas to New York when a flight attendant approached the thirty-eight-year-old newsprint saleswoman and asked if she would like to be upgraded to first class. Leeds didn't need a second invitation, and followed the airline employee to the front of the plane. She slipped into a brown leather seat next to Donald Trump.

What allegedly happened next is now well known: After introducing themselves, the two ate their dinners in silence. When the meal service was over, Trump raised the armrest between them and "suddenly turned on me and started groping me and kissing me," Leeds, now in her seventies, told us during an interview in her apartment on the Upper East Side of Manhattan. "He hadn't said anything."

Leeds recalled wondering why neither the flight attendant nor the man across the aisle intervened, though she acknowledged that she did not ask for help. She said the touching and kissing "went on for a little while, and it was when he started putting his hand up my skirt that I just ripped myself out of the seat, stood up, grabbed my purse, and went stomping to the back of the airplane," where she remained for the rest of the flight. After landing, "I stayed there and waited for the entire plane to clear because I didn't want to take the chance of running into him," she said. "I then got off the plane and went my merry way."

She didn't say much about it at the time; women who are groped or grabbed or kissed often don't, even now, and back then the culture of silence was even stronger. "When it originally happened, I didn't complain to the airlines, I didn't tell my boss. You didn't make a big deal about it," she said. "As a woman on the road then . . . you got a lot of attention from the guys. Ninety-nine percent of it was benign. But Trump was the exception, and I'll never forget it."

Leeds may have been stoic about the incident with Trump, but that's not to say she wasn't affected by it. "I was completely shocked and felt very vulnerable," she said. Also like many victims of sexual assault, Leeds vividly remembers random details of the encounter. "I had a brown wool suit on with a silk blouse that had a tie on it," she recalled. "I loved that suit. But I never wore it again."

As much as she might have wanted to put Donald Trump in her rearview mirror, she wasn't able to. One night about two years later, she was sitting behind a table handing out seat assignments at a gala being held at Saks Fifth Avenue for the Humane Society of New York, where she was working at the time, when in walked Trump. Leeds recognized him as the man who had groped her on the plane.

"Up to the table comes Donald Trump with his wife, Ivana, who was very pregnant, and I handed him his table assignment, thinking 'I remember you,'" Leeds recalled. "He looked at me, and then he said, 'I remember you,' and then he said, 'You're the cunt on the airplane.' It was like I suddenly was all by myself. It was like everyone just disappeared and I was standing there all alone. He's looking at me and I'm looking at him and I'm thinking 'Holy mackerel,' and he takes the chip and he goes on."

———

Leeds's accusation dates back to even before the birth of Ivanka, Donald's second child, when he and Ivana were ascendant in the media and there was little public sign of trouble in their marriage. If Leeds was one of the first women to feel the unwelcome embrace of Donald Trump, she was far from the last. Making unwanted physical advances became a Trump trademark, according to many women, and one that has continued to define him. The alleged assaults tended to take place in clusters, particularly around the time of his divorce from Ivana and after the births of his fourth and fifth children, Tiffany and Barron.

Leeds told a few people about the encounter during the 2016 presidential campaign, and came forward publicly by contacting the *New York Times* after Trump denied during a televised debate having ever groped anyone. She wasn't the only women to go public. In November 2016, after the *Washington Post* published an article disclosing the existence of a tape recorded in 2005 while Trump was preparing to film an episode of *Access Hollywood* in which he boasted that his fame allowed him to sexually assault women, many stories about Trump's sexual misconduct came to light. And they continue to. The accounts span nearly four decades and bear a striking resemblance to one another. Reading them in the aggregate, patterns emerge. Forcible kissing. Groping. Genital grabbing. Barging in on sleeping women. And, all too often, an utter indifference to women's volition or boundaries.

As we detail in previous and later chapters, much of Trump's alleged sexual misconduct was connected to his activities in the modeling and beauty pageant worlds. But other allegations against Trump were more random and isolated events. A number of the following stories have been told already, some with less detail; other women spoke with us for the first time. Many of the women we spoke with said they kept silent about the encounters out of shame or a fear of not being believed, and for a good number of them— though not all—their encounters with Trump were traumatic. A handful of women simply brushed off his advances without much thought, while others went on to date him.

———

In terms of timing, Jessica Leeds's accusation, dating back to the late 1970s was an outlier. The first cluster of Trump's alleged gropings dates to the early 1990s, around the time his marriage to Ivana collapsed, and starts with a young model named Kristin Anderson. She says that around that time—she hasn't given a specific year— she was out with friends at the China Club, a nightspot in the basement of the Beacon Hotel on Seventy-Fifth Street and Broadway where professional athletes from the Rangers came to party after winning the Stanley Cup in 1994 and where the Yankees celebrated after winning the 1996 World Series. Anderson, an aspiring model in her early twenties, was perched on a velvet couch in the club when a man sitting next to her slid his hand up her skirt and touched her vagina through her underwear. Shocked, she jumped up and turned to see Donald Trump, she told the *Washington Post*. She and her friends were "very grossed out and weirded out," she said. "It wasn't a sexual come-on. I don't know why he did it. It was like just to prove that he could do it and nothing would happen. There was zero conversation. We didn't even really look at each other. It was very random, very nonchalant on his part."

———

Jill Harth knows exactly when she had her first run-in with Trump: December 1992. She and her then-boyfriend George Houraney had traveled to New York from their home in Florida for a business meeting with him. The couple of thirteen years ran a small company together, American Dream Enterprise, that staged events such as music competitions, auto shows, and a "Calendar Girl" beauty contest. This was several years before Trump would make his own foray into the beauty pageant business, and the couple was hoping to do a deal with him to hold some of the events at his casinos in Atlantic City, to raise their profile. Harth and Houraney met with him in his Trump Tower offices, and during the meeting Trump allegedly asked Houraney if he was sleeping with Harth, who was thirty at the time. When Houraney said yes, Trump demanded: "Is it just for the night, or what?," according to a lawsuit Harth filed against Trump in federal court in 1997.

The next night, the three had dinner together at the Plaza hotel; Trump was dating Marla Maples at the time, but didn't bring her along. During dinner, Trump repeatedly put his hands up Harth's skirt, trying to touch "her intimate private parts," she alleged in her lawsuit. "You know, there's going to be a problem," he told Houraney that night. "I'm very attracted to your girlfriend." The couple returned to Florida, but Trump continued to call Harth, telling her he wanted to sleep with her.

The couple and Trump agreed to work together, and the following month he invited them to Mar-a-Lago, his Palm Beach estate, for a dinner to celebrate their new partnership. He asked them to bring some "Calendar Girls" with them (Harth's lawsuit alleges Trump asked them not to include any black contestants). While giving Harth a tour of the estate that evening, he allegedly pinned her against the wall of his daughter Ivanka's bedroom. Harth said she had been studying the decor of the opulant room, the centerpiece of which was an intricately carved gilded canopy bed enclosed in cream shantung silk edged in little pom-poms, and was stunned when Trump started kissing and groping her, "touching her intimately," according to the court filing. "It was a shock," Harth said in 2016. "I pushed him off me. And I was, I said to him, 'What are you doing? Why are you doing this?'" Trump was twice her weight, and she was worried he would rape her. She was so fearful that she began vomiting profusely as a defense mechanism. She felt "degraded and humiliated as a female," the lawsuit said. She ran out of the room.

Harth thinks Trump couldn't believe she was resisting him. "Donald gets what he wants," she said in a 2016 interview. "I believe, in his mind, he was—this was a come-on for him, some kind of romantic overture. Whereas for me, it was unwanted and aggressive, very sexually aggressive."

Harth and Houraney had planned to spend the night at Mar-a-Lago, as had some of the "Calendar Girls," but after Trump forced himself on Harth, she wanted to get out of there, so she and Houraney left. Evidently unchastened, Trump started stalking Harth, according to her account, urging her to leave Houraney. "He constantly called me and said: 'I love you, baby, I'm going to be the best lover you ever had. What are you doing with that loser, you need to be with me, you need to step it up to the big leagues,'" Harth said. His apparent desire for her didn't stop him from asking her to provide him with "access" to a seventeen-year-old beauty contestant from Czechoslovakia, the lawsuit alleges. The lawsuit also says that

Trump called some of the "Calendar Girls" over a period of several years, offering career advancement in exchange for sexual favors. Harth's lawsuit said he harassed her for six years.

Harth wasn't the only woman who had had an unwanted encounter with Trump the night of the "Calendar Girl" party, her lawsuit contended. After Harth and Houraney's departure, some of the women who had come with them stayed and spent the night as originally planned. In the predawn hours, Trump allegedly snuck, uninvited, into a room where one of the women was sleeping, just as he had allegedly done with the supermodel in the Plaza hotel. This time, though, there was no man in his way, so he crept into her bed. "You said you don't sleep with men on the first date," Trump allegedly told her. "Now it's the second date and here I am!" She managed to kick him out

During the course of their business partnership, Harth had multiple business meetings with Trump, and he continued "to try to jump her," Nicholas Kristof wrote in a *New York Times* column based on an interview with Harth in 2016. "He'd say, 'Let's go in my room, I want to lie down,' and he'd pull me along," Harth told Kristof. "I'd say, 'I don't want to lie down,' and it would turn into a wrestling match. . . . I remember yelling, 'I didn't come here for this.' He'd say, 'Just calm down.'"

Trump ended up walking away from the partnership, and in 1995, the same year Houraney and Harth married, he filed a breach of contract lawsuit against Trump that also included Harth's allegations of sexual harassment. In April 1997, Harth filed a second lawsuit, later withdrawn, which alleged that Trump had sexually harassed her and wanted her to be a "sex slave." At the time, Trump and Houraney were negotiating an agreement on the first lawsuit, and one of the conditions of that settlement was that Harth withdraw her legal action, which she did. In July 1997 Trump and Houraney reached a deal.

After the settlement, Trump invited the couple to a party, at which he was so charming they thought maybe he had changed, Kristof wrote. When the couple divorced not long after, Trump started calling Harth again. In 1998, newly single and trying to find a job and rebuild her life, Harth started dating him. He was separated from Maples at the time.

Kristof asked Harth why she would date a man who allegedly had harassed her and, according to her lawsuit, tried to rape her. "I was scared, thinking, 'what am I going to do now?'" she claimed. "When he called me and tried to work on me again, I was thinking maybe I should give this a try, maybe if he's still working on me, I should give this rich guy a chance." But Harth found Trump "a disappointing boyfriend, always watching television and rarely offering emotional support," Kristof wrote. Trump wasn't able to give her what she needed. "It was a hard divorce, and I was in a nonstop crying jag," Harth told Kristof. "You know what he was thinking? He wanted me to get a boob job. He made an appointment for me to get a boob job, a doctor in Miami." Harth stopped seeing Trump, although years later she tried to get a job on his presidential campaign.

———

In either the fall of 1995 or the spring of 1996, the advice columnist E. Jean Carroll claims that she was making her way out of the Bergdorf Goodman department store on Fifth Avenue when she ran into Donald Trump. "I am surprised at how good looking he is," she recalled in *New York*. Trump told her that he needed to buy a present for someone and asked her to help him. She agreed and the two made their way to the lingerie section. He picked up a see-through lilac-gray lace bodysuit and ordered her to try it on. Bantering, she told him it was his color and insisted that *he* should try it on. The two jokingly made their way to a dressing room, and things got serious.

"The moment the dressing-room door is closed, he lunges at me, pushes me against the wall, hitting my head quite badly, and puts his mouth against my lips," Carroll wrote. She was shocked, but continued laughing. "The next moment, still wearing correct business attire, shirt, tie, suit jacket, overcoat, he opens the overcoat, unzips his pants, and, forcing his fingers around my private area, thrusts his penis halfway—or completely, I'm not certain—inside me."

After a struggle, Carroll managed to push Trump off her, she wrote, and fled.

When Carroll's allegations were published in June 2019, Trump denied them. "She's not my type," he said.

———

Entrepreneur Lisa Boyne accepted an invitation from her pal Sonja Morgan (now of *Real Housewives of New York* fame) in 1996 and found herself at dinner with Trump, with whom Morgan had been friends dating back to his marriage with Ivana. For Boyne, the evening was unpleasant from the moment Trump picked her up in his limo. "He was a douche bag," she told us. "He took all the air out of the limo. He wouldn't let anyone talk." They got to Raoul's, a French bistro and celebrity haunt in SoHo that the New York glitterati "made their living room" for decades, in the words of the *New York Times*. Boyne and her party slid into a booth in the back corner under a huge painting of a nude woman lying on her back, her arm flung across her head and obscuring her face. Trump sat at one end and renowned modeling agent John Casablancas at the other. "When we got to the restaurant . . . John Casablancas sits down," Boyne recounted to us. Boyne said she knew who Casablancas was due to his public affair with Stephanie Seymour, whose relationship with him began when he was forty-two and she was sixteen. Boyne said she found Casablancas "creepy." Boyne, Morgan, and a handful of models were sandwiched between the two men.

Trump started asking Boyne which of the models she thought he should sleep with. "This is a conversation I felt like I was having with a twelve-year-old boy," she said. "'Who do you think the hottest girl is?' 'Rate all these women I'm dating.'" Trump didn't hit on Boyne. "I'm not a model. He wasn't interested in me," she told the *Huffington Post*.

If the women wanted to get out of the booth, the men made them walk across the table. Trump "stuck his head right under the women's skirts" and commented on whether or not they were wearing underwear and on their genitalia, Boyne told the *Huffington Post*. "It was the most offensive scene I've ever been a part of. I wanted to get the heck out of there." Boyne says she left before the appetizers arrived.

In the spring of 1997, Cathy Heller was at Mar-a-Lago with her husband, her three kids, and her in-laws for Mother's Day brunch. Trump came over to their table to greet them, just as he had the other guests. Heller stood up, planning to shake his hand. "He took my hand, grabbed me, and went for the lips," she said. Heller turned her head when she realized what was happening, so his kiss landed on the side of her mouth. Trump was angry that she had twisted away, and walked off. "I remember she was really freaked out," said another relative who was at the brunch. "He was very forceful."

Karena Virginia's incident with Trump took place in the late summer of 1998, shortly before he met third wife Melania. Virginia was waiting for a car to pick her up from the 1998 US Open.

The twenty-seven-year-old pharmaceutical rep had brought some clients there and was leaving the grounds of the tournament when she encountered Trump. "Hey, look at this one. We haven't seen her before," Trump said to the men he was with, Virginia recounted at a 2016 press conference with lawyer Gloria Allred, who represents several of Trump's accusers. Virginia said Trump walked up to her, put his arm around her, and grabbed her breast. "I felt intimidated and powerless," she said. Her car arrived and she got in and left.

———

The period before Trump proposed to Melania brought another wave of allegedly unwanted touching from Trump. One of those incidents happened during a Mar-a-Lago New Year's Eve party in the early 2000s. Karen Johnson spoke publicly about the events of that night for the first time in an interview with us. Johnson said she was at Trump's Palm Beach estate that night with her husband, who was suffering from multiple sclerosis, and another relative. The family visited the seaside club regularly; Johnson and her husband had even held their wedding reception there a few years earlier. Trump, whom she didn't know before her wedding, had "chased some of my bridesmaids around," said Johnson, but he had been "nice" to her.

At the New Year's Eve party, Johnson, wearing a black Versace dress, danced with her friends. Shortly after glittering balloons fell from the ceiling at the stroke of midnight, her husband said he wasn't feeling well and the relative was ready to go. Johnson decided to make a quick trip to the restroom before they headed home. "I hadn't seen [Trump] that whole entire night," said Johnson, who was in her late thirties at the time. "I was just walking to the bathroom. I was grabbed and pulled behind a tapestry, and it was him. And I'm a tall girl and I had six-inch heels on, and I still remember looking up at him. And he's strong, and he just kissed me," she recounted to us. "I was so scared because of who he was. . . . I don't even know where it came from. I didn't have a say in the matter."

Johnson said Trump then grabbed her hand and said, "You have to help me greet these guests out," explaining that Melania was upstairs. "So I stood next to him while he greeted some guests out the door," Johnson said. She didn't let on that anything was amiss because she didn't want to create an awkward situation. "I was afraid to say what had happened," she said. "I didn't even know how it happened."

Documentation and photographs further corroborate Johnson's description of the evening. A friend also said Johnson told him about the encounter years before Trump ran for office.

In the days after the incident, Trump began pursuing Johnson. "He started calling me. I answered my phone and he said, 'Do you know who this is?' And I knew his voice. And I was wondering how he got my phone number," she said. He called her regularly for the next week or two, she told us, offering to fly her up to New York to visit him. Johnson told Trump she couldn't because she was taking care of her dying husband. "Don't worry about it, he'll never know you were gone," she said Trump told her. "He said he'd have me back by six o'clock. This was like crazy. He was going to fly me to New York for the day to see him. I said, 'No, no, no.'" But Trump persisted. When he was in Florida, he called and said he would send a car to bring her to Mar-a-Lago. "I kept saying, 'No, no, no,'" she said. "I was scared. I didn't know what to do."

In time, Johnson said, the calls stopped. She never went back to Mar-a-Lago. She eventually told the relative who was with her at the New Year's Eve party what had happened, but she never told her dying husband.

Years later, Johnson was shocked to hear Trump describing on the *Access Hollywood* tape exactly what he had done to her. "When he says that thing, 'Grab them in the pussy,' that hits me hard because when he grabbed me and pulled me into the tapestry, that's where he grabbed me—he grabbed me there in my front and pulled me in," she told us.

———

In 2003, Melinda "Mindy" McGillivray was working as an assistant for a photographer friend of hers at a Ray Charles concert at Mar-a-Lago and was backstage with a small group that included Trump and Melania. "The next thing you know I feel a grab," she told Megyn Kelly on NBC's *Today* show. "I stand there, I'm stunned. I'm speechless. I don't even know what to do or say in that moment." She elaborated to the BBC: "It was like someone was trying to feel whether a fruit was ripe at the store." It made her feel "violated, entirely violated," she said. "To see someone who resembled my father grab me like that was just deplorable." The encounter left her feeling overlooked and unimportant. "He didn't even acknowledge me," McGillivray, who was twenty-three at the time, told Kelly. "It made me feel very small, inferior. It made me feel like I was objectified."

It was in 2005, however, the year that Trump married Melania and she became pregnant with their son Barron, that the bulk of the alleged sexual assaults that were made public during and after Trump's presidential campaign took place. Rachel Crooks was a lanky, athletic, six-foot-tall twenty-two-year-old who had recently moved to New York from her hometown in Green Springs, Ohio, and was working as a receptionist that year in the Bayrock Group offices on the twenty-fourth floor of Trump Tower. Crooks said she often saw Trump walk past the glass doors of her office on his way to the building's residential elevator, and the two had waved to one another a few times. One morning, she decided to introduce herself to him. "I don't know what motivated me," she told us in an interview at her sister's house in Ohio. "I just remember feeling very confident. Like, he does business with Bayrock. He knows everyone in the office but me. There's no reason he shouldn't know me—I thought it was awkward. We had seen each other regularly through the door, so I just went up to him outside the elevator."

She said she offered Trump her hand to shake. He grasped it and held it in the air as he started kissing her, first on one cheek, then on the other. "He kept asking me questions and then pulling me and doing it again," she said. "He asked where I was from and said, 'Oh you should be modeling. I have my own modeling agency.'" Crooks said she hardly had time to react. "It happened so quickly. I was just so surprised. I didn't understand what he was trying to do. Ultimately, he pulled me in and kissed me on the lips, and I was very upset. The only thing I can think that ended the encounter was that his elevator arrived, thankfully."

Crooks had been totally unprepared for Trump's advances. "I didn't have any notion of him being the womanizer he is," she said. "I just thought he was a successful New York businessman." She ran into an empty office and called her sister. "Nothing like that had ever happened to me."

Sometime later, Crooks said, Trump went into the Bayrock office and asked for her phone number. She asked him what he needed it for, and he said he wanted to give it to his modeling agency. "That was the last time I personally interacted with him," she said. "Any other time after that I just resorted to, if I saw him coming down the hall to the elevator, the kitchenette was right over here so I would leave my desk and go. But it was hard because I was answering the phones and I was tied to the desk. I just tried to be out of sight." Crooks never heard from the modeling agency.

———

Jennifer Murphy was in Trump's office for an interview that same year. She had competed in one of his beauty pageants and had been a contestant on *The Apprentice* and was looking for a job. When their conversation was over, Trump accompanied Murphy, in her mid-twenties, out. "He walked me to the elevator, and I said goodbye," she told *Grazia* magazine in 2016. "I was thinking, 'Oh, he's going to hug me.'" Instead, he pulled her face in and kissed her on the lips. "I was very taken aback by that at the time," she told *Grazia*, although she later told CNN's Erin Burnett, "It didn't really bother me."

And it was also in 2005 that Juliet Huddy had lunch with Trump. When he and the former Fox News anchor had finished their meal in Trump Tower, he planted one on her lips, too. "He said goodbye to me in an elevator while his security guy was there," Huddy said in a December 2017 interview. "Rather than kiss me on the cheek he leaned in to kiss me on the lips." But she wasn't particularly put out, either. "I wasn't offended," she said.

Proximity to his new wife doesn't seem to have been much of a deterrent for Trump that year. Natasha Stoynoff had gone to Mar-a-Lago on assignment for *People* to interview Donald and Melania together for a feature story marking their one-year wedding anniversary. Melania was very pregnant at the time. When she took a break to change into a different outfit for more photos, Trump told Stoynoff there was a "tremendous" room in the mansion he wanted to show her. "We walked into that room alone, and Trump shut the door behind us," Stoynoff recounted in a 2016 article in *People*. "I turned around, and within seconds he was pushing me against the wall and forcing his tongue down my throat."

Trump was big and fast, Stoynoff said. She says she was saved by a butler who came into the room to tell Donald that Melania was on her way down to resume the interview. "I was still in shock and remained speechless as we both followed him to an outdoor patio overlooking the grounds," Stoynoff wrote. "In those few minutes alone with Trump, my self-esteem crashed to zero. How could the actions of one man make me feel so utterly violated?"

Trump seemed oblivious to the emotional damage he had wrought. "You know we're going to have an affair, don't you?" he said to Stoynoff while settling on a love seat and waiting for Melania to join him. "Have you ever been to Peter Luger's for steaks? I'll take you. We're going to have an affair, I'm telling you." Melania returned and Trump went back to playing the devoted husband.

Barron Trump was born in early 2006; that year Ninni Laaksonen, Miss Finland 2006, appeared on *The Late Show with David Letterman* in New York with Trump and three other Miss Universe contestants. As they were being photographed outside before the show, Trump groped her, she told the Finnish newspaper *Ilta-Sanomat*. "Trump stood right next to me and suddenly he squeezed my butt. He really grabbed my butt," she said, according to a translation of the Finnish article in *The Telegraph*. "I don't think anybody saw it but I flinched and thought: 'What is happening?'"

As Trump's fame grew as a result of the success of his reality show *The Apprentice,* which first aired in 2004, stories of Trump groping women in public diminish. One former *Apprentice* contestant, Summer Zervos, says that Trump assaulted her in private settings on several occasions in 2007, however. The first time was when the former contestant met Trump in his office to get career advice. He kissed her multiple times on the lips without her consent, she said in a press conference with Gloria Allred. According to her account, Trump called her several times after that meeting. The two then met at the Beverly Hills Hotel. Zervos thought they would be going to a restaurant for dinner to discuss business opportunities, but instead she was escorted by staff to one of the bungalows, where Trump was evidently staying. In the hotel suite, he immediately started kissing her with an open mouth, she contends.

Zervos walked away from Trump and sat in a chair and tried to strike up a conversation. He asked her to come sit next to him, and when she did he grabbed her shoulder, started kissing her aggressively, and put his hand on her breast, she said at the press conference. She got up, and he tried to pull her into the bedroom, saying, "Let's lay down and watch some telly telly," Zervos recounted. He put her in an embrace and she tried to push him away, saying, "Come on, man, get real." He mimicked Zervos's words back to her while "thrusting his genitals" at her, she said. When Trump denied her allegations and called her a "liar," she filed a defamation lawsuit against him, which, as of June 2019, his lawyers continued to fight.

More recently, another woman filed a lawsuit against President Trump, this one for a sexual assault that allegedly happened during his presidential bid. Alva Johnson, who had joined the Trump campaign in 2016 in Alabama, working as director of outreach for the state, had gone to Florida to manage the recreational vehicles that served as their mobile offices there. Trump had come to Florida for a rally on August 24, 2016, and was in one of the RVs taking pictures with volunteers. He was trying to make eye contact with her, she noticed, so she spoke to him when he passed her on his way out of the vehicle. "I've been on the road for you since March, away from my family," she told him, according to a lawsuit she filed against him in February 2019, which was first reported in the *Washington Post* and the *New Yorker*. "You're doing an awesome job. Go in there and kick ass."

Trump "grasped her hand and did not let go," the lawsuit alleges. He leaned toward her, "close enough that she could feel his breath on her skin," the suit says. "He's coming straight for my lips," she said. "So I turn my head, and he kisses me right on the corner of my mouth, still holding my hand the entire time. Then he walks out." Johnson called her boyfriend, her stepfather, and her mother to tell them what happened. "She was hysterical," her mother told the *Washington Post*. Other campaign employees who had been in the RV at the time said they didn't see what Johnson described and dismissed her allegations. She continued to work for Trump through his election, attended an inaugural ball, and applied for two jobs in the administration, neither of which she was given.

The action was dismissed by a federal judge, who said he found the lawsuit to be too political but said her lawyers could redraft the case and could continue with discovery. Trump's lawyers later released a video of him kissing Johnson on the cheek that both sides say corroborates their version of events.

————

Trump has repeatedly denied all of the accusations in this chapter that had previously been made public. He has said the sexual misconduct allegations against him are made up and politically motivated. He has accused women who have made accusations against him of seeking fame. He has said the allegations don't make sense—he never would have been in a nightclub alone, for example, or that an accuser is not physically attractive enough to warrant his attention. "Look at her. I don't think so," he said of one. "Believe me, she would not be my first choice," of another. But what hurts accusers even more than Trump's verbal assaults is being treated as though they are worthless.

Being touched "like you're some kind of stuffed animal on the couch" makes a woman feel "inconsequential," said Kristin Anderson of her encounter with Trump at the China Club. "It's really not nothing, and it sends an awful message to women that they're nothing." Sexual misconduct makes women question themselves. "The stigma of abuse is very real," Anderson said. It can be quite embarrassing to reveal how you somehow found your sweet self in the middle of a big, bad, abusive mess. It is far easier to just keep quiet, ignore it, and move on, but not in the long run."

"I really felt like I must be putting out this vibe that he thinks he can do this," Rachel Crooks said she thought after Trump kissed her outside her office in Trump Tower. "I didn't really think about his thought process. It was much more that I was embarrassed that he thought I was so insignificant or that I was putting off this dumb-girl vibe. That was my thought process, that he thinks I'm just some dumb bimbo looking to meet him for money."

When Karena Virginia talks about being groped by Trump at the US Open, the word *shame* comes up repeatedly. She felt shame when it happened and shame when she came forward, she told the *New Yorker*. She worried about how she dressed after Trump grabbed her breast, hoping to avoid attracting any more unwanted attention, she said in the *Huffington Post*.

Karen Johnson, who alleged that Trump groped her and grabbed her by the genitals at the New Year's Eve party at Mar-a-Lago, hesitated to tell anyone about her experience. "I feared that because I had been a dancer many years before they would say to me, 'Well, you must have asked for it,'" she told us. "What he did was very traumatizing to me," Johnson added. "And it still is. You know, I didn't ask for that. I was literally just walking through a room . . . no matter what my past is I don't deserve to be treated that way." Despite her fears about not being believed, she is clear that she didn't bring the assault on herself. "This is about a monster, an immature child running around who has no respect for anybody but himself and his giant ego," she said.

As one of the oldest accusers, Jessica Leeds has some perspective. "I spout off about a lot of these men [who are accused of sexual impropriety], and a lot of them are wealthy, powerful, or consider themselves important. They work for major companies. For them it's like scratching an itch. It doesn't mean anything. But the psychological damage they can do to the person they are inflicting aggression on is profound."

Jill Harth may well have been right when she said Trump thought of his actions as a romantic overture. The accounts of the women he interacted with paint a picture of someone who either does not realize his advances might not be welcome or does not care, someone who sees women as objects with no agency and whose desires are of no consequence.

"To me, this is a feature of his narcissism or maybe his sociopathy, that he doesn't seem to care what kind of an impact he's having," said Dr. Sue Kolod.

"They aren't real people, they're like cardboard characters dressed up in beautiful bodies," Dr. Justin Frank said. "It has to do with his lack of empathy and a disregard for women's boundaries." That kind of dehumanization is at the core of predatory behavior, Frank said. A trait of sexual predators is that "they have no concern about the effect they have on somebody else, they have no concern about the damage they do," Frank said. By turning women into objects, Trump can liberate himself from needing to consider the impact of his actions. "He really is free from any kind of guilt or concern."

FIVE

ICARUS FALLS

"It's all in the hunt and once you get it, it loses some of its energy."
—DONALD TRUMP, 2005, IN *TRUMP NATION*

There had been whispers, of course. Buzz about relationships with Catherine Oxenberg; Robin Givens; Peggy Fleming; Carol Alt; Carolyne Roehm, wife of businessman Henry Kravis; Georgette Mosbacher, who was married to businessman and politician Robert Mosbacher, and others. By 1989 there was seemingly enough smoke to give Ivana Trump reason to at least start looking for the fire extinguisher; instead, she turned a blind eye. "[Gossip columnist] Cindy Adams had asked me if the rumors were true, that Donald was cheating on me," Ivana wrote in her 2017 book, *Raising Trump*. "I was so angry that she'd even suggest it that I didn't speak to her again for years. Apart from gossip, which you always have to take with a kilo of salt, I had no reason to suspect him of straying. Donald hadn't lost weight or changed his hair. He wasn't dressing better or making mysterious charges on the credit card. He acted exactly the same as he always had at home."

Ivana acknowledged in her book that she, too, had heard the chatter, but wrote that she hadn't seen any other evidence of Donald's infidelity. And she had already dismissed so much: the insults, the pressure in 1987 to sign a new prenup, even her husband's repeated suggestion, starting as early as 1986, that he would like to have an open marriage. She brushed it all off—until a point.

That breaking point had a name: Marla Maples, or, as Ivana prefers to call her, "the Showgirl." Ivana says Trump's affair with Maples, a model and aspiring actress, was the final straw for her marriage because her trust was broken. "Trust, for me, is everything," she told ABC News in a 2017 interview.

How and when Trump met Maples, who had been her high school's homecoming queen, was 1984 runner-up for Miss Georgia USA, and won the 1985 Miss Hawaiian Tropic "bikini contest," is unclear. Trump had reason to be vague about their meeting, because the timing of it could have been the difference between whether the 1987 prenup he had Ivana sign would be valid or not.

The stories of Trump's first encounter with Maples, who was born in 1963 and is seventeen years his junior, are myriad. Maples said on *The View* that she met Trump when she was twenty. The *New York Post* reported that they met at a tennis match in Atlantic City in 1985 but started their affair two years later. Trump biographer Michael D'Antonio said Maples was introduced to Trump in 1985 by former sports agent Jerry Argovitz, who had been a judge in the Hawaiian Tropics pageant and had brought her to Trump Tower.

Maples's former manager, Chuck Jones, dates their relationship to 1987. In an interview for this book, Jones said that Maples hung around Trump Tower hoping to meet the real estate titan and eventually wound up bumping into him on the street, but they didn't really get acquainted until later. "It was his wealth and his fame. She had apparently been doing her homework on him," said Jones, who would later go to jail for breaking into Maples's house and stealing dozens of her shoes and boots and who, years after that incident, was also convicted of harassing her.

According to Jones, Maples had learned that another Jones client, Lionel Hampton, was going to be performing at the Rainbow Room in December 1987, and she asked Jones to get her in. "She said, 'Well I want to meet Donald Trump. And he's going to be there,'" said Jones, who has rarely spoken publicly about Maples since serving his sentence. "And I said, 'Marla, Trump's married! Her name's Ivana.' And she said, 'Not for long.'"

Nevertheless, Jones brought Maples to the event. They were sitting at a table with Hampton and Rainbow Room manager Tony May when Trump and Ivana walked in. "They sat in a table right across from our table," Jones said. "The dance floor was in between. And right away, [Trump's] eyes lit up when he saw Maples."

Maples wrote her number on a piece of paper and slipped it into Trump's pocket, Jones said, but Trump didn't notice. He was intrigued enough by her, however, that when he went to his office the next day, he ordered his assistant Norma Foederer to track down Maples's contact information, not realizing he already had it. Two weeks later, according to Jones, Maples called him from the St. Moritz hotel on Central Park South, which Trump owned at the time. "I said, 'Marla, who's paying for this?'" Jones recalled. "And she said, 'I've got to tell you. I met Donald Trump. And I'm staying here as his guest.'"

Jones's account differs from the most widely disseminated version of the Trump-Maples courtship, which has them spotting one another on the street and then starting up a telephone relationship before they begin meeting in person, reportedly on occasion in the pews of the Marble Collegiate Church, the same place where Trump made his vows to Ivana. When Trump and Marla's relationship became a sexual one is anyone's guess, but "by '88 I knew I truly loved this guy," Maples once told *New York*.

The couple tried to be discreet, at least at first. When Maples attended the 1987 boxing match between Mike Tyson and Tyrell Biggs at the Trump Plaza in Atlantic City, she did so accompanied by her ex-boyfriend Tom Fitzsimmons, a former New York policeman who worked as Trump's bodyguard for a while and regularly served as cover for their relationship. Trump also enlisted Alan Lapidus, the architect on the Trump Plaza Hotel and Casino, as a beard, as well as others in his employ. Lapidus recalled having dinner with Marla one evening and then driving off with her in a limousine. After traveling a few blocks, the car pulled up next to an identical one, in which sat Trump. Marla switched cars and Lapidus went home to his wife. "Donald used a lot of us that way," Jack O'Donnell, former president and chief operating officer of Trump Plaza, said in an interview for *The Trump Dynasty* documentary on the A&E network.

Trump put Marla up in various Trump properties, from the St. Moritz hotel in Manhattan to the Trump Castle in Atlantic City, so he could easily see her on the sly. "We wound up comping all of her services and stays and food, whatever it might be," O'Donnell said. Sometimes Marla would attend events he was at with Ivana, with a date as cover. For a while, Trump thought he had it all. "Beautiful wife, beautiful girlfriend, everything beautiful," he told Nancy Collins of *Primetime Live* in 1994. "Life was a bowl of cherries."

In March 1988, Trump fulfilled a long-held dream of his by buying the Plaza hotel in Manhattan and, a few months later, he installed Ivana as president. No longer having to worry that his wife might turn up in Atlantic City at any minute, Trump started getting careless about being seen with Marla there. That June, at the Mike Tyson–Michael Spinks boxing match in Atlantic City, they sat in the same row, with only Fitzsimmons between them. In photos taken that evening, they both lean in toward Fitzsimmons, making it clear they are all there together. Indeed, a month later the *New York Post* ran an item saying that a "shapely blonde" had been seeing a married New York tycoon and had been shopping in the stores in Trump Tower telling shopkeepers to "charge it to Donald."

That same month, *Penthouse* publisher Bob Guccione tried to blackmail Trump, threatening to expose his affair with Maples unless he stopped trying to block the sale of a $40 million Atlantic City property to a Trump rival, according to a lawsuit written about David Cay Johnston, Pulitzer Prize–winning journalist, author, and Trump biographer, when he was covering the Atlantic City casino industry for the *Philadelphia Inquirer* in the late 1980s and early 1990s.

Trump was seen out and about with Maples in Atlantic City so frequently that their relationship had become an open secret. "It wasn't a very well-kept secret in Atlantic City," O'Donnell said. "Let's face it, when the room service guy goes up to deliver dinner for two and Donald Trump is one of the people, the secret doesn't last long."

"I learned about Marla Maples nine months or so before it became public," Johnston told us in an interview at a New York hotel. "I saw her in Trump Plaza with security people and went, 'Who's that?' And Trump's guys trusted me enough that they told me. . . . And I knew his marriage to Ivana was in big trouble." Johnston decided not to publish the scoop because his beat was business, not gossip, and, as he put it: "Purported billionaire, rich guy, has a girlfriend. If there's a news story it's rich guy *doesn't* have a mistress."

But he was right about what it signaled for Trump's marriage to Ivana, which had been deteriorating in public view. In a *Vanity Fair* article written during the couple's separation, longtime Trump chronicler Marie Brenner reported that, starting in the mid-1980s, the two "never seemed to touch each other or exchange intimate remarks in public." And while Ivana had continued to be laudatory of her husband, he no longer lapped up her devotion. "He seemed to be tired of hearing Ivana's endless praise; her subservient quality appeared to be getting to him," the article noted. Ivana, on the other hand, said she didn't notice her husband's disaffection. "I really wasn't aware of growing apart," she told Barbara Walters in a 1991 interview. "I wasn't aware of problems. Every marriage takes a give-and-take."

That's what she said publicly. The private story was another one entirely. Despite her outraged reply to Cindy Adams, Ivana had had enough misgivings of her own to pay New York's celebrity divorce attorney Raoul Felder a visit in 1989. "I can say that she didn't have anything bad to say about him," Felder told us in an interview in his memorabilia-laden Madison Avenue office. "But it was about a potential divorce." Ivana admitted to Felder that she was having private investigators follow her husband.

Whatever her motivation for seeing Felder, Ivana didn't file for divorce after their meeting. And Trump continued his affair with Maples. In the summer of 1989, Trump moved her into his yacht, the *Trump Princess*. "Donald was not really very discreet about it," said Roger Gross, managing editor of *Casino Journal*. "He had her stay on the *Trump Princess* all summer except when Ivana came." Later that year, when Marla needed new digs, Trump temporarily moved her into Trump Tower, into an apartment just four floors below the triplex he shared with Ivana and their children. And in mid-December he took her to a Rolling Stones concert. Her usual beard, Fitzsimmons, had his own date. Although Marla walked in a few feet behind Donald, it became clear that the two were together.

That fall, the Trump Organization suffered a major tragedy. On October 10, 1989, three top Trump executives—Atlantic City gaming division chief Stephen Hyde, Trump Sports and Entertainment president Mark Grossinger Etess, and Trump Plaza executive vice president Jon Benanav—had taken a helicopter into Manhattan for a meeting with Trump. On their way back to Atlantic City, the helicopter they chartered crashed, killing everyone on board. Trump learned of the accident when a reporter called him to get his reaction. Members from his staff gathered in his office, as the calls from journalists kept coming. With a reporter on speakerphone set on mute, Trump turned to a vice president who was in his office and said, "You're going to hate me for this, but I just can't resist. I can get some publicity out of this." As recounted in Harry Hurt's book *Lost Tycoon*, Trump took the phone off mute and told the reporter he had intended to get on the helicopter with his executives but had changed his mind at the last minute. The New York *Daily News* splashed the story of Trump's supposed close brush with death on its front page the next day.

That was around the same time that Trump's overleveraged empire started taking on water. He was accruing staggering amounts of debt, which would swell to $3.4 billion by 1990, much of it in the form of junk bonds. His personal stake was $832.5 million, according to the *New York Times*. His yacht was losing money. The Plaza hotel was losing money. His airline was losing money. The Castle Casino, Trump Regency, and Trump Plaza Casino in Atlantic City were all losing money. His empire was on the verge of collapse.

Amid the business turmoil, Trump grew bolder in his outings with Maples. That December, he spent Christmas with his extended family at his parents' house in Queens and, the next day, sent Ivana and the kids to Aspen on their annual ski trip. He told Ivana he had some work to do and would join her in a few days. Instead, on December 27, he flew a Trump-branded 727 down to Chattanooga,

Tennessee, where he was greeted by Maples's clan. He agreed to pose for group photos with them, Hurt wrote.

A few hours later, Trump and Maples jetted off to Aspen, the town where he had first wooed Ivana. He secreted Maples in a condo not far from the hotel his family occupied. Bringing his mistress to Aspen was a fateful decision that would result in a confrontation between his wife and mistress that was the best Christmas gift that New York gossip pages could ever have wished for.

————

The legendary Marla-Ivana showdown took place on December 30, 1989, a day before the thirteenth anniversary of Trump's proposal of marriage to Ivana. She had gotten a hint of what was coming a day earlier when she picked up the phone in their hotel and heard Donald on an extension. "He was talking about Marla," Ivana said later in an interview with Barbara Walters. "And I really didn't understand. I never heard a name like that in my life. And I came to Donald. I said, 'Who is Moola?' And he said, 'Well, that's a girl which is going after me for last two years.' And I said, 'Is that serious?' And he said, 'Oh, she's just going after me.'"

The day of the confrontation, Ivana was skiing and saw Donald with a dark-haired woman, whom Walters said Ivana was told was a friend of "Moola's." Later that day, Ivana and Donald were having lunch at a mid-mountain eatery called Bonnie's when she spotted the same woman in the food line. "I said, 'I understand from my husband that you have a friend which is after my husband for last two years,'" Ivana told Walters. "I says, 'Will you give the message that I love my husband very much.' And that was it and I walk outside. And I didn't know this Marla was standing behind this girl in line but because I never met her, I had no idea. And Marla just charged right behind me."

The ensuing exchange between the women has been widely documented, including by the two of them.

"Do you love your husband?" Marla asked the stunned Czech, whose kids were next to her watching the encounter. "Because I do."

Ivana says that she responded by saying: "Get lost. I love my husband." According to several media accounts, what she actually said was: "You bitch, leave my husband alone."

If the scales fell from Ivana's eyes in that moment, Maples had her own revelation. "When we saw each other in Colorado, Ivana and I, it was just a moment of both of us wanting to know the truth," Maples later told *New York*. "It was good that the truth became known, but that was also when the real pain began. I realized that we had both been deceived."

The confrontation may have been devastating for the two women involved, but Trump seemed decidedly less emotional about it when he described it to Nancy Collins during the *Primetime* interview. "Ivana and I were standing near the restaurant putting on our skis when Marla came out of Bonnie's and suddenly the two women were standing next to each other," he recounted. "You could tell there was conflict, friction, but no hair pulling. I'm standing there like an idiot and this not very attractive man, probably three hundred pounds, says to me: 'It could be worse, Donald. I've been in Aspen for twenty years and never had a date,' which really gave me perspective."

After all the years Donald and Ivana Trump had spent chasing press ink, the media wasn't about to turn away from this story. The *Chicago Tribune* published a version quoting a decorator who said he saw Ivana and Donald walking away from Bonnie's together. "She was talking and he was trying to shush her," the bystander told the paper. "They both stopped to put on their skis. . . . She was facing us and he had his back to us and it's now clear that they're fighting. She's waving her hands and yelling at him. And now every-body decides, 'This is interesting,' and we all go over to the railing. It goes on for twenty-five minutes. It went on forever! Every now and then she tried to make up and put her arms around him, but he pulled back, he wouldn't respond. He finally skied off, and everyone started clapping and cheering. She smiled and waved to the crowd and skied away in his direction. But then I saw them near the next lift and they were still going at it."

People published a slightly more tongue-in-cheek rendition. "Trump, who was sitting within earshot putting on his skis, took off down the mountain," the magazine wrote. "Wrong move: Ivana is an excellent skier; Donald is not. When the formidable Czech pushed off in hot pursuit, fascinated observers swear they saw her whip in front of Donald and then ski backwards down the slopes, wagging her finger in his face."

What was entertainment for the rest of the world was devastating for Ivana. "I was shattered and shocked," she wrote in her book. "Put-ting on a brave front for the kids during those first few days was one of the hardest things I've ever done." When she and Trump returned to Manhattan, they initially continued to share a bed, she wrote.

Around the same time, *Playboy* ran an article about Trump in which he refused to answer a question about whether he was faithful to his wife and said that "any man enjoys flirtations." He is pictured on the cover next to a crouching model who appears to be wearing nothing save the jacket of Donald's tuxedo. The interview was con-ducted in October 1989 but wasn't published until late the following January. It was one more nail in the coffin of the Donald-Ivana union.

In early February, Ivana called New York *Daily News* gossip queen Liz Smith and said she needed to meet her urgently. When Smith arrived at the Plaza hotel suite in which Ivana was waiting for her, the jilted Mrs. Trump threw herself into Smith's arms. "Donald didn't love her anymore," Ivana sobbed to Smith. "Donald hadn't wanted to sleep with her, saying he couldn't be sexually attracted to a woman with children. . . . She had gone to California 'to have some work done,' but Donald didn't even like her after that."

Ivana had decided it was time for a separation. Smith broke the news on February 11, 1990 on the front page of the Sunday edition of the New York *Daily News* with the headline "Love on the Rocks," while Donald was on a business trip in Japan. Ivana was devastated at Donald's betrayal, according to Smith's account, noting that Trump would agree to stay married to her if Ivana would agree to an open marriage. "Ivana had too much self-respect for that," Smith wrote.

Trump called Smith from his plane during his return flight before he even touched down in New York. She got his side of the story, either from him, a spokesman traveling on the plane with him, or from him pretending to be his own spokesman, which was a common move of his. Trump often called reporters, sometimes using the name "John Barron," pretending to be a PR agent in his employ. "Ivana Trump did not help build the Trump empire," Smith wrote an anonymous source told her. "She doesn't know that much about business. Donald just let her run the Plaza Hotel to keep her busy." When he returned to New York, Donald moved out of the Trump triplex and into another apartment a few floors down.

The next day, the *New York Post* had its own banner head-line: "SPLIT." For the tabloid, the scandal took precedence over the release of Nelson Mandela after a quarter century in a South African prison, which was relegated to small type on the bottom of the front page. Over the next three months, the Ivana-Donald-Marla triangle dominated the front pages of the New York tabloids, with the *Daily News* serving as Ivana's proxy and the *Post* Donald's. To readers of the *Daily News,* Ivana was a woman wronged, and for readers of the *Post* she was a gold digger after Trump's money.

It wasn't just New York tabloid readers who were treated to the tawdry details of the bitter ending of the Trump fairy tale. The saga made headlines in *Newsweek, Time, People, Forbes, Vanity Fair*, the *New York Times*, the *Los Angeles Times*, the *Washington Post*, the television networks, and in newspapers and magazines in the Middle East, Europe, and Australia.

And what juicy headlines they were. On February 16, the *New York Post* screamed "Best Sex I've Ever Had," on its cover, a quote purportedly from Maples that she later denied uttering. A reporter who worked at the *Post* at the time has since speculated that Trump impersonated Marla on a phone call. The revelations rolled on with the relentlessness of tsunami waves: Trump had been stashing Marla at the St. Moritz hotel; Trump had been hiding her at Trump-owned properties for three years, including at the St. Moritz, where she had stayed in suite 414 for several months and, briefly, at Trump Tower, just three floors below the apartment where his wife and children were living. Liz Smith later told *Vanity Fair* that the Trump divorce was "the most extraordinary thing I ever witnessed, next to Elizabeth Taylor and Richard Burton."

The airing of such sordid and intimate tidbits might make most people uncomfortable, but not Trump; he reveled in the attention. "He's getting a kick out of it," a buddy of his told *New York*. "If you look at it from his point of view—somebody who's not concerned about how he's seen morally—it's a big coup."

Maples was making covers, too, but she was nowhere to be found. She had gone into hiding, donning a red wig and white straw hat, first at the Southampton home of a friend of Tom Fitzsimmons, then in Atlantic City, then in Guatemala with a pal in the Peace Corps. In her absence, the gossipmongers set on her friends. Photographers and reporters began following her family. Eventually Trump and her father told her she needed to come home.

Maples finally emerged on April 19, giving ABC's Diane Sawyer an interview and *Primetime* its best ratings to date by telling the whole world that she loved Trump. She followed that with an appearance at the White House Correspondents' Dinner, but turned down a spread that Trump arranged for her to do in *Playboy*.

————

The Trump divorce proceedings were as much a public spectacle as the final days of their union. If Donald had been derogatory of Ivana before, now he took his gloves off. The legal proceedings dragged on, and played out in the public eye. Ivana tried to get her prenup revoked, citing Donald's infidelity, and Donald insisted that he had been totally faithful and still loved Ivana. The couple's lawyers volleyed barbs in the press and in the courts for more than a year, not reaching a settlement until March 1991. Their divorce decree was granted exactly a year later on grounds of "cruel and inhuman treatment." "Donald, during the divorce, was brutal," Ivana said. "He took the divorce as a business deal, and he cannot lose. He has to win."

Ivana had proven herself a worthy contestant, pulling aside the veil on the man whose image she had helped create to show a cruel and violent abuser. According to a sworn deposition Ivana gave as part of her divorce that was made public in Harry Hurt's *Lost Tycoon,* Trump had been physically abusive to his wife on at least one occasion.

In her deposition, Ivana said that in 1989, after seeing the results of Ivana's visit to the plastic surgeon in Los Angeles, Trump decided to visit the same doctor for scalp reduction surgery, a procedure in which a doctor slices out a hairless section of scalp and sews together the remaining skin to cover bald spots.

Between the headaches from his newly tightened scalp and the aching suture itself, the surgery left Trump in agonizing pain, according to Ivana's account in the court deposition. He turned his rage on Ivana. "Your fucking doctor has ruined me," the documents say Trump shouted at her. He grabbed her and began tearing clumps of her signature platinum locks out of her head. He then ripped her clothes off, unzipped his pants, and forced himself inside her for the first time in more than a year. "According to versions she repeats to some of her closest confidants, 'he raped me,'" Hurt wrote.

Donald Trump's legal team supplied Hurt's publishers with a statement from Ivana, which was included in the front of the book, saying that she had not meant the word *rape* to be interpreted in a literal or criminal sense. On the occasion in question "Mr. Trump and I had marital relations in which he behaved very differently toward me than he had during our marriage. As a woman, I felt violated, as the love and tenderness which he normally exhibited toward me was absent," the statement said.

Ivana's statement in the book is preceded by one from Hurt in which he notes that "the statement by Ivana Trump does not contradict or invalidate any information contained in this book."

Years later, Ivana confirmed the account contained in Hurt's book to a journalist, who asked not to be identified. Ivana was in Jamaica for a charity ball in early 2011 and referred to being raped. "She said at one point he had wanted to have sex with her and she didn't and he just forced her," the journalist said in an interview for this book. "She claimed that when he got upset he would become violent with her."

Ivana did not respond to our requests for comment.

The alleged rape incident didn't become public until Hurt wrote about it in his 1993 book the year after the divorce was finalized, but even before people knew about it, popular opinion largely favored Ivana. "There is enormous sympathy for her," *Newsday* columnist James Revson said. "You couldn't measure with an eyedropper the sympathy for him in this town." Liz Smith made the case in more glorified terms. "Ivana is now a media goddess on par with Princess Di, Madonna, and Elizabeth Taylor," she wrote.

Even Trump's parents took Ivana's side. Donald may have been reveling in all the attention, but Fred Trump was not nearly as thrilled. "If you don't stop what you're doing, it's going to give me a stroke," he told his son, according to Hurt's book. Mary was also distraught. "What kind of son have I created?" she lamented to Ivana.

Donald was unmoved by his parents' entreaties and unfazed by the bad press. "Whatever the media says now is irrelevant," he said. "The negative publicity has absolutely no effect on my life at all."

But those who knew him say it did. "I think that was the turning point from when he was considered serious by other developers and other people in the business," Barbara Res, a former Trump Organization executive, told the *Washington Post*. "After that I don't think he was considered a serious businessman . . . when he broke up with Ivana and did the *Playboy* and all that. I think that was the beginning of the end of him being a serious businessman . . . and he moved into being a cartoon."

The transformation took place on a personal level as well. Trump became more sexist, more openly objectifying, Res said. She recounted a meeting they had with a potential architect for a project the company was undertaking in California. Out of the blue, "[Trump] says, 'I hear that the women of Marina del Rey . . .' And he starts talking about women's bodies. And that was just, it was a shock to me and a shock to the architect. We were just, 'What is he saying?'"

Res said she saw an ugly side of Trump emerge. "He used to be deferential to women," she wrote in the *Guardian*. "He had tremendous respect for his mother, and I think this influenced his treatment of women. . . . Over the years, I saw him change. As Trump became more famous, his behavior toward women worsened."

SIX

LUST AND MARRIAGE

"You know, it doesn't really matter what [the media] write as long as you've got a young and beautiful piece of ass."
—DONALD TRUMP, 1991, *ESQUIRE* INTERVIEW

In the wake of his split from Ivana, Trump still had Marla Maples—whether or not he wanted her. He had broken it off with her several times during his drawn-out divorce proceedings, but she clung to him like a downed aviator to a life raft during those turbulent years, and somehow they always ended up back together. "It was a wrong time for me to have a relationship," Donald said in an interview for Lifetime's *An Intimate Portrait* in 1995. "At the same time, it was great to know somebody was there, and she was there like nobody I've ever seen." Still, he seemed to know the limitations of his feelings for Maples. During their on-again, off-again phase, Trump told people that what he felt for her was "more like lust" than love.

Even while Donald and Ivana's divorce was playing out in the press, his relationship with Maples was garnering glossy magazine pages of its own. In 1990, *Vanity Fair* ran a profile of Maples calling her the woman "primed to be the next Mrs. Trump." Now twenty-seven, the Georgia Peach, as the press liked to call her, had finally found the fame that she had come to New York seeking. She began carrying around glossy photographs of herself that she would sign on demand.

Whatever his true sentiments for Maples might have been, Trump clearly liked what having a leggy blonde on his arm—and in the tabloids—did for his image. In late 1992, when Maples had joined the cast of *The Will Rogers Follies* on Broadway, Trump would often pop over from Trump Tower to the Fifth Avenue salon where she had her hair blown out before the show, standing next to her chair and looking around to see who was noticing him with the young flaxen-haired belle. Whatever issues they had in their relationship, Marla was an ego-boosting prop for the now middle-aged titan.

And he liked the Pygmalion aspect of their relationship. "I'm a great star maker, which I've done with Ivana and Marla," he told Nancy Collins in 1994, shortly after he married Maples. Maples was well aware that Trump was grooming her. "Once we started going out in public, an image was expected," she said. "The hair and the makeup and the designer dresses and you become a caricature of yourself. And I think what he loved about me the most was that I wasn't part of that world. But once we were together publicly, he wanted to change me into that social animal."

———

The spiritually minded Marla put forward a blissed-out image of herself, but the reality was far more tempestuous. From the very beginning, the couple's relationship was "marked by jealous temper tantrums and frequent breakups," Trump biographer Edward Klein wrote in *Vanity Fair*. "They might love each other, but they enjoyed torturing each other, too. . . . Every time Donald dumped Marla and went off to have his picture taken with some model, people thought he had the upper hand. But the truth, it turned out, was far more complicated than that.

"Marla knew how to push Trump's buttons. She taunted him in public for being overweight. She played with the hair on his head, lifting it up and exposing his scalp, and poking fun at his efforts to hide his hair loss. She derided his sexual prowess in front of his friends and associates."

And she could seem unstable. "She was very emotional," Chuck Jones, her former manager, said. When they were fighting, Trump never knew what Maples might do, friends said.

Never known to be faithful, Trump acted out his indecision with ferocity. It was during the interim between the Aspen face-off and his marriage to Marla that the alleged incidents involving Kristin Anderson, Jill Harth, and the supermodel in the Plaza hotel all took place. It was also around that time that Trump is said to have impregnated several women and facilitated the terminations of those pregnancies. "There are women who have had abortions paid for by Donald Trump. I don't have the medical records to prove that, but they've told girlfriends about it," said former Pulitzer Prize–winning *Philadelphia Inquirer* reporter David Cay Johnston. "It's one of many things that's sort of common knowledge about Donald." Johnston said he never published the names of the women who received abortions because he was unable to obtain both their permission and their medical records. Johnston said, however, that he knows the identities of the "brand-name" women, whom he says would be familiar figures to the public. When *New York Times* reporter Maureen Dowd asked Trump flat-out if he was "ever involved with anyone who had an abortion," he sidestepped, responding: "Such an interesting question. So what's your next question?"

This was also around the time that Trump was reportedly chasing young models at the Look of the Year modeling contests and

going to wild, cocaine-fueled parties. And he had at least two relationships that overlapped with Maples, including one with *Playboy*
Playmate Barbara Moore and another with model Rowanne Brewer,
which landed him yet again in the tabloids. Rumors circulated that
Trump asked the Elite agency to arrange for Brewer to have an HIV
test, "for the obvious reasons," biographer Harry Hurt wrote.

Trump met Brewer—now Rowanne Brewer Lane—at a pool
party at Mar-a-Lago in 1990. According to accounts of the festivi-
ties, dozens of bikini-clad models were lounging around the pool,
but Trump's eyes were on Brewer, who had been sent to the event
by her agency and hadn't brought a bathing suit. When Trump
learned that, he set out to right that wrong. He took her by the
hand, led her into a room, and opened a drawer containing a stash
of swimsuits. Brewer picked out a bikini and went into the bathroom to put it on. "I came out and he said, 'Wow,'" Brewer told
the *New York Times*. Trump was so taken with her that he wanted
to show her off to the crowd. "He brought me out to the pool and
said, 'That is a stunning Trump girl, isn't it?'" she said. The two
dated for several months. Maples saw Brewer Lane as a threat, and
the model was the subject of many of Maples and Trump's fights,
people close to Marla said.

Marla's mother, Ann, took to attending the Mar-a-Lago pool
parties when her daughter wasn't around to keep an eye on Trump,
veteran Palm Beach journalist Wayne Grover said in an interview
for this book. Ann "wanted her daughter to be married to a billionaire," Grover said, adding that he never witnessed Trump behaving
badly with the women at his parties. "I never saw him do anything
other than to smile [at the women] and say how hot some of them
were," Grover said.

Trying to follow the Trump-Marla breakups and reunions could
have given an observer whiplash. The tabloids documented all of

it—with Trump's apparent complicity. In June 1991, the *New York Post* reported that Trump had booted Marla from his condo and had taken up with Italian model Carla Bruni (though Bruni repeatedly denied any involvement with him, reportedly saying he was too tacky to date and letting him know she wanted nothing to do with him). When Sue Carswell, a reporter from *People,* left a message with Trump's people to follow up on the story, she received a phone call from a man identifying himself as John Miller, Trump's publicist. Carswell thought the man sounded an awful lot like Trump, so she taped the call and then called Maples and played the recording for her. Maples started crying, recognizing the voice as that of her recent ex. Trump's alleged publicist also bragged to the reporter that in addition to living with Maples, Trump was dating three other women, according to a transcript of the call obtained by the *Washington Post.* The "publicist" called other reporters as well, telling them that Trump now had a bevy of beauties on his dance card, naming everyone from Madonna to Kim Basinger.

But Maples was the one in the headlines, and it was Maples whom Trump had so famously left his wife for. It would be hard for Trump to end it with her without damaging his public image even more than he already had over the prior few years. Marla, though, didn't make it easy for him to stay. Friends said Trump was starting to notice her "idiosyncrasies," and that she was always wanting to know where he was and whom he was with. But whatever misgivings Trump may have had about her, he couldn't quite wrest himself free of her.

In July 1991, a week after Marla had fled to morning show host Kathie Lee Gifford's Connecticut house following yet another tiff with Trump, he phoned in to *Live with Regis and Kathie Lee* to announce the couple's engagement. While the Giffords had been in Washington, D.C., Trump had made his way up to their home and proposed to Marla. Later, reporters noticed that Marla was sporting a 7.5-carat, emerald-cut diamond from jeweler Harry Winston on her left hand. At the time he was $3.4 billion in debt, $832.5 million of which he was personally liable for, and lenders had put him on an allowance of $450,000 per month, leading them to query where he got the money to pay for the $250,000 ring. He said he borrowed it in exchange for free publicity. When journalist David Cay Johnston started making inquiries about the ring, though, Trump promptly wrote a check to Harry Winston. "That goes to an important principle about Donald: He doesn't pay for anything he doesn't have to," Johnston told us. "He's literally said to people with things like dresses for wives and whatnot, 'I don't pay for things, people give them to me.' He thinks he's the king of England."

Whatever euphoria their engagement may have brought to Trump and Maples, it didn't last for long. On September 14, at the Miss America Pageant in Atlantic City, the problems underpinning their relationship were on public display. Trump had insisted that he wanted to "see the bodies that won the swimsuit contest." Carolyn Sapp, twenty-four-year-old Miss Hawaii, who would go on to win the contest, stood up to be ogled by Trump, who acted as though he didn't know her. That was confusing to Sapp, who said that Trump had met her a year earlier when she was staying in the Plaza hotel and had repeatedly asked her out (she declined). She approached Trump, "very brazen," Maples said later, and asked him: "Do you remember when we met?" Maples decided to put a stop to the encounter. "What are you doing flirting with my fiancé?" she demanded, insisting afterward that she had been teasing. Trump, though, continued to talk about how great Sapp's body was and by the end of the pageant what may initially have been playful indignation on Maples's part had become serious anger.

Five days later, at one of her performances of *The Will Roger Follies*, Marla bumped into someone she knew during a break and lingered for some time talking to him. "Donald got very mad," Marla said. "He said, 'I was waving for you to come to me, and you didn't come.'" On September 22 the couple was back in *Daily News* headlines: "Here we go Again ... Trump Dumps Marla."

Maples may have been stung by being publicly discarded so many times, but she knew how to get her own back. In October 1991, the *Deseret News* reported that Maples was spotted in Oregon holding hands with singer Michael Bolton. Friends said that even while Maples was seeing Bolton, she was using Trump's American Express card for her shopping excursions—including to buy gifts for Bolton's kids.

Trump didn't like being made a fool of so, as he had done with Ivana, he hijacked the narrative.

"She was very hurt," Trump later said. "Michael Bolton calls Marla and says, 'Marla, I'd like to take you out.' And he falls madly in love with her. Now, I say to myself, Wait a minute. I don't like this. Michael Bolton—he's got the No. 1 fucking album in the world, *Time, Love and Tenderness*, and what that does to a guy like me, a competitive guy, it's like an affirmation that the girl has to be great, because the No. 1 singer has fallen for her. There's nothing wrong with what she's doing. I left her. Not only that. I left her like a dog.

"So what happens is, I say, 'What the fuck is going on?' I do a Trump number on her. All-enveloping. I call her. She says, 'How could you have left me the way you did?' She decides to go to Hawaii with me instead of to Europe with Michael Bolton. In Maui, this guy finds out where we are, and starts sending flowers. Yellow roses with a note: 'I've got Georgia on my mind. Love Michael.' She's torn. I've left her twice. But she drops him and comes back to me."

Trump's hatred of losing compelled him to win Maples back—possibly against his own self-interest. He remained suspicious of her and asked someone close to her to report back to him on her movements. The friend declined.

———

Despite the dazzler he had put on Maples's finger, Trump was proving remarkably slow to get to the altar. The duo kept headline writers busy throughout 1992 with their ongoing series of breakups and reconciliations. Finally, Marla found a way to turn up the heat: In early 1993, she got pregnant. The couple had gone through a period when Trump wasn't calling Maples as much as he normally did, and Maples knew what that likely meant. When she found out Trump was going out to California for a celebrity golf tournament, she and her mother decided to go, too. Maples prepared for her trip by going off her birth control pills, according to a source with direct knowledge, and did so secretly to force Trump to finally settle down with her.

Once again, Trump found himself in a situation he had to spin to safeguard his nobody's-fool reputation. Maples hadn't trapped him, because he knew that she had gone off the pill, he told *Vanity Fair*. "We've been together for six years. If she wanted to do that—get me by getting pregnant—she could have done it a lot sooner," he told the glossy. "We had just gotten back together and she wasn't using the Pill and I knew it. I don't feel as though I was trapped. Trapped would have been not to tell me she wasn't on the Pill. I'm not the kind of guy who has babies out of wedlock and doesn't get married and give the baby a name. And for me, I'm not a believer in abortion."

That was what he told *Vanity Fair*. He gave a different account to radio host Howard Stern. "At the time it was like, 'Excuse me, what happened?' Trump said in an interview taped after he and Marla had welcomed daughter Tiffany into the world. "And then I said, 'Well, what are we going to do about this?' She said, 'Are you serious? It's the most beautiful day of our lives.' I said, 'Oh, great.'"

Friends later said that Trump worried the baby wasn't his. And despite his proclamation to *Vanity Fair* that he wouldn't let his child be born out of wedlock, he hemmed and hawed about what to do—and made sure he had plenty of female company while he was trying to make his decision. In March 1993 he began an affair with twenty-four-year-old Barbara Moore, *Playboy*'s 1992 Miss December, that lasted about six months. The two met at Trump Castle in Atlantic City, where Moore was walking in a fashion show with a group of other Playmates. Trump invited all the girls up to his suite for drinks after the event. "You have to remember that long ago . . . he was thought of as somebody a lot of women wanted," Moore said in an interview for this book. There was a pianist playing in the room, and Trump and the models had gathered around to listen to the music. "Everyone was fawning all over [Trump]," Moore said, remembering that she was wearing a gold leather dress—just Trump's taste. "Everybody wanted his attention, and he liked me. . . . It was exciting, having this powerful man interested in me."

The two went off to the private part of his suite and talked for hours, Moore said. Trump was interested in all the details of how she had become a *Playboy* model. "It made me feel special that he cared," she said. "It also made me think that he cared about your mind, and he wanted to know he was with someone who was a smart woman that stimulated him." They spent a romantic—and erotic—night together that stretched into the early hours of the next day. Afterward, Trump had a security guard walk Moore back to her room, which made her feel cared for. "He said he would call me, which he did right away, actually, the next day when I was back in L.A.," she said. Moore felt like she was on top of the world. A few months earlier she had been a relative unknown in a small town, and now she was a *Playboy* Playmate, living in Los Angeles and hanging out in the Playboy Mansion and getting daily phone calls from Donald Trump inviting her to visit him. "It was just like, wow, my life was really changing," she said.

Moore didn't give much thought to whom else Trump might have been seeing, and had no idea he was engaged to Maples, she said. Nor did she consider their relationship exclusive. "He was in New York and I was in L.A. I just thought it was a spark of a new fun romance that was exciting to me. . . . I just didn't have a lot of expectations," she said. She was also a bit intimidated because he was so much older than her—he was forty-six at the time, more than two decades her senior—and she didn't have a lot of life experience. When Trump invited Moore to Mar-a-Lago in late April, she suggested he also fly in a Playmate friend of hers from Texas. That way, she'd "have someone to hang out with if he were busy with phone calls, meetings or whatever, because it was like a five-day trip," she said. Moore had no idea that he and Marla Maples had held a press conference announcing her pregnancy less than three weeks earlier.

Mar-a-Lago was grandiose and impressive, Moore said. The outdoor arcade was covered in ornate tiles and Oriental carpets were laid on the ground. Each of the bedrooms in Trump's private quarters had its own theme. One of them had twin beds, murals of frogs on the wall, and a giant stuffed frog. A bright yellow room that had been Ivana's favorite had a sitting area, makeup area, and giant closets. Perhaps the biggest surprise was Trump's room, the decor of which was contemporary in design and devoid of gilt. "Every other room I've seen of his is gold, but that room," Moore said. "He changed his room to make it modern and painted it poopy color beige, and I thought, 'Oh my gosh, you ruined it.' It had so much history, that house. I thought he was one of those that takes the history of something and ruins it."

Moore saw different sides of Trump during her time with him. When she first got there, before her friend arrived, Trump told her he wanted to go golfing. She didn't know how to play, so she just tagged along. "He was very, very sweet," she said. "I was pretty shy and uncomfortable on the golf course. I didn't know what to talk about with him." Later, though, after Moore's friend arrived, the two women had to walk over huge cobblestones to get to dinner. "It was very hard with the high heels and I almost fell and slipped backwards, and he was laughing and said, 'Oh yeah, those always get all of the women.' And that kind of bugged me, because I was almost falling down. 'Come and help me,'" she said. But she saw Trump's warm side again at that very dinner when Trump invited a midwestern couple who was there to build a spiral staircase in the estate to join them for dinner. "I thought that it was really nice that he included them, because he was supposed to be with us," she said. "It wasn't like, 'Oh, I've got these two Playmates, now I'm going to be a weirdo with them, or talk weird or be weird sexually.'"

After dinner Moore was in the kitchen, where she saw a passport-size photo of a young blonde woman in a fancy frame. "[There were] no other pictures [of her], and I didn't even know who that was, but there were huge paintings of Ivana all throughout the house," Moore said. The picture, she realized much later, was of Marla.

Just as Ivana had, Moore found Trump to be down-to-earth. "He loved people that were just normal and not wealthy," she said. "I think that's why people identified with him and voted for him. He was really like one of those good ol' boys, normal types." She saw a depth to him, but had a hard time connecting with him on a sexual level. "I think it was his age," she said. "Maybe it was just that. I don't really like to talk about the actual intimacy. I can say it wasn't so passionate. It was normal."

The two only got together a couple of times after that—once when Trump brought Moore to see him in Trump Tower and another time that summer when she was in New York for a modeling job. She called him and asked if she and a friend could come visit him. He said yes, so they went up to his apartment in Trump Tower. "It was so weird because we hadn't seen each other in a while and then it was more of an animal attraction," she said. The two started kissing, and things got so steamy that they stopped caring that someone else was in the room and started having sex. "My friend was like, 'I guess it's time for me to leave,'" Moore said.

And then, around September, Trump just stopped calling. His daughter Tiffany was born the following month. Moore didn't know the real reason their relationship ended until recently. "I thought it just fizzled out. I did not know there was so much going on, that he got someone pregnant, and he had to marry her," she said. "Who knows what would have happened if that didn't happen to him?"

All the while, Marla had been pressuring Trump to make their relationship legal. Gossip columns reported that the two would have an "intimate wedding" over the Fourth of July weekend, either in New York or Paris. And the two did jet off to Paris, checking into the Ritz hotel. "There was a photo of him pushing his cart out of the airport, and Marla's carrying her wedding dress over her shoulder in a see-through plastic container," said Wayne Grover, who was covering the trip. "I knew it wasn't going to happen because you have to, at the time, have been a resident for ninety days to get married. He knew that and I knew that. Eventually Marla was told that and she went home disappointed."

When they got back to New York, Maples, now six months pregnant, turned to the press to pressure Donald to put a ring on it. She taped an interview with NBC's *Today* show, telling them that Trump had "just a little fear" about getting married. "We get down to making the commitment, and he will be a day away, and he'll go, 'Can we wait another week?'"

———

Dalliances and indecision aside, when the time came for Maples to give birth to Tiffany, Trump proved himself surprisingly attentive. Unlike Ivana, who had wanted to retain an air of mystery and sexuality, and current wife Melania, who has never let him see her use the toilet, New Age–minded Marla wanted Donald in the delivery room with her holding her hand. And not just him. Her mother was there, her friend Janie Elder was there, her manager's fiancée was there, as was a woman named "Aiko, who calls herself a nurturer, and who specializes in prenatal care and birthing, and who gives massage and prays with you," Maples said. "There were a lot of times I yelled, 'Pray for me *now*!' And Donald was going to the doctor, 'Can't you give her something?' because he couldn't stand me in pain, and me telling Janie, 'Don't you dare allow him to give me anything.'"

The room in Saint Mary's Hospital in West Palm Beach was filled with candles, soothing aromatherapy scents, and calming music, according to an episode of Lifetime's *Intimate Portrait* of Marla. She and Donald kissed as she gave birth, and Donald cut the cord, Maples told Lifetime. "I was very nervous, because she was in a lot of pain," Donald later told the New York *Daily News*. "I tried to convince her to take something, but she wouldn't. I asked the doctor to convince her, but he knew Marla was determined not to take any drugs. She's so strong, such a strong woman. I'm amazed."

On October 13, 1993, Tiffany Ariana Trump was born, binding Donald and Marla together for life. And yet, he still hadn't married her. Maples was growing increasingly frustrated with Trump's unwillingness to commit. Worse, Christmas was approaching and she didn't want to go visit her family with her new baby while still unmarried. She looked for spiritual guidance—"Arthur Caliandro and I prayed together over the telephone," she said, referring to the minister of Marble Collegiate Church—and then took matters into her own hands. She issued Trump an ultimatum: marry her by the end of the year or she and her daughter would be gone. "I felt it was now or never. If we didn't make this commitment now, before the holidays, it would never happen. I didn't see any reason to wait, and I didn't see why he should wait."

Resolving to tie the knot again was not easy for Trump, and he continued to hem and haw for a while. "Mom, I'm going to have to make a decision about Marla," Trump told his mother, Mary, over lunch one day. "She stuck by me through the worst. She's been loyal. The obvious decision is to marry her." Mary Trump told her son that Ivana would probably still take him back. Fred Trump was no cheerleader of Marla's, either. Maples lamented to Caliandro that she thought the senior Trump was the biggest obstacle to her walk down the aisle, and he "reportedly confirmed she was on the right track." At the same time, neither parent was thrilled about their son fathering a child outside of marriage. Maples's parents were none too pleased, either.

Honor and traditional values might not have been the only considerations pushing Trump toward commitment. He was considering taking part of his empire public with an initial public stock offering, and he thought that his suffering reputation as an unfaithful husband and father of an illegitimate child was damaging his business prospects.

So marry Maples he did, but not before a showdown over the prenup. "This was the big battle all along," Maples told *Vanity Fair*, saying that, in the end, they found a compromise. If they divorced before their five-year anniversary, she would get a reported $1 million. After five years, that amount reportedly increased to $5 million. "So that way, I feel that we have what he needs right now for his business. And then, in five years, I have what *I* need for a true marriage," she said at the time. Legal experts cast doubts on Maples's sunny interpretation. "Let me tell you, it will either be extended after five years, or Trump is out of there," one told *Vanity Fair*.

At long last, on December 20, 1993, nearly a year after the Georgia beauty queen had gotten pregnant, Donald Trump and Marla Maples were united in matrimony, he wearing a tuxedo by Brioni and she a white satin sheath dress by Carolina Herrera and a $2 million tiara loaned to her by Harry Winston. This wedding was big and brash and considerably more opulent than Trump and Ivana's nuptials had been. The couple eschewed Marble Collegiate Church, the alleged site of their early meetings and Trump's first trip to the altar, opting instead to hold the ceremony in the Grand Ballroom at the Plaza hotel, the former realm of the former Mrs. Trump. In addition to the 1,300 invited guests, among which were New York mayor David Dinkins, Howard Stern, Evander Holyfield, Rosie O'Donnell, and O. J. Simpson, were seventeen television crews, the usual crush of gossip writers, and ninety paparazzi, according to the wedding announcement in the *New York Times*. The VIPs were separated from less illustrious friends and family by a velvet rope. The shindig was the closest thing to a royal wedding New York had seen. "This is the equivalent of Westminster Abbey tonight," *Lifestyles of the Rich and Famous* host Robin Leach said. "It's Charles and Diana all over again." Howard Stern gave the marriage four months.

All the fanfare, though, didn't diminish the reticence that had led Trump to take so long to get to the altar in the first place. He didn't want to give up his freedom, he had told *Vanity Fair* while he was wavering. And he didn't seem more convinced once he had made his decision. "I was bored when she was walking down the aisle," he later told biographer Timothy O'Brien. "I kept thinking, 'What the hell am I doing here?'"

The marriage never seemed to gel. The two were together when they were in Mar-a-Lago at the same time, but they spent a lot of time apart and in New York Marla had her apartment in Trump Parc on Central Park South and Donald had his a few blocks away in Trump Tower, just a few floors below the family triplex where Ivana and the kids were still living.

Trump was no more faithful to Marla after taking his vows than he had been before. He continued to harass Jill Harth and the women from her Calendar Girls beauty contest, according to her lawsuit, and before Tiffany's second birthday he had had an affair with New Zealand model Kylie Bax. And he reportedly continued his old modelizing habits. Author Laurence Leamer wrote in his book *Mar-a-Lago* that staff said there were often models traveling with Trump on his plane.

The trouble in their relationship was apparent to people around them. Model Maureen Gallagher remembers a night at Mar-a-Lago when the tension between Trump and his new wife was palpable. "She was bickering with him in public, and that's one of those things—you don't fuck with him in public while people are watching," Gallagher told us.

Apparently life with Donald wasn't all Marla had hoped it would be. In mid-April 1996, she was discovered by police, sandy and disheveled, at 4 a.m. on a beach a few towns away from Mar-a-Lago in the company of Trump bodyguard Spencer Wagner and wearing only spandex leggings and a jogging top. Trump was in New York at the time. It wasn't long before the press got wind of the story. When a reporter called Trump to get his reaction, Trump threatened to sue. Later, repeating the explanation that Marla had given him, Trump told the reporter that Marla had been with a girl-friend and had to pee, and that Wagner was only standing by to make sure no one caught her.

Trump hewed closely to his standard playbook, doubling down on his dubious version of events in an interview a week later. He said that he stood by Marla. "Any man would be shocked to hear his wife was stopped by the police at 4:00 a.m. with another man on the beach—but I am not just any man, and Marla is not just any woman. I love Marla, and I trust her," he said.

Wagner's ex wife Mary Miller, who was already divorced from Wagner at the time but who remained close with him, thinks something is fishy about the whole story. It just didn't fit with the man she knew. "He was never a playboy or a silly guy like that," she told us during an interview in Colorado. "He was always responsible. I just don't see it. I really don't. He loved his job and he liked Donald Trump. He knew his career would be over because no one else would hire him if he got caught having sex with someone's wife." Before the story broke in the media, Wagner had warned her not to believe what she was going to hear and read.

Miller said that Wagner would often take Maples and her friends to party in Miami. She thinks that maybe Maples had had too much to drink and needed to throw up. Miller doesn't believe the two had gone to the beach to have sex. "Spence, when he has sex, it's really quick, so he wouldn't have to go that far to do it," she said. "They could have done it, three seconds, anywhere."

During the ensuing media frenzy after the bizarre story emerged, Trump put Wagner up in a house he owned near his Palm Beach estate and had Mar-a-Lago staff bring him food. One day, Wagner just disappeared.

Miller said that Trump fired Wagner a few weeks after the incident. "Spence said he no longer worked there and he was going to look for work," she said. As he was leaving Trump's house, a car ran a red light and hit Wagner's Camaro. "They had to use the Jaws of Life to get Spence out," Miller said. "Spence said he felt it was an attempt to kill him and he became very paranoid after that."

Wagner never provided any proof that Trump or anyone else tried to have him killed.

Around the same time, Wagner asked Miller to go to a pool hall in Delray Beach with him. Miller said when they arrived, Maples was there. "He went over to talk to her," Miller said. "I have no idea what they talked about."

A short time after Wagner was fired, the *Globe* published an interview with him in which he said that he had indeed had a tryst with Maples that night. Trump sued him for violating his confidentiality agreement while continuing to insist that the affair never happened. "Everybody knows that the story is not true," Trump friend Richard Fields told the Associated Press. But the *Globe* stood by its reporting, saying they were convinced Wagner was telling the truth because he was interviewed for "many many hours" and took a lie-detector test, "which he passed with flying colors."

But Wagner's career as a bodyguard was finished. He became so fearful that Trump was after him that he wound up in a mental institution, Miller said, adding that she lost touch with him after that. In 2012 he died of a drug overdose.

Marla got a reckoning of her own. In May 1997 Trump dialed the *New York Post* and gave them an exclusive story. Marla learned about it the next day, when she opened the door of her apartment and saw the headline: "Donald is Divorcing Marla," according to an account by the late Trump biographer Robert Slater. The announcement was well timed—for Trump. Had they stayed married longer, he would have had to pay her more in the divorce, according to their prenup.

Apparently the ennui Trump felt watching Maples walk down the aisle never dissipated. "Marla's a good girl, and I had a good marriage with her, but it's just that I get fuckin' bored," Trump told journalist Michael Gross after their divorce. "One of those little things."

New York Post columnist Cindy Adams said the marriage had been doomed from the beginning. "He basically didn't want to get married," she said of Trump. "It was lust, not really love. She loved him very much. But Donald is somebody who's in love mostly with himself."

Like Ivana, Maples fought Trump in court to get more than she had agreed to in their prenuptial agreement, but eventually accepted a reported $2 million. "After giving Donald two years to honor the verbal commitments he had made to me during our 12-year relationship, I decided to walk away completely under the terms of the prenuptial agreement that had been placed before me just five days before our 1993 wedding," the *Post* quoted her as saying in June 1999.

Despite the energy she had put into getting Trump to settle down with her, Maples expressed relief when the marriage was over. "Donald was never the man I wanted to marry," she said. "Donald was obsessed with me and was always running after me. I couldn't get away." Maples had thought she could change Trump, but she never managed to. "After I became a mother I was less willing to put up with his behavior," she said. "I finally found the courage to walk away and stay away."

SEVEN

SWAGGER, STRUT

"I think the only difference between me and the other candidates is that I'm more honest and my women are more beautiful."
—DONALD TRUMP, 1999, TO THE *NEW YORK TIMES*

Even before he put the Trump brand on young models, Donald had found another business that ensured he would have a steady supply of eager beauties in his life. In 1996, Trump purchased the Miss Universe Organization, which also operates the Miss USA and Miss Teen USA pageants. "It's a very, very great entertainment format," he said at the time. "It gets very high ratings, it's doing very well and we'll make it even better." (In fact, the ratings were sinking and would decline even further by the time Trump was forced to sell Miss Universe in 2015 after NBC, which co-owned and broadcast the pageant, cut ties with him in response to incendiary comments he made about Mexicans while announcing his presidential candidacy.)

The current incarnation of the pageant was launched in 1952 by California-based Pacific Knitting Mills, the manufacturer of Catalina Swimwear. It was first televised in 1955 by CBS, which aired the event for nearly fifty years until Trump struck a deal with NBC in 2002. The pageant was a "sick puppy" when Trump bought it, he said, and he had an improvement plan in mind: "I made sure the women were really beautiful because they were getting a little bit not as beautiful. They had a person who was extremely proud that a number of women had become doctors. And I wasn't interested," he said on Howard Stern's radio show. "I made the bikinis smaller and the heels higher," he told David Letterman in 2010. Despite those viewer-baiting changes, Trump didn't leave the outcome to chance. On more than one occasion he intervened to get the final candidates he favored.

Trump made his vision for the pageants clear as soon as he took control. The first woman to be crowned Miss Universe during the Trump era was Alicia Machado, who competed as Miss Venezuela. After winning the pageant, she was expected to go on a media tour and attend fashion, society, and charity events as an ambassador for both the organization and her native country, but she put on weight—12 or 18 pounds in her telling and 48 in Trump's. She realized she needed to get the situation in hand, so she asked the president of the Miss Universe Organization to get her a doctor to help her with diet and exercise. The organization agreed, brought Machado to New York, and put her up in a hotel. Trump saw an opportunity for publicity.

The next day, the eighteen-year-old Machado donned a white T-shirt and black leggings and laced up her sneakers over the slouchy socks that were popular at the time. Employees from the Miss Universe Organization brought Machado to a gym—where she was ambushed by journalists from dozens of media outlets who had, unbeknownst to Machado, been invited by Trump to watch her exercise. "I was about to cry in that moment with all the cameras there," Machado said. "I said, 'I don't want to do this, Mr. Trump.' He said, 'I don't care.'"

As Machado pasted on a smile and jumped rope, did leg lifts on the floor, and pedaled a stationary bike, cameramen filmed away.

Trump stood next to her in his blue suit and posed for photos. "This is somebody who likes to eat," he told the assembled reporters. Machado sat on the bike sandwiched between Trump and the trainer who had been hired to work with her as the two men discussed Machado's ideal weight in front of the reporters. Trump further humiliated Machado in the following year's Miss Universe competition, during which viewers were invited to call in and vote on whether or not the pageant's winner should be obligated to maintain her appearance during her reign.

Machado pushed back. In a joint CBS interview with Trump and Machado before the 1997 pageant, at which Machado would be passing on her crown, Trump told the reporter that Machado had "had a little problem . . . where she gained a little weight." She interrupted him, protesting, "I don't think so."

Even while busy fat-shaming Machado, Trump was working on getting her into bed. When asked years later by Telemundo if Trump had ever tried to sleep with her, Machado replied: "Yes, in many situations. But I've never talked about it." She told the interviewer that Trump also made other women in the pageant uncomfortable with his advances.

Trump's degradation of Machado took a toll on her. She said that she developed an eating disorder and suffered psychological trauma because of it. Machado was surprised when Hillary Clinton revived the incident during the 2016 presidential campaign, but she wasted no time in speaking out against Trump. She said he had derisively called her "Miss Piggy," "Miss Eating Machine," and "Miss Housekeeping" in reference to her Latin American roots. Machado appeared in a pro-Hillary ad, saying that Trump used to yell at her, telling her she looked ugly and fat.

———

Trump's interest in beauty pageants goes almost as far back as his interest in models. Ron Rice, the founder of Hawaiian Tropic, started holding the Miss Hawaiian Tropic beauty contest in the mid-1980s and before long Trump was being invited as a VIP guest and sometime judge. "He'd come to our pageants because he enjoys being around the girls," Rice said. Marla Maples was a finalist in the US version of Miss Hawaiian Tropic in 1985, though the two didn't meet then. That was the same year that Trump bought the Mar-a-Lago club in Florida, and he soon started asking Rice to pad the guest list for events there. "He'd call me up and say, 'I'm having a big party. Bring your girls in,'" Rice said. "So I'd bring in a bunch of models. Sometimes he gave us rooms at Mar-a-Lago."

Those shindigs were a point of pride for Trump for years. In 1993, West Palm Beach mayor Nancy Graham found herself seated next to the developer at a business luncheon. He started bragging about the parties to her, continuing even when the person at the rostrum started speaking, she said. "He talked about the food and the chefs and all the planes bringing all these women from everywhere," Graham told the paper. "The whole thing was about the beauty of these women. . . . I thought it was really stupid. Why would you sit there for an hour and brag about something like that? To a woman."

Trump liked hanging out at the Miss Hawaiian Tropic contest, but with Miss Universe he had a bigger and flashier pageant that he could call his own. Once he took it over, he was hands-on. From the very beginning, Trump exercised what he saw as the owner's prerogative. "I'll go backstage before a show, and everyone's getting dressed and ready and everything else," Trump told Howard Stern during a radio broadcast in 2005. "No men are anywhere, and I'm allowed to go in because I'm the owner of the pageant and therefore I'm inspecting it. . . . 'Is everyone okay?' You know, they're standing there with no clothes. 'Is everybody okay?' And you see these incredible-looking women, and so I sort of get away with things like that."

Interviews with women who competed in the pageants confirm that Trump's comments to Stern were more than just bluster. Victoria Hughes was Miss New Mexico Teen USA in 1997. The contestants, who were as young as fourteen, rehearsed for two and a half weeks so the show would be ready when it was aired on national television. As Hughes recalled, the girls were in the changing room shortly before the show was set to begin, when their chaperones told them to get dressed quickly because a guest was coming to wish them all good luck. They didn't know whom to expect. "The curtain opened and there was Donald Trump grinning ear to ear," said Hughes, who at nineteen was the oldest girl there, having been born on the cutoff date for eligibility. "Many ladies were caught off guard," Hughes said. "We all should have been notified that the owner, a man, was going to see us. There were 51 young ladies back there, all in various stages of dress. . . . He didn't stay long but he made sure that he made his presence known."

The pageant contestants were not professional models who were used to being seen in their underwear, and Trump's appearance created a stir. "There was talk about why he was even let in at all, and the bad timing it all was," Hughes said in an interview for this book. "In my own opinion, he never should have been let in at all. If he wanted to offer us his praises for the show, he really could have done it at a different time."

"I remember putting on my dress really quick because I was like, 'Oh my God, there's a man in here,'" said Mariah Billado, who was Miss Vermont Teen USA at the same pageant. Billado said she told then-fifteen-year-old Ivanka, who cohosted the event that year, what had happened. "Yeah, he does that," Billado said Ivanka replied. (In 2016 the Trump campaign dismissed Billado's accustation, saying they "have no merit.")

Trump even evaluated Ivanka's physical appearance during the event. He was sitting next to the reigning Miss Universe, Brook Antoinette Mahealani Lee, when Ivanka took the stage. "'Don't you think my daughter's hot? She's hot, right?'" Lee said he asked her. "I was like, 'Really?' That's just weird. . . . That's creepy."

Victoria Hughes recalled bumping into Trump at various events for years after the competition. "He was always very flirtatious and very touchy," she said. "He seemed to think the world revolved around him and that women wanted him to pull them close or give them kisses on the cheek. As far as he was concerned, he walked on water and women should bow down to him. Unfortunately, many always did."

Adult contestants have similar stories to tell. Temple Taggart competed in the 1997 Miss USA pageant as Miss Utah. Trump introduced himself to her with the same greeting many other women report getting from him. "He kissed me directly on the lips," Taggart told the *New York Times*. "I thought, 'Oh my god, gross.' He was married to Marla Maples at the time. I think there were a few other girls that he kissed on the mouth. I was like, 'Wow, that's inappropriate.'"

Tasha Dixon, who was eighteen when she appeared as Miss Arizona in the 2001 Miss USA, said that Trump invaded their dressing room, too. "He just came strolling right in," she told a local television station in Los Angeles. "There was no second to put on a robe or any sort of clothing or anything. Some girls were topless. Other girls were naked." Heightening the discomfort, employees of the Miss Universe Organization urged the contestants to lavish Trump with attention when they saw him, Dixon said. She thinks that Trump bought the Miss Universe Organization with a specific purpose in mind. "I'm telling you, Donald Trump owned the pageant for the reason to utilize his power to get around beautiful women," she said. "Who do you complain to? He owns the pageant. There is no one to complain to. Everyone there works for him."

At times, Trump's gaze was more targeted. Samantha Holvey told CNN that when she was twenty and competing in the 2006 Miss USA pageant, Trump made pointed visual inspections of all the contestants. "He would step in front of each girl and look you over from head to toe like we were just meat, we were just sexual objects, that we were not people," she said. "You know when a gross guy at the bar is checking you out? It's that feeling." Being ogled by Trump made Holvey feel "the dirtiest I felt in my entire life." She and her fellow contestants were also invited to private parties filled with "old, rich, drunk guys ogling all over us," Holvey said.

Not only was there no one to whom the contestants could address their grievances because Trump was the boss, but the girls were also mindful that they needed to stay on his good side if they wanted to remain competitive. What "the Donald" thought mattered—a lot. It could be the difference between winning and not winning. George Wayne, longtime *Vanity Fair* celebrity journalist, was on the panel of judges at the 2008 Miss USA pageant in Las Vegas, alongside former Mrs. Paul McCartney Heather Mills, Project Runway winner Christian Siriano, Olympic gold-medal swimmer Amanda Beard, Kelly Clarkson, and others. The judges were put up in suites at the Hard Rock Hotel in Vegas for several days before the event while they attended preparatory meetings. The judges for the live event didn't see the contestants ahead of time, so hadn't yet met the girls when, the day before the pageant, Trump arrived and put in his two cents. "He basically told us in his own inimitable fashion who he wanted to win the pageant: Miss Oklahoma," Wayne said in an interview for this book. "We were aghast."

The panel ended up choosing Crystle Stewart, an African American woman from Texas. "It was the perfect fait accompli," Wayne chuckled.

The *Vanity Fair* columnist saw Trump again the following week at Ivana's wedding to Rossano Rubicondi, which she held at Mar-a-Lago. Wayne asked Trump what he thought of his new Miss USA. "He gave me that look and just walked out," Wayne said. "He didn't say a word."

That Trump was involved in the selection wasn't a secret. "It's just kind of common knowledge that he picks six of the top fifteen single-handedly," Michael Schwandt, a choreographer for the Miss Universe pageant, said in a 2009 interview with Guanabee.com. "His reason for doing so, as he told me and he's told the girls before, is that he left it all up to preliminary judging in the past and some of the most beautiful women, in his opinion, were not in the top fifteen and he was kind of upset about that." Only the top fifteen contestants compete in the televised event. They are selected by a different group of judges, which includes employees of the Miss Universe Organization and Trump himself.

Schwandt said that the day before the live broadcast Trump would have all the girls line up in alphabetical order and say their name, age, and where they came from while he observed. Schwandt later retracted his story, though Guanabee's editor stood by it. And the organization itself effectively confirmed his account. "In the 2009 Miss Universe competition, a preliminary panel of judges selected nine of the top 15 and members of the Miss Universe Organization, including owner Donald J. Trump, selected the remaining six," the Miss Universe Organization said in a statement. "This system has been in place since 2005 and has always been fully disclosed to the contestants, their directors, the judges and the viewing audiences."

TMZ later obtained audio that backed up Schwandt's account. In it, Trump asked the girls which of their competitors was the most beautiful and, taking their suggestions, sorted them into two lines. "You know why we do that, because years ago when I first bought it, we chose 10 people. I chose none," he explained. "And I get here, and the most beautiful people were never chosen. And I went nuts. So we call it the Trump rule. It's the Trump rule and we get to choose."

He went on to plug his son's eligibility in the audio. "Eric Trump, I have a son, he's very handsome, he's 6′6″ and he was number one in his class in school," Trump told the girls. "But he's not allowed to see you because he's a judge. I don't know why a judge is not allowed . . . can NBC explain that to me please?"

Former contestants described the same process. In her memoir, *Still Standing*, 2009 Miss California USA Carrie Prejean said that during their dress rehearsal the contestants were instructed to put on the revealing outfits they wore in the opening number and line up for Trump onstage. He gave them the kind of inspection he would have learned in military school, looking each one of them up and down and jotting notes on a little pad. He asked one of the contestants who she thought was the most beautiful woman in the room. When she suggested she liked one of her competitors because the woman was sweet, Trump replied: "I don't care if she's sweet. Is she hot?" Prejean recounted. "It became clear that the point of the whole exercise was for him to divide the room between girls he personally found attractive and those he did not," Prejean wrote. "Many of the girls found the exercise humiliating. Some of the girls were sobbing backstage after he left, devastated to have failed even before the competition really began to impress 'The Donald.'"

The 2013 Miss Washington USA, Cassandra Searles, felt degraded by her involvement in the pageant. In a 2016 post on

Facebook, she called Trump a misogynist and said that he treated her and her fellow Miss USA contestants "like cattle," lining them up "so he could get a closer look at his property." She later added a comment to her post saying, "He probably doesn't want me telling the story about that time he continually grabbed my ass and invited me to his hotel room." Paromita Mitra, Miss Mississippi USA in 2013, added her own comment. "I literally have nightmares about that process," she wrote.

Shi Lim, Miss Universe Singapore 2013, said the contestants were well aware that the list of finalists was up to Trump. "We called it the Trump card," she said. Kerrie Baylis, Miss Universe Jamaica 2013, said that she thought the finalist list resembled the countries that Trump did or wanted to do business with.

In their book *Russian Roulette,* journalists Michael Isikoff and David Corn detailed how the process unfolded in the 2013 pageant, which was held in Moscow. Trump had a special room backstage, which was arranged in accordance with his requirements. It was stocked with Nutter Butter cookies, white TicTac mints, and Diet Coke. The walls were devoid of distracting pictures, the room was immaculate, the soap was unscented, and the hand towels were rolled, not folded. It was in this sanctum that Trump watched videos of the girls who had been chosen as finalists and reviewed the judges' decisions. He didn't hesitate to overrule them.

"If there were too many women of color, he would make changes," the authors wrote, quoting someone who worked at the Miss Universe Organization. "He often thought a woman was too ethnic or too dark skinned," said another employee of the organization. "He had a particular type of woman he thought was a winner. . . . he liked a type." That type, the staffer said, included Eastern European women. Trump was also said to eliminate women "who had snubbed his advances," the authors wrote.

Did Trump actually have sex with contestants? He bantered about it with Howard Stern in 2005, the same year he married Melania. "It could be a conflict of interest," he told Stern. "But you know, it's the kind of thing you worry about later, you tend to think about the conflict a little bit later on." A few minutes later as Trump, Stern, and his sidekick Robin Quivers were joking around, Trump suggested that sleeping with the girls might be his "obligation."

———

Just as he eschews boundaries in his life, Trump disregards boundaries in his businesses. One bleeds into the next, and they are mutually reinforcing. It was perhaps inevitable, then, that once he started his modeling agency, he began funneling women he liked from Miss Universe to Trump Model Management. He did the same thing after he started on *The Apprentice*, NBC's hit business reality show that Mark Burnett created and Trump began hosting in 2004, making him a household name. Jennifer Murphy, whom Trump once referred to as "one of the most beautiful women I have ever seen," represented Oregon in the 2004 Miss USA pageant. During the event, she spoke to Trump about the possibility of being a contestant on *The Apprentice*. She participated in the reality show the following year. And models from Trump's agency appeared on the show parading outfits designed by contestants.

"He came in to *The Apprentice* believing his own hype. He has a problem with that," Katherine Walker, the show producer for the first five seasons of *The Apprentice,* told us. "That's his Achilles' heel. Once it's not about him, he can't function. Trump Organization, Trump Tower, Trump, Trump, Trump. That's a huge weird psyche thing." Trump's TV stardom expanded his ego and his confidence in the hunt. "All the women on *The Apprentice* flirted with me—consciously or unconsciously," he wrote in his 2004 book, *How to Get Rich.* "That's to be expected. A sexual dynamic is always present between people, unless you are asexual."

Trump's objectification of women permeated the set, both in the boardroom and behind the scenes. Summer Zervos, a contestant in season five, accused him of sexual misconduct and filed a defamation lawsuit against him in 2017. Murphy, who appeared in season four, said he kissed her on the lips when she met him in Trump Tower to solicit his help with her job hunt. In a 2014 episode of *Celebrity Apprentice* he told former *Playboy* model Brande Roderick: "It must be a pretty picture, you dropping to your knees."

Trump was apt to define the women by their physical attributes. In the fifth episode of season one, he was trying to figure out whom to cut that week. (Each week, the two teams were given a task to perform and at the end of the episode Trump would cut a contestant from the losing team with his signature phrase, "You're fired!") Trump asked Walker, the only high-level female producer that season, for advice. "He turns to me directly and asks, 'Who should I fire?' He asked me this twice, three times," Walker said. "Now, this is something we're definitely not doing, FCC regulations, which I honored . . . I told him, 'It's your prerogative.' It was far more interesting to give him that leeway."

Walker told Trump he should ask each member of the team that question because they all felt that one member had caused them to lose their task that week. Trump understood exactly whom she was talking about. "He said, 'You mean the one with the . . .' and he put his hands out in a gesture to signal the girl with the giant breasts," referring to contestant Kristi Frank, Walker told the Associated Press. "He didn't even know her name." Still, Frank had gotten Trump's attention. "He definitely liked big breasts and, that's the thing, she had them," Walker told us. Trump axed Frank at the end of the episode, but after growling "You're fired!" at her, he tried to soften the blow by saying that, out of all the women on the show, she was the one that he would have chosen to marry. "It makes me a little sick," Frank told the Associated Press. "It's kind of sweet, but it makes me feel like, 'OK, he's checking me out again.'"

That behavior was routine for Trump. "There were times when I heard him say somebody was hot or had a great ass," Walker said. It was easy to predict which women Trump was going to prefer. "He definitely has a type . . . Stormy Daniels, Melania, even his daughter, kind of baby-doll perfection," Walker said. Ivanka, though, was in a class of her own. "He clearly has some fascination with his daughter that crosses the line," Walker opined during an interview in a noisy coffee shop in Long Beach, California.

Trump's appetite for women sometimes got in the way of the smooth running of the show, Walker said. At one point, she had to have a one-on-one talk with him. "There had been a team of women that had basically been bamboozling him about this girl, who was very thin and flighty. It was a very hard boardroom and these other women were manipulative and they got her fired for 'being crazy,'" Walker said. The producers thought it was great. Walker, not so much. "She's not crazy," she told the producers. Trump came to see Walker and asked her opinion on the situation.

"Quite frankly, sir, it sucks," she said she told him.

"Ride with me," he responded.

"So I go in the elevator with him and just his bodyguard. I head up to the twenty-fifth floor to talk with him. And I said to him, 'They bamboozled you and you have to be careful with these women in the future,'" she said. She explained to him that the risk was that the viewing audience would start to think that he could be played by attractive women. "He seemed to listen," she said. "I think he trusted me."

Contestants on the show said that Trump's preoccupation with women could manifest itself at any time. Randal Pinkett, who won season four, said that the men would sometimes find themselves alone with Donald because, for a period, the competition was men versus women. "Donald would take the occasion to talk about specific women; Jennifer Murphy in particular was one of his favorites," Pinkett said in an interview for this book. "He would talk about the women he thought were attractive. He would ask if we would sleep with them. He would indicate that he would like to sleep with them—who he found attractive, who he found sexy or whatever."

Trump had married Melania earlier that year.

Pinkett said he found Trump's behavior appalling and unprofessional. "It wasn't a dating show," he said. "It wasn't a social endeavor. Not that that behavior is appropriate in a social environment or when you're dating someone, because it's not. But in a professional environment it's unacceptable. To me, it's demeaning to women. It's disrespectful to women . . . to be reduced to a conversation about looks, attractiveness, and sex, to me, is totally inappropriate and disrespectful."

Surya Yalamanchili had a similar impression when he appeared on season six, which filmed in Los Angeles. He wrote in *Politico* about a night at the Playboy Mansion, to which his team of mostly women were invited as a reward for having won the competition one week. After being greeted by Hugh Hefner's three girlfriends, the contestants sat down by the fireplace for a chat with Hef, whose history with Trump dated back to 1990, when the now-president appeared on the cover of *Playboy*, the very magazine he ogled as an adolescent. They were then led outside for a pool party, where dozens of *Playboy* bunnies, some wearing fuzzy tails and rabbit ears, were waiting to party with them.

At the end of the evening, Yalamanchili found himself chatting with Hefner, Trump, and another contestant. "With a wry smile, Trump looked at Hefner and said, 'It's hard for me to tell which of these girls are yours, and which ones are mine,'" Yalamanchili wrote. "The women on my team were well-credentialed business executives, people Trump had supposedly hand-picked for their skills. In that moment, the only real difference to Trump between them and the scantily clad Playmates who were there for his entertainment was that some of the women were 'his,' and some weren't."

In season ten, the contestants were sent out to buy new clothes. The men went to Brooks Brothers and Pink and Lord & Taylor, but Trump wanted the women to wear shorter skirts and to show more cleavage, so they were sent to Forever 21, competitor and U.S. Air Force veteran Gene Folkes said. When they came back, Trump asked one of the women to come around to his side of the board table and twirl for him to show off her new outfit.

It wasn't only the men whom Trump would query about who they found attractive and who they would want to sleep with—it was the women, too. Sometimes his questioning went even further; he once asked a female contestant her breast size, Folkes told us in an interview. "I think what was most surprising, though, is the aggressive nature by which he approached women specifically," Folkes told us. "He has this way of talking to women. It's not even condescending, it's just disregarding."

The way he referred to women was similar, Folkes said. "It's like Tourette syndrome; you could be there talking about bananas, and he's talking about someone's breasts."

Proximity to the women didn't deter Trump from discussing their desirability. "We were in the boardroom one time figuring out who to blame for the task, and he just stopped in the middle and pointed to someone and said, 'You'd fuck her, wouldn't you? I'd fuck her. C'mon, wouldn't you?'" a former crew member told the Associated Press, speaking on condition of anonymity because of a nondisclosure agreement. "Everyone is trying to make him stop talking, and the woman is shrinking in her seat."

But the negative view of Trump was far from universal. Contestant Jennie Finch, a US softball player and two-time Olympian, had only good things to say about him. "He was extremely supportive," she told the Associated Press. "You could tell there was so much respect there on all sides, especially with the female athletes. Obviously, he was complimentary, but never in an inappropriate way." Poppy Carlig, the contestant who was asked to twirl, said she thought the request was just "playful banter." Nor did she read anything creepy into Trump telling her she reminded him of Ivanka. On the contrary. "I thought that was really touching because I know how much he values his family."

Pinkett acknowledged that Trump's relationship with women can be complex and that during his time working at the Trump Organization as the winner of *The Apprentice* he witnessed the positive relationships Trump had with his senior female employees, including Carolyn Kepcher, who was a judge on *The Apprentice* and whom he had elevated to the highest level of his organization. "You look at how much he respects his daughter, as an example," Pinkett said.

But that doesn't mean that Trump can't also be sexist, Pinkett argued. "I saw a great statement on Twitter of all places that said, 'Saying that you treat women fairly so therefore you can't objectify them is like saying you're a serial killer but you also have friends who are alive.' So I don't accept the argument that has come from people like Ivanka, who points to herself and . . . others who he's elevated as if that's some defense that he can't be sexist. I don't buy that argument. You can do both and those can coexist, but the fact that you've elevated women is not a pass for the bad deeds and bad behavior toward other women."

Walker said that Trump always treated her with respect. At the same time, she has no problem believing some of the accusations against him. "Is it possible for some men like him to respect some women and completely objectify others? Absolutely," Walker said. "He can compartmentalize."

And Trump didn't treat all the women who worked on the show with the same respect he afforded Walker and Kepcher. He had what Walker called "an uncomfortable crush" on a female camera operator during season one. Employees of the show told the Associated Press that Trump made lewd comments about her, said she had a nice rear, and compared her looks to Ivanka's. "It was uncomfortable because he constantly was obsessed with her," Walker said. The camera operator left the show for the next four seasons, returning only for *Celebrity Apprentice,* but many on the crew found it unpleasant to listen to the comments he made both to and about her while she was there.

Trump's behavior grew more flagrant over time. "When he realized that he could get away with it—maybe by the third season—that's when he started hitting on the [production assistants] and stuff," Walker told us.

When asked about Summer Zervos, Walker paused, her eyes flitting for a moment to another point in the cafe. "I absolutely believe her," she said firmly, returning her gaze. Season five of the show was shot in Los Angeles and Trump would always stay at the Beverly Hills Hotel when he was in town. "He was in our casting all the time."

Trump's behavior was not unusual in the entertainment industry, in Walker's experience. On the contrary—on the creepiness scale, he was pretty ordinary by Hollywood standards. "I think the problem about him, what's not average about him, is he's actually very insecure on some level. Stormy Daniels got that," she said. "To me, this is a guy who gets a little bit of power, he's always thinking about kissing a girl because he's got so many weird insecurities. So what does he do? He takes advantage of this girl Summer."

Zervos was hoping Trump would help her get a job, which made her vulnerable because she needed something from him. "For him to be in that position, it's a feeling on his part that, 'Just give me a kiss and I'll give you that information,'" Walker said. "That's classic low-end behavior.... My point is, if you really want to stop him, you must ignore him. And that's a narcissist."

Pinkett told us that he, too, finds Zervos's story credible. "Then you see the *Access Hollywood* tape, it's no surprise," he said. "It's no surprise to extrapolate that Donald would invite Summer Zervos to his hotel and proposition her. It's no surprise when you look at Stormy Daniels or [Karen] McDougal. The list goes on and on and on—and these are just the examples that we know. How many women came forward to tell their stories? How many women haven't stepped up—for a variety of reasons, which I can understand? I'll just say where there's smoke, there's fire."

Pinkett and five other former contestants on the show were so disturbed when Trump announced his candidacy for president that they spoke out against him publicly. "Because our allegiance to our country supersedes our relationship with Donald, we see today as an act of patriotism and not disloyalty," Pinkett said in a press conference, representing the group. "We believe the American people have a right to be as informed as they can be in this election regarding Donald's qualifications as the Republican Party's front-runner and leading candidate to become president. Today we denounce Donald's campaign of sexism, xenophobia, racism, violence, and hate as a unified team."

Trump dismissed the former reality show contestants who publicly opposed him as a bunch of "failing wannabes."

EIGHT

THE NUPTIALS WILL
NOT BE TELEVISED

*"You've got to deny, deny, deny and push back on these women. If you
admit to anything and any culpability, then you're dead. . . . You've got
to be strong. You've got to be aggressive. You've got to push back hard.
You've got to deny anything that's said about you. Never admit."*
—DONALD TRUMP, DATE UNKNOWN, AS QUOTED IN *FEAR*, BY BOB WOODWARD

"How do the breasts look?"
—DONALD TRUMP TO HOWARD STERN IN 2005

I n 1998, Sam Mendes packed the old Henry Miller Theater at Forty-
Third Street and Broadway with round black cabaret chairs and
tables dotted with red tasseled lamps and installed banquettes and
a bar, thus transforming it into the Kit Kat Klub for the second
Broadway revival of *Cabaret*, a musical about the rise of Nazis in
1930s Germany. "It's rough, it's dirty, it's in your face," Mendes said
of the new Weimar-styled nightclub-cum-cabaret-cum-theater.
Perhaps fittingly, it was there that Donald Trump, who would
eventually have his own political rise, met an inscrutable twenty-
eight-year-old brunette with steel-blue eyes who would be the star
of the second revival of his role as married man.

The third Broadway staging of *Cabaret* was a huge hit and opened the door to Mendes's career as a film director—and it seems Trump has had success his third time around as well. In Melania Knauss, he found his best match, a woman who seemed to combine Ivana's Eastern European love of a strongman with Maples's homey attitude.

Donald Trump is a creature of habit, and the story of how Donald Trump met the Slovenian model rings familiar. In 1998, when he had been separated from Maples for about a year, he went to the Kit Kat Klub for a party for a Victoria's Secret model with Norwegian heiress Celina Midelfart, who was in her mid-twenties and living in Trump Tower while studying at New York University, as his date. According to Trump's account, he was meant to be introduced to another model that night, but Knauss caught his eye. "I went crazy," he told Larry King during an interview the CNN host conducted with newlyweds Donald and Melania in 2005. "There was this great supermodel sitting next to Melania. I was supposed to meet this supermodel. They said, 'Look, there's so and so.' I said, "Forget about her. Who is the one on the left?' And it was Melania." Melania was twenty-eight at the time and had been invited to the party by her friend and agent, Paolo Zampolli. When Midelfart absented herself to use the restroom, Trump seized the opportunity to hit on Melania.

After chatting her up, Trump asked Melania for her number, but she refused to give it to him, asking for his instead. She was impressed when he gave her *all* his numbers—the office, Mar-a-Lago, all of it, she later told *Harper's Bazaar.* Their courtship began with a few dinners in New York. It didn't take more than a month before she was boarding his private jet to fly to Mar-a-Lago.

Another common thread in Trumpworld is the lack of a single, clear narrative around the meeting of his wives. His first encounter with Melania is no exception. According to *Golden Handcuffs* author Nina Burleigh, Melania and Donald met much earlier, well before he separated from Marla. Melania had arrived in the United States in 1995, and either late that year or early the following year she posed for the nude photos that were leaked to the *New York Post* during Trump's presidential campaign. "But the photographer for that shoot, Alé de Basseville, a French guy, is on the record with a 100% backing that he and everyone at that shoot knew [of a relationship between the two in 1996] because she told them that her boyfriend was Donald Trump and he remembers it specifically," Burleigh said. "He thought that it would increase the value of his photoshoot to this French magazine that was going to print them. And he wanted to tell the editor, you know, this is Donald's girlfriend and it was '96. He says that Paolo Zampolli said to him, 'You can't do that because he's still not untethered from his wife.'"

Another source, Mary Miller, the ex-wife of the bodyguard of late-night-romp-on-the-beach-with-Marla fame, told us that Melania was already in the picture when Maples and Wagner made headlines.

———

Of course, Melania wasn't the only woman in Trump's life during his separation from Marla. In addition to Midelfart, Trump was also seeing two well-known biracial models, Maureen Gallagher and Kara Young. Gallagher, who had never publicly acknowledged her romance with Trump before being interviewed for this book, dated Trump in the late 1990s, after he had already started seeing Young. Gallagher said she found the titan genuine—and genuinely interested in her as a person. "We had really great conversations, we talked about all kinds of stuff—mostly about sports and dreams and hopes and where we're going with this whole thing," she said. "He wanted to push me. He always wanted to push me to do better." According to Gallagher, she and Trump would have dinner in the private dining room at Mar-a-Lago, and sometimes she would go down on her own and stay in Ivanka's room. "I could always use the spa," she said. And when she decided to move to Miami, he took care of that for her, flying her bike and everything she needed down to Palm Beach and then trucking it down to Ocean Drive in Miami for her.

Gallagher said her relationship with Trump was steamy. "It was crazy," she said. "We had lots and lots of sex. Tons, you know. I did a lot of work. . . . He says all kinds of shit when he's in the throes of it. It didn't make any sense to me." Gallagher declined to give his exact words, but said Trump's banter in bed was "sweet and kind." And she enjoyed her time with him. "He was very sexy, you know? We usually hit the sheets, and for a long time, too. And then he'd go fix his hair for half an hour. It was all very romantic," she added with a laugh. "He was gentle, kind of taken by me. It was like, 'Wow, you're really good at this.'"

Gallagher had other men in her life, too, and wasn't looking to settle down with Trump, so was unable to give him the kind of affirmation he seemed to need. "He said to me, 'You love me, don't you? You're in love with me?' And I was like, he's a megalomaniac. I didn't know what to say. I was like, 'I like fucking you.' I was like, 'I don't spend enough time with you to be in love with you.' I told him straight up . . . I'm having fun."

Their relationship ended when Melania came on the scene. Gallagher bumped into them once after they had started dating at a Halloween party at Lotus, a restaurant and club in the Chelsea neighborhood of Manhattan. Gallagher was wearing a very short red rubber dress and walked by the couple. "I looked at him and he looked at me like, 'Don't say anything.' So I didn't," Gallagher told us. "But she could feel it. She knew. You know, she's no baby doll, either. She's been around." Still, Gallagher knew that was probably the end of her and Trump. "I went to myself, 'Okay, the game's all over now.' No chasing stuff or things like that. [Melania] nailed him to the cross." Trump never called Gallagher again.

Trump's relationship with Young was something different. She was the one Trump really fell for. He saw Gallagher behind the scenes. He took Young out in public. And it was Young who had Trump's credit card. "I knew everyone in SoHo. They were like, 'She was just here with his card,'" Gallagher said.

Trump and Young began popping up as an item in the gossip columns in the summer of 1997, after he saw her at a party in the Hamptons and tracked down her phone number. She had been dating celebrity reporter A. J. Benza, but he had moved to Los Angeles earlier that year and the two had started seeing other people. "He and I—what's the word?—we crossed over," Benza told us. "And suddenly we both realized, and when that happened there was a big to-do. And I had to call him privately one time," Benza said. "I said, 'Who's seeing Kara—me or you?' He didn't know how to answer that. He said, 'A.J., you're a good guy. I saw her last night, we went to Le Cirque.' And I said, 'I just want to let you know that I saw her last week in California.'"

Trump, who likes to brag about stealing other men's girlfriends, made sure to rub that in Benza's face when Benza was on the Howard Stern show in 2001 promoting his book, *Fame: Ain't It a Bitch?* Trump called in to the show during Benza's interview, telling Stern: "I stole his girlfriend, but I didn't know I was stealing your girlfriend. I've been successful with your girlfriend, I'll tell you that."

Benza hit back, saying that Trump had had hair plugs and would send Young clippings of newspaper articles about himself on which he circled his name and wrote "billionaire." "He's out of his mind," Benza said on the show.

Trump parried: "I'm doing you a favor, A.J. She didn't love you. A.J. doesn't like Trump for one reason: I stole his girlfriend. I took her away like he was a dog. . . . While you were getting on that plane to go to California thinking that she was your girlfriend, she was some place that you wouldn't have been very happy with."

Benza threatened to attack Trump with a baseball bat, and things continued to degenerate from there:

Benza invoked Ivanka: "I can't wait till your little daughter gets a little older for me."

Trump: "Hey, A.J., I guarantee you have zero chance. A.J., any girl you have, I can take from you—if I want. Any girl you have, I can take from you. You're full of shit. So any girl you have, I can take. That I guarantee. And that was proven before."

Meanwhile, Stern's producers managed to get Young on the phone. "They shouldn't fight each other because it's something that's old, because they have very big egos," she said when on the air.

Trump wasn't letting go. He kept insisting that Young admit she left A.J. for him. "I started going with Kara while you and Kara were fully in bloom and fully going out, and then Kara left you. Is that correct, Kara?"

"I think it's sad that two grown men are doing this," Young replied.

But Young knew that it was more than just two men fighting over a trophy. Trump's feelings for Young had been so real that he had asked her to marry him before they had even been together a year, Benza revealed to us in an interview for this book. Young, whose son from her first marriage was still an infant at the time, turned Trump down. "I do know he wouldn't take no for an answer for a while," Benza said. "And he made numerous attempts."

Of all the women Trump dated after Maples, it was Young whom Melania viewed as the biggest threat. "She knew Donald thought differently about [Young] than the way he casually would date other women in the city," Benza said. "Melania knew he treated Kara differently. This was a girl he stayed home with, ate at home with and watched movies. . . . It was very domesticated."

———

Ivana thought Trump wanted his professional equal for a wife, and Marla presented herself as sweetness and light. Melania is none of those things, and seems comfortable with Trump's portrayal of her as a sex object. She doesn't flinch when he does things like call for her by hollering "Where's my supermodel?" However she may feel about her husband's representation of her down inside, she plays the role of the ideal Mrs. Trump impeccably. Whatever one may read into her grimaces and disappearances when he behaves badly, she keeps her true feelings to herself.

There is no doubt that Melania knew exactly what she was getting into when she married Trump. "He was known as a ladies' man," she told Barbara Walters in an interview the couple did during the campaign. Trump had cheated publicly on his previous two wives and made his disregard of fidelity clear in his 2000 book, *The America We Deserve*. He wrote there that monogamy in marriage is not the most important family value, placing it behind one's relationship with one's parents and siblings. "A lot of people want to say that being monogamous is the only value. They don't understand that family values means having a context, having a place where you belong, having people who really know you and to whom you're accountable," he wrote.

Melania seems to have been willing to accept that. "I think the mistake some people make is they try to change the man they love after they get married," she said. "You cannot change a person. You accept the person."

The two fulfilled each other's needs: She was a stunning model, and he was a charming and successful man. He made no bones about her sexiness being important to him. Howard Stern once asked Trump if he would stay with Melania if she were disfigured in a car accident. "How do the breasts look?" Trump asked Stern.

"The breasts are okay," Stern replied.

"That's important," Trump concluded.

Trump had no qualms about publicly objectifying Melania, and she was happy to play along. When Trump called in to Stern's show on November 9, 1999, Stern asked him to "put that broad in your bed on the phone." Trump did, and Stern began peppering Melania with a series of creepy questions, beginning by asking what she was wearing. "Not much," she replied, going on to tell Stern that the two had sex "even more" than every day. "I have my pants off already," Stern smarmed. After Stern repeatedly told Melania how perfect, how hot, how flawless she was, she said, "Do you want to speak with Donald?" Trump took the phone back and told Stern that Melania was "actually naked," adding, "It's a thing of beauty."

Trump gave Melania security—something she needed, because at twenty-eight she was becoming too old to be a successful model. "She ran into Donald just at the right time," a friend of hers told the *New York Post* after their engagement. "She was just about out of money, at the end of her rope and about to move back to Eastern Europe." Melania found plenty to like in Trump. "He's a very successful businessman, he's very charming. He's very smart, the energy between us is unbelievable," she said in 1999. But there was more to it, she said: "I think you can't be with the person if it's not love, if they don't satisfy you. You can't hug a beautiful apartment, you can't hug an airplane, you can't talk to them."

Donald was clear-eyed about his appeal for Melania. "Do you think my wife is with me because I look good? She's with me because of the money," *The Apprentice* contestant Gene Folkes told us Trump said once. And Melania knew what she was for him. When asked by a student in an NYU business school class she was addressing in 2005 if she would have married Trump if he wasn't rich, she responded: "If I weren't beautiful, do you think he'd be with me?"

"Of all three women, Melania handles Donald the best," former Trump Organization executive Louise Sunshine said. "She's very independent. He's very independent. She doesn't hesitate to tell Donald good from bad, right from wrong."

Still, their relationship wasn't always smooth sailing. They hit a rough patch shortly after they met when Trump rekindled things with Kara Young, a source close to Young told us. "Melania came home and saw [what was] not her makeup on a bathroom towel. She flipped out. A big fight ensued," Young's friend said. "They flew her back to Mar-a-Lago." The source told us that Melania was allegedly suffering from a health issue and had gone down to Mar-a-Lago to recuperate. She eventually forgave Trump. Melania's former roommate said they broke up over "trust issues" after he went "back to his old ways."

They were back together within six months.

In 2000, Donald broke up with Melania, reportedly because she wanted nothing to do with the presidential run he was considering. That separation didn't last long, either, and the following year, two and a half years after they first met, she ditched her one-bedroom, $2,500-a-month rental and moved into his Trump Tower triplex.

Despite the occasional squall, the Donald-Melania pairing was much less stormy than his time with Marla had been. That's largely down to Melania's unflappable disposition. Friends describe her as serene, and Trump's older children referred to her as "the Portrait" because she spoke so little. She proved herself to be equally as discreet when it came to bodily functions. During a January 2004 appearance on Howard Stern's show, Trump reminded Stern that he said he had never seen his girlfriend do anything "bad." Stern initially didn't grasp what Trump was talking about.

"That's true, she would never even do another chick," Stern responded.

"No, but not even that," Trump corrected. "You said you've never even heard her fart. Is that true?"

"Not only is that true," Stern affirmed. "She doesn't make doody."

"I'm going to say, I could say the exact same thing about Melania," Trump replied.

Melania confirmed the importance of retaining an aura of mystery around her toileting in a 2015 interview with *People* in which she asserted that separate bathrooms are the key to a happy marriage.

Surely that wasn't the clincher, but the germaphobe-in-chief popped the question just a few months after his conversation with Stern. In April 2004, Donald proposed to Melania at the Costume Institute Gala at the Metropolitan Museum of Art with a twelve-carat, emerald-cut diamond set in platinum with tapered baguettes on either side. In Trump's view, she had earned it.

"She's shown she can be the woman behind me," he told gossip columnist Cindy Adams. "We're together five years, and these five years for whatever reasons have been my most successful. I have to imagine she had something to do with that."

If press reports—or the lack, thereof—are any indication, Melania didn't give Trump a hard time over the prenup, either. The two walked down the aisle on January 22, 2005; he was fifty-eight and she was thirty-four. They took their vows at the Bethesda-by-the-Sea, an Episcopal church in Palm Beach, in front of five hundred guests, among them Hillary Clinton, Katie Couric, and Billy Joel. It was a more intimate crowd than had attended his wedding to Marla but it was by far his most over-the-top wedding. Trump reportedly wanted to accept an NBC offer to broadcast the wedding live, but Melania nixed the idea. Melania wore a beaded couture Christian Dior dress with a thirteen-foot train and sixteen-foot veil. The dress, which dexterous hands spent 550 hours adorning with 1,500 crystals and pearls, cost upward of $100,000. Donald stayed true to character and wore a black Brioni tux.

They exchanged their vows on their knees, sotto voce. "We had a little smile, but we were serious, because they are serious words," the first-time bride said. When he was permitted to kiss his new wife, he did so three times. "We completely forgot everything around us," Melania said. "It was just us two. It was beautiful." Despite all the pomp, the ceremony was filled with touches that had deep meaning for Melania. There was a candle in the church that had been lit only one other time before—at her baptism in Slovenia. And instead of flowers, she carried rosaries that were family heirlooms. All four of Trump's children were included in the ceremony.

The reception was held—of course—at Mar-a-Lago and was, as one would expect, lavish. The whole extravaganza was attended to by 45 chefs, 28 seamstresses, and 100 limousine drivers, and 10,000 roses, hydrangeas, gardenias, and peonies—all white—were transported from New York in refrigerated trucks. Melania reportedly oversaw every detail, including the size of the dinner plates. Violins played as guests ate lobster and caviar and drank Crystal champagne. Joel, Elton John, Paul Anka, and Tony Bennett performed.

As party favors, some wedding guests received envelopes containing about a dozen black-and-white nude photos of Trump's model bride, according to journalist John Connolly.

The couple honeymooned at Mar-a-Lago.

———

Melania may have had a better understanding of who her husband was and what his limits were, but in one respect she made the same mistake as his previous two wives had: she got pregnant. In addition to having told Ivana he couldn't be sexually attracted to a woman who had had children, Trump made clear to radio shock jock Howard Stern that he was no fan of what pregnancy did to a woman's body. "I've seen beautiful women that for the rest of their lives have become [a] horror after giving birth," he said in one of the many interviews with Stern over the course of nearly two decades. He agreed to have a baby with Melania on the condition that she promise to get her antepartum body back.

So get pregnant she did, and the *Access Hollywood* tape in which Trump boasted about sexually assaulting women was made just a few months after she conceived. Melania chose to see the beauty in her blossoming, appearing in *Vogue* in a gold bikini when she was seven months pregnant. "I think it's very sexy for a woman to be pregnant," she told the fashion bible. "I think it's beautiful, carrying a baby inside."

All Donald could see was her growing body. "You know, they just blow up, right?" he said on *The Howard Stern Show* in 2005. "Like a blimp—in the right places. In her case, the right places. I mean, she really has become a monster—in all the right places. I mean monster in the most positive way. She has gotten very, very large—in all the right places." He told Stern he would give her one week to lose the baby weight.

On March 20, 2006, Melania gave birth to Barron William Trump after eight hours of labor. Twenty minutes after Barron's arrival, Trump called in to MSNBC's *Imus in the Morning* to announce the birth of his fifth child.

———

Three months after Barron was born, Trump flew to Los Angeles to tape an episode of *Celebrity Apprentice* at Hugh Hefner's Playboy Mansion, where he met a sweet-faced *Playboy* Playmate and former pre-K teacher named Karen McDougal. When the party was winding down, he asked for her number and the two began talking on the phone. Before long, they were dining in a bungalow at the Beverly Hills Hotel. "We talked for a couple hours—then, it was 'ON'! We got naked + had sex," she wrote in a journal that the *New Yorker* obtained. When she was leaving, Trump offered McDougal money. "I looked at him (+ felt sad) + said, 'No thanks—I'm not 'that girl.' I slept w/you because I like you—NOT for money'—He told me 'you are special.'"

The two went to carry on an affair for ten months, having sex on "many dozens" of occasions, sometimes unprotected, and seeing one another at least five times a month, she told CNN's Anderson Cooper, occasionally lowering her nickel-size ultramarine eyes in the uncomfortably frank interview. They hooked up all over the country, in hotels, at Trump golf courses, at his house in Bedminster, New Jersey, and he even took her to the Trump Tower apartment he shared with Melania, she said. They got together whenever Trump went to Los Angeles, always at the Beverly Hills Hotel. During their relationship, McDougal met members of Trump's family and was even photographed with Melania and Ivanka while wearing a pink bustier and bunny ears, and on another occasion with Eric. Trump didn't show any reluctance to be seen with her in public, she said.

McDougal said she had no idea he was with other women, aside from Melania, during the time they were together. He told her she was "beautiful like Ivanka" and "a smart girl."

McDougal fell in love with Trump, and she believes he did with her as well. "There were real feelings between the two of us," McDougal told Cooper. "He's so sweet. What everyone sees on TV, I didn't see that in that man, because that man was very sweet, very respectful, very loving, very kind and caring. That's the man I saw." Trump told McDougal he loved her "all the time," she told Cooper, and said he was remodeling an apartment in New York for her. She said that "maybe" she had hoped the two might get married someday.

Trump was less flagrant about his relationship with McDougal than he had been during other affairs. This time, to avoid getting caught, Trump sometimes had McDougal pay for her own flights and expenses when they would see one another and would later reimburse her. McDougal broke off the relationship in April 2007 because she felt guilty about Melania and because she had been offended by some of the things Trump had said. McDougal said it was possible Melania knew about their relationship, but she couldn't say for sure.

NINE

YOU GET WHAT YOU PAY FOR

"You have to treat 'em like shit."
—DONALD TRUMP, 1992, NEW YORK MAGAZINE

"Haven't we all? Are we babies?"
—DONALD TRUMP, 2008, ON HOWARD STERN (WHEN ASKED IF
HE'D EVER HAD A THREESOME)

Barron Trump was days short of turning four months old when Trump jetted off to Nevada for the American Century Championship in July 2006. In the sixteen years since NBC had launched the celebrity golf tournament, held at the Edgewood Tahoe Golf Course nestled on the shore of Lake Tahoe, it has come to be known as a star-studded affair with plenty of partying. This year was no exception. Other celebrity participants that weekend included Dan Quayle, Ray Romano, and Lance Armstrong. There was top-notch talent from the porn world in attendance as well.

Trump arrived on a Thursday, according to a *GQ* reconstruction of the weekend. He had invited Karen McDougal, his mistress of one month, to meet him at the event, but she wasn't supposed to get there until Saturday, so he had some free time on his hands. Trump hit the links, and after finishing his round headed over to the hospitality room where the event's sponsors bestowed swag on celebrity participants. One of the companies with a booth in the room was Wicked Pictures, a Los Angeles–based pornographic film studio. Jessica Drake and Stormy Daniels were two of the actresses manning the booth that day.

Drake started talking to Trump. "He flirted with me and asked me to walk along the golf course with him, which I did," she said at a press conference during the 2016 presidential campaign arranged by lawyer Gloria Allred. During their walk, Trump asked the adult film actress for her phone number, which she gave him.

While on the golf course, Trump spotted Stormy Daniels, who at the time was one of the most famous actresses in the porn industry, having just broken into the mainstream with a role in *The 40-Year-Old Virgin,* a Judd Apatow movie with a celebrity ensemble cast topped by Steve Carell. "I want to come talk to you later," Daniels said Trump told her. Later, back in the hospitality room, he asked her to give him her phone number and to have dinner with him. When she agreed, he told her to meet him in the Harrah's hotel penthouse, where he was staying.

By coincidence, that afternoon Daniels bumped into a friend, fellow porn star, and neighbor named Alana Evans, who had come up to Tahoe with friends for a weekend getaway. Evans's friend, another porn star named Cindy Crawford, was getting a tattoo on her ankle when, to her surprise, Evans saw Daniels walk by outside. She called to Daniels, who crossed the street and joined Evans and her friend in the tattoo parlor. Daniels told Evans about meeting Trump and his dinner invitation, and said she was excited to go out with him. Daniels said Trump was going to be throwing a party, and invited Evans to come along.

Daniels—whose real name is Stephanie Clifford—went back to her hotel to change into a clingy gold dress with a plunging neckline. She then headed over to Harrah's and up to Trump's suite, thinking they'd be going out to dinner, and was surprised to find him in black silk pajamas. He said they'd be dining in his room, she told gossip website The Dirty, which first broke the news of the encounter. She told him to put some clothes on. At the time, Daniels was twenty-seven and Trump was sixty.

That was also the night of the infamous spanking incident. Trump showed her a magazine that he was on the cover of, Daniels told Anderson Cooper during an interview on *60 Minutes*. Daniels was unimpressed. "I was like, 'Does this—does this normally work for you?' And he looked very taken—taken back, like he didn't really understand what I was saying. Like, I was, 'Does, just, you know talking about yourself normally work?' And I was like, 'Someone should take that magazine and spank you with it.' And I'll never forget the look on his face," she said. "And I said, you know, 'Give me that,' and I just remember him going, 'You wouldn't.' 'Hand it over.' And—he did, and I was like, 'Turn around, drop 'em.'"

Trump lowered his pants a little, turned around, and Daniels gave him a few swats. "And from that moment on he was a completely different person," Daniels said. That's when the normal conversation started. Trump asked Daniels questions about the porn business. He was impressed with her business acumen and started talking about getting her on *The Apprentice*. He talked about his family and showed her a picture of Melania and Barron, she wrote in her book *Full Disclosure*. He also told her she was beautiful and reminded him of Ivanka.

Daniels asked Trump about his hair. "He told me he was afraid to cut it or he'd lose his money," she told The Dirty.

At some point when she was with Trump in his suite, Daniels texted Evans urging her to come join them, but Evans was with Crawford, who had not been invited and who had had too much to drink, and Evans didn't feel comfortable leaving her friend behind. When her texts didn't get the response she wanted, Daniels upped the pressure on Evans and started calling, asking her to come over. During one of the calls, Daniels had the phone on speaker and Evans could hear Trump talking. "'Come on, Alana, come and have some fun with us. Let's party,'" Evans told us Trump said. "At that point, it's like, oh, no, there he is, it's totally real now. But that's the other thing. When Stormy and him are calling me, there's no noise. There's no music, there's no sound. It's just the two of them. This isn't a party."

When Evans realized that there was no one in the room but Daniels and Trump, she got scared. "Girls like me, things happen to us. We disappear all the time," Evans explained during a long interview for the book in San Diego. "Me, in the scheme of things, compared to someone like Donald Trump. . . . No one would have even batted an eye if something would have happened. My own personal life, I don't date men like that. I don't date drug dealers. I don't date gangsters. I don't date any man of questionable power, because it's dangerous."

Evans called her then-boyfriend to ask him what he thought. "He was straight up like 'I don't think you should do that,'" she said. "Not because there was a jealousy issue or controlling or I'm not allowed. . . . We're in porn. We don't have that type of traditional relationship. It was really like, from him, that's not a place you want to be. . . . He was like '[Trump] is bad news.'"

Evans turned off her phone to avoid Daniels's phone calls.

———

At some point during her evening with Trump in his suite, Daniels got up to go to the bathroom. When she came out, Trump was sitting on the bed in his underwear and undershirt. He kissed her, and they had sex ("one position, no condom," according to an email she wrote to The Dirty, which also gave an unflattering description of Trump's manhood). When they finished, Trump told her he wanted to see her again. She asked about his wife, and he told her not to worry about it, saying that he and Melania kept separate bedrooms. Daniels signed one of her DVDs for Trump and left.

Later that evening, Trump called Jessica Drake, the first porn star he had chatted with that day, and invited her up to his room. She didn't feel comfortable going alone, so she brought two friends. Trump, back in his pajamas, "grabbed each of us tightly in a hug and kissed each one of us without asking for permission," Drake said during the press conference with Gloria Allred. She elaborated later in an interview with the BBC. "He grabbed me in more of a forceful way and he kissed me on the lips," she told the British broadcaster. "It was almost like a pounce. It didn't feel good to me. It didn't feel consensual to me."

Trump spoke to the three women for a little while, querying them about their personal relationships and asking Drake questions about shooting porn. The women left after less than an hour. When Drake had returned to her room, a man called her and told her Trump wanted her to go back to his suite. She said she didn't want to. Then Trump called her and asked her to come have dinner with him and invited her to a party. When she said no, he asked, "What do you want? How much?" she said. She told him she had to go back to Los Angeles so he would leave her alone, but he still wasn't taking no for an answer. She received yet another phone call from a man, possibly Trump but possibly someone else, who said that if she would accept the invitation, Trump would pay her ten thousand dollars and let her use his private jet. She declined.

Evans called Daniels Friday morning and asked how the evening had gone. "Well, picture this: Donald Trump chasing me around his hotel room in his tighty-whities," Evans said Daniels told her. "She then told me that he offered her keys, basically tried to give her one of his condos in Florida. . . . He was trying to gain her favor, big time."

Daniels saw Trump again later Friday night at a party at a club inside the hotel, where Trump introduced her to Steelers quarter-back Ben Roethlisberger (who, two years later, would settle a lawsuit filed against him by a Harrah's casino hostess who alleged he raped her during the 2008 tournament). Trump had to leave and asked Roethlisberger to look out for Daniels. When Daniels decided it was time for her to call it a night, the football player walked her up to her room. When they got there, he asked her for a kiss, she wrote in her book. When she said no, he said, "Come on," she wrote. Spending a night with Trump hadn't been an issue for her, but Roethlisberger felt different to her. "I was terrified. I am rarely terrified," she wrote. After she went into her room and locked her door, he stayed outside knocking for several minutes. Eventually, he left.

———

Karen McDougal arrived at the tournament on Saturday morning, as she and Trump had arranged. She had no idea that he had been with other women before she got there, and once she arrived he was as solicitous to her as ever, leaving her only to play golf. "I went to every event, every after thing, parties, daytime things, I was there," she said in her interview with Anderson Cooper.

The overlap between McDougal and Daniels didn't end that weekend. After the tournament was over, Trump began calling Daniels, always from a blocked number. He would say they should get together to talk about her appearing on *Celebrity Apprentice*. She could get in touch with him either by calling his assistant or his bodyguard, and he always took her calls. If he couldn't, he would call back within minutes from a blocked number.

A week after the golf tournament, Trump invited Daniels to the Miss Universe pageant in Los Angeles. McDougal was there, too, and went to the after party. The following January, he brought McDougal to the Hollywood launch party for Trump Vodka, where she sat with Don Jr. and his wife, Vanessa. Trump had invited Daniels as well. They met again a short time later, when Daniels was in New York for work and called Trump. He invited her to come see his office in Trump Tower.

And then came the famous meeting in the Beverly Hills Hotel. It was July 2007, a year after Trump and Daniels first met at the golf tournament, and Trump was renting one of the hotel's famed bungalows. Once again, they had dinner in his room. The TV was visible from the dining room table and he was watching *Shark Week*. "He is obsessed with sharks. Terrified of sharks. He was like, 'I donate to all these charities and I would never donate to any charity that helps sharks. I hope all the sharks die,'" Daniels said in a 2011 interview with *In Touch*. He still hadn't figured out how to get her on *Celebrity Apprentice,* he told her. "I was pretty annoyed. He kept rubbing my leg and was like, 'You know, you're so beautiful. I love your little nose, it's like a little beak.' I go, 'Did you say a beak? Like, what the f—?'"

She avoided sex with him by telling him she was having her period and left a short time later.

That was the last time Daniels saw Trump. The next time they spoke, he told her he hadn't been able to get her on the show. She began avoiding his calls after that.

———

When it comes to women, Trump has a type—or two. Two of his three wives fit into the exotic category—Ivana and Melania (as did his mother, whose native tongue wasn't English). And while he married Maples, she best exemplifies the type he tends to go for in women he doesn't plan to settle down with: curvaceous and blonde. "Clearly his type is fake blondes with boobs, with that tall, slender shape. And it is crazy because he talks about his type all the time and he compares a lot of them to his daughter, which is creepy," Alana Evans said.

He has a type when it comes to occupation as well. "He likes dancers, he likes porn stars, he gets all kinds—in the past—of young models from different nightclubs in New York. He's infamous in my industry for this kind of behavior," Evans said. "Way before Stormy."

Trump has also shown a willingness to pay for sex. Drake and McDougal may be the only women who have publicly said that he offered them money, but stories about him doing so have been making the rounds for decades. "Donald has a magic number and I've heard it from more than one girl," Evans said. "Jessica Drake dropped the ten-thousand-dollar number. Other girls that I've talked to, that's the amount of money that he's offered. Those aren't going rates for porn girls. Normally if a porn star is an escort, she's getting like a thousand dollars for an hour. So for someone like him to out of the ballpark offer like ten grand, he knows in a likelihood they're not going to say no."

The stories about Trump and porn stars date back decades. "It goes back to the eighties," Evans said. "In my world, Donald Trump is someone who has been talked about prior to being president. There's friends I've worked with who have told me this directly. . . . I heard it for years."

Evans said she knows of at least three porn stars who claimed they were paid to have sex with Trump—two of whom she said told her directly. "They were some of the biggest in the industry and they were known for being very dominating," she said.

One of those people posted her story on Evans's Instagram page. Evans told her to take it down, because she feared for her friend's welfare. The alleged encounter took place in the mid-2000s, around the same time Trump met Stormy Daniels. The woman was working as an escort and a client had booked her for an hour at a rate of ten thousand dollars. Evans's friend said she was waiting at the hotel for her client, and when she opened the door men in suits came in and swept the room, making sure no one else was there. "She actually thought she was getting busted," Evans said. The men left and Trump walked in. The rendezvous didn't last more than fifteen minutes and then Trump left, Evans's friend told her.

The other encounter was a little earlier, likely right before Trump met Melania, Evans said. A tall, slender, foreign woman with dark curly hair, pale skin, and light eyes who primarily worked as an escort but had also done some adult films—which is how Evans knew her—was at a bar in a Trump building with another friend of Evans. Trump, who had made an appointment with the escort, came down and met the two of them in the bar. Evans's friend stayed there while the other woman went upstairs with Trump. "They had a friendship," Evans said. "It wasn't a one-time thing."

The third woman Evans heard was with Trump was a dominatrix adult film star whom Evans had met several times. "She's definitely a boss over him, one hundred percent," Evans said. "You wouldn't need a paddle with him, you wouldn't need a whip. It was the strength and the personality that he responds to. So I think what he looks for in women is that. If you can't bring that, he's going to automatically dominate you, because that's just what he does."

———

John Tino didn't just hear about Trump having sex with porn stars—he alleges he saw it firsthand. Between 1981 and 1983 Tino worked in a private brothel in Times Square above a theater that showed porn movies and had live sex shows. The private club—which he said was known as the "VIP Room"—was on the second floor. There was a private entrance around the side so clients could drive right up, enter, and go up the stairs without being seen.

Like much of the porn and sex industries in that era, which were controlled by the mafia, Tino's club was allegedly run by a crime family captain who was killed in a mob hit a few years later. Tino said he was tapped by the crime boss, whose name we are withholding, to run the VIP Room for him. The VIP Room was reserved for special clients and consisted of a few rooms with beds in them. The bathroom was in the hall. The rooms were kept meticulously clean and were always stocked with clean towels and candy bowls filled with condoms and K-Y jelly. The rooms were nicely wallpapered, and in each one hung a scented cardboard pine cutout like you'd see in a taxi and a mirror, right in front of the bed. And in each room was a hidden camera. The rule was, a light in the room had to stay on at all times.

Tino's job was to collect the sealed envelopes of cash the clients handed him (the regular rate was $1,500 an hour, though it could go higher), to escort the clients to their bedrooms, and then to go sit in a locked room and watch the clients on monitors to make sure none of the girls was being roughed up. Videos of all the encounters were recorded on black-and-white tape, with no sound. "You didn't know if one of these actors, whoever they were, were going to get crazy and start beating the girls," Tino said during one of several interviews for this book. "I had a piece, I had a baseball bat. It was a Ruger and a baseball bat."

Every night when the VIP Room shut down, Tino would collect the tapes and put them in a bag or a box. The following morning he would go downtown to his boss's office and deliver the tapes to him.

The secret club was frequented by a few celebrities, and a client they called "the real estate guy," Tino said, referring to Trump. Most of the women who worked there were porn stars, though not all. Trump preferred a woman who primarily performed live sex shows with her husband, though she acted in the occasional adult film as well.

Trump always wore a tie. He was cocky and aloof. He never drank alcohol. And he always asked for the same woman, whom Tino had nicknamed "Tri." Trump was at the height of his game at the time. He was getting ready to open Trump Tower and had become a local celebrity. Ivanka was a baby and Ivana was pregnant with or about to get pregnant with Eric, the couple's third child. But Trump was also grappling with a family tragedy. His brother, Freddie, had died in September 1981, in his early forties.

While Tino saw Trump at the club on multiple occasions, there is one that stands out in his mind. Around the fall of 1982, the boss called Tino and said he needed to see him. "I'll never forget it," Tino said. "He says, 'The real estate guy is coming. He wants Tri and he wants another girl—a young girl—for a ménage à trois.'"

The woman was initially reluctant. "When I told Tri, she said, 'What the fuck? No.' But I said, 'You gonna tell [him] no? 'Cause I'm not going to tell him no for you,'" Tino said, referring to his powerful boss. "The money was good for her. She said, 'What the fuck.'"

One night, a young-looking girl showed up at the club. "The first time I saw her there was when she was in the room," Tino said. The way she was dressed reminded him of Jodi Foster in *Taxi Driver*. "I was disgusted . . . [My boss] told me, 'You've got to pay special attention to this because if he tries to hurt [her].' He said, 'I don't think he will, but I don't need that.'"

Tri asked the girl how old she was. She said she was a teenager, Tino said. The real estate guy spent an hour in the room. After that,

Tino asked his boss to give him a job somewhere else. "I needed to get a little change," he said.

Tino bumped into the real estate guy one day in a completely different setting. He had gone to a union hall in Manhattan, and Roy Cohn walked in with Donald Trump. "He was having work done," Tino said. "He was having the concrete, S&A." S&A, which was mob controlled, supplied the concrete for Trump Tower. "When they came in, Trump looked at me. And then his demeanor went all business. I didn't acknowledge him."

Since those days, Tino did a few stints in jail, after which he changed his name. His boss from the Times Square club and many of the other mobsters who were around at the time are dead and no one knows what has become of the tapes.

Tino has tried to tell this story to reporters on multiple occasions. None of them was ever able to track down the woman known as Tri, nor the teenage girl. Tino has redoubled his efforts because he has been diagnosed with terminal cancer. He doesn't want to take what he knows about Trump to his grave. "That's why I'm telling you this now," he told us. "He's the president."

———

A few days before I, Barry Levine, talked with John Tino, a trusted source passed me his name and telephone number and briefly filled me in on his claims.

John's story, I was told, had been known to some reporters in New York investigating Trump during the 2016 campaign. But none of them decided to publish his account.

Two of them told me they believed John but their editors declined to run it without more evidence to corroborate his account of what he witnessed with the porn actress herself. And that is what we tried to find.

"See if you can find the porn star," I was told. "The story really lives and dies with her. But everyone who's worked it believes she's dead. So all you're left with is this old wiseguy's story. And to make matters worse, by the way, the old wiseguy is dying, too."

I saw a brief mention about the story on Twitter from 2017. I was not the only one, it seemed, who wanted to prove this man's story. One person tweeted something of a warning: "And hurry. John Tino is very sick with cancer. . . ."

Another tweeted whether there was "tape" of Trump with the possibly "underage girl" and the "porn girl."

I immediately knew a polygraph test would be out of the question because the meds would interfere with the test's ability to detect deception in Tino's answers. A polygraph expert confirmed to me that would be the case and said the ill mobster would certainly not be a candidate for the test, which police often use.

When I reached him on the phone, Tino acknowledged he was battling late-stage liver cancer and said he had been receiving drug therapies.

In the same breath as insisting to me his truthfulness over witnessing Trump and this porn actress and what he believed could be an underage girl, he volunteered: "I've been coughing up blood. But if you want to make your way out to see me, I promise you I'll sit and answer all your questions for as long as you need.

"It's my dying wish to tell this story to the public," he continued. "I have nothing to gain by doing this."

That conversation with Tino, it turned out, would be the first of dozens of conversations I would have with this man over the next eight months.

Over this period of time, while his medical condition continued to worsen, his story about Trump has never changed and his belief in what he saw has never wavered. While he's done time in prison for

Ladies' man —Trump was given that citation by his peers at the New York Military Academy. The woman seen with him in this staged yearbook photo was a school secretary. (Seth Poppel/Yearbook Library)

"He was a good-looking guy. And a douche," Candice Bergen recalled of her date with Trump when she was eighteen. She is seen here a year later, in 1965. They both attended the University of Pennsylvania. (CBS/Getty Images)

Australian golfer Jan Stephenson sits on the beach in 1976—the year she and Trump stopped dating. The breakup opened the door for him to marry Ivana. (LPGA/Getty Images)

During the 2016 campaign, the *Daily Mail* turned up an "extraordinary trove" of hundreds of Trump family photos found in a Palm Beach, Florida, thrift shop. The pictures date to the late 1970s, during the earliest days of his marriage to Ivana. One, the *Mail* says, shows Trump channeling Burt Reynolds—"the quintessential *Cosmopolitan* centerfold—as he relaxes in his robe" on the couple's bed; a second shows Trump and Ivana with his father Fred at a party; another shows the young dad holding daughter Ivanka; and a fourth shows Ivana lounging in the sun. (Courtesy of DailyMail.com)

Trump and his mentor, the notorious Mob-
connected New York lawyer Roy Cohn, attend
a news conference in 1984. (Bettman/Getty Images)

The seedy Doll Theater in Times Square
fits the description of the building
where mobster John Tino claims Trump
allegedly engaged in a threesome
involving a teenage girl in the early 1980s.

Aerial view of Mar-a-Lago
in Palm Beach in 1988.
(Russell C. Turiak)

Some model parties took place on the
Trump Princess, seen here in 1989.
(Russell C. Turiak)

While married to Ivana, Trump hid his affair with Marla Maples in relatively plain sight. Here they attend a fight in Atlantic City, New Jersey, in June 1988. Marla's "beard"—Tom Fitzsimmons— sits between them. (Jeffrey Asher/Getty Images)

Marla Maples (in black) stands between Trump and Ivana during the infamous "wife-mistress" confrontation in Aspen, Colorado, in December 1989. (Alpha photo)

After Marla left, Trump and Ivana had additional words. "As far as I was concerned, the marriage ended that day," Ivana said in her book, *Raising Trump.* (Russell C. Turiak)

The *New York Post*'s famous cover on February 16, 1990. Marla later said, "I never said that, someone else said that. Is it true? I'm not going to talk about that." (New York Post)

Trump is pictured with Rowanne Brewer in New York in 1990. They dated when he was separated from Ivana and on the rocks with Marla. (Russell C. Turiak)

In 1992, Trump dated Guess model Anna Nicole Smith, who he said had the "best body, best face, best hair." (© 2007 RICHARD BOCKLET/Ace Pictures, Inc.)

Trump photographs aspiring *Playboy* model Bridget Marks at the magazine's fortieth anniversary party in May 1993 in New York. When he was running for president, Marks said: "I thought he was thoughtful. I thought he was respectful." (Ron Galella/Getty Images)

Trump touches the stomach of Marla Maples as he confirms published reports that she's pregnant with his baby on April 7, 1993. (HAI DO/Getty Images)

Just eighteen days after the pregnancy announcement, Trump had *Playboy* Playmate Barbara Moore stashed at Mar-a-Lago. Here, she sits on a sofa in her bikini, surrounded by pictures of Trump on April 25, 1993. (© 2018 Barbara Ann Moore)

Moore snapped this candid shot of Trump relaxing at Mar-a-Lago. (© 2018 Barbara Ann Moore)

Trump posing with models, some of them in their early teens, at a promotional event for the 1992 Elite "Look of the Year" contest in New York.

At a Mar-a-Lago party in January 1993, Trump pushed model Kelly Hyler into the pool. She attempted to return the favor, but Trump's security guards stopped her. "She had her arm around his neck, but she was playful, I remember," said the photographer Lannis Waters. (© The Palm Beach Post/ZUMA Wire)

Barbara Pilling provided this modeling shot of herself, showing her at age seventeen—the year Trump hit on her at a New York club. "He said, 'You're absolutely gorgeous, you're just like Marilyn Monroe but with dark hair,'" Pilling said. "I remember my booker was . . . like, 'Er, no,' and rolled his eyes." (Marc Baptiste/Courtesy Barbara Pilling)

Stacy Wilkes, a contestant in the 1991 Elite "Look of the Year" contest, provided this modeling photo, showing her as a sixteen-year-old when Trump, as a celebrity judge, allegedly body-shamed her. "I mean there was no way to be skinnier for me," she said. (Courtesy of Stacy Wilkes)

While his parents look on, Trump stares at Marla on their wedding day at The Plaza Hotel in New York on December 20, 1993. When their affair became public, his mother Mary was said to have asked Ivana, "What kind of son have I created?" (Time & Life Pictures/Getty Images)

Ivanka (*center, in white*), a teenager, sits on her father's lap during a Beach Boys concert at Mar-a-Lago in January 1996. Trump has a history of making "creepy" comments about his eldest daughter's looks. (Davidoff Studios Photography/Getty Images)

Alicia Machado, the 1996 Miss Universe, laughs with Trump at Mar-a-Lago. He ended up fat-shaming the Venezuelan beauty and also tried to sleep with her, she claimed. (Davidoff Studios/Getty Images)

Kara Young and Trump attend a movie screening in New York in 1998. Their relationship turned serious. Her ex-boyfriend, A. J. Benza, claims Trump even secretly proposed marriage to the model. "She could have been First Lady," Benza told us. (New York Daily News Archive/Getty Images)

Model Maureen Gallagher is seen on the runway for a Christian Dior show in 1992. For a time, Trump was dating both her and Young. (Roberto Rabanne)

Before Melania emerged as his fiancée, Trump's steady girlfriend was Celina Midelfart (*left*). Here, in February 1998, the Norwegian heiress attends a birthday party in New York for Trump's ex-wife, Ivana. Ivanka poses with them. (Photo by Ron Galella/Getty Images)

Some seventeen years before winning the White House, Trump and then-girlfriend Melania Knauss appear presidential in front of a U.S. flag for *New York* in 1999. That year, Melania said Trump "would be a great leader" and she could see herself as a first lady, saying, "I would be very traditional, like Jackie Kennedy and Betty Ford."

(George Holz/Getty Images)

Trump and Melania pose with future convicted sex offender Jeffrey Epstein and British socialite Ghislaine Maxwell at Mar-a-Lago in February 2000. Trump eventually barred Epstein from Mar-a-Lago because he allegedly sexually assaulted an underage girl at the club, according to court documents.

(Davidoff Studios Photography/Getty Images)

Left to right, Kylie Bax, Trump, Bill Clinton, and Melania pose together at the U.S. Open tennis tournament in New York in September 2000. Bax, a New Zealand supermodel, once dated Trump. When the *Access Hollywood* tape emerged years later, she was quoted as saying, "I'm sorry, but he is a man." (Clinton Presidential Library)

A few years before seeing Stormy Daniels, Karen McDougal, and Summer Zervos at the Beverly Hills Hotel, Trump was photographed there with Melania for the 14th Annual Night of 100 Stars Gala in February 2004. Pictured with the couple is *Lolita* actress Dominique Swain. (Victor Spinelli/Getty Images)

The private entrance to Trump's favorite bungalow—22—at the Beverly Hills Hotel. The bungalow was also said to be Frank Sinatra's favorite. (Barry Levine)

Trump poses with Stormy Daniels on July 13, 2006, in Lake Tahoe. She recalled in her book *Full Disclosure:* "He had a red cap, a Trump crest as a placeholder for the MAGA slogan not one of us could see coming." (© Stormy Daniels)

Stormy Daniels (*right*) in the sparkly dress she allegedly wore the night of her sexual encounter with Trump in 2006. She wore the same "little gold dress" that year to her friend Alana Evans's birthday party at the Vanguard nightclub in Los Angeles. (Courtesy Alana Evans)

Hugh Hefner presents "Playmate of the Year" Karen McDougal at the Playboy Mansion in May 1998. She ended up meeting Trump there eight years later, which resulted in an alleged ten-month extramarital affair. "I didn't know he was intimate with other ladies. I thought I was the only one," she told CNN. (Brad Elterman/Getty Images)

A former contestant from *The Apprentice,* Summer Zervos, sued Trump for defamation after he repeatedly denied her claims of sexual misconduct. "I wondered if the sexual behavior was some kind of test," she said. She's seen here at a press conference in 2016. (Frederick M. Brown/Getty Images)

Rachel Crooks claimed Trump inappropriately kissed her by an elevator in Trump Tower in 2005. Here Crooks holds a snapshot of herself from that time, when she worked as a receptionist in the New York building. (The Washington Post/Getty Images)

Activists rally at a protest against Trump, then the Republican presidential candidate, for his "treatment of women" in front of Trump Tower in New York in October 2016. (Drew Angerer/Getty Images)

At a rally in Lewis Center, Ohio, in August 2018, attendees hold placards reading "Women for Trump." (Bloomberg/Getty Images)

THIS CHECK IS PRINTED ON CHEMICAL REACTIVE PAPER WHICH CONTAINS A WATERMARK AND HAS MICRO PRINTING IN THE SIGNATURE LINE

DONALD J. TRUMP
725 5TH AVENUE
NEW YORK, NY 10022

CAPITAL ONE, N.A.
57 WEST 57TH STREET
NEW YORK, NY 10019   60-791/214   NO. 002821

CHECK DATE
08/01/17

CHECK AMOUNT
****$35,000.00**

PAY   **THIRTY FIVE THOUSAND DOLLARS AND NO CENTS**

TO THE
ORDER OF   MICHAEL D COHEN ESQ
10A
NEW YORK, NY 10022

Before going to prison, Michael Cohen presented into evidence at a congressional hearing in February 2019, a $35,000 reimbursement check he said Trump gave him to help cover the $130,000 Cohen had paid out in "hush money" to Stormy Daniels. (Exhibit from House Oversight Committee)

felonies involving larceny during a life in organized crime, there's no indication from publicly available records that he's ever been in a mental health facility.

I also had individuals connected with law enforcement review Tino's records and they found no issues with the veracity of his account. One told me, "The stuff he got nailed on, while felonies, were pretty lightweight. He's certainly no killer."

The only agreement I made with Tino in connection to reporting about him for this book is that I agreed not to reveal his former last name, which is known to police and federal authorities, along with the state in which he was convicted.

When I traveled to Tino's nondescript home a few hours outside of New York City, I was met by an intelligent but frail man with a tremendous conviction for the truth.

Over the course of several hours, I also got a crash course in the mob complete with seeing his battle scars from surviving a past gunfight.

Then, over the months, through dozens of calls only to find that most of the people who associated with Tino are dead—either from natural causes or victims of mob violence themselves—I was able to locate two individuals who confirmed his work at the secretive sex den. Both of these individuals specifically remembered him by his mob nickname, "Blue Eyes."

One of the individuals, who is in his late eighties, said of Tino: "I remember 'Blue Eyes' from the office. He worked for us. He would come by. [—] had him running a place in Times Square."

The man said he recalled Tino regularly bringing in tapes but "I don't remember what happened to them. It was so long ago."

Leads that Tino's boss, before his death, moved the tapes to a storage facility in Manhattan never checked out and the whereabouts of the tapes today are unknown.

Tino, and others, have speculated that the tapes, possibly retained for blackmail or otherwise, could have been destroyed by Tino's boss or other mobsters because at the time of his disappearance and slaying, federal prosecutors were also investigating Tino's boss for his involvement in child pornography.

Another theory, according to Tino and others, is that the tapes could have been confiscated by federal authorities and could still be sitting in an evidence box somewhere.

Details of search warrants connected to Tino's boss, those that have been made public, are inconclusive.

The other source, who had been associated with a crime family other than Tino's and worked for another major mobster who operated sex establishments in Times Square like Tino's boss, claims he remembered being told by Tino about the circumstances of these allegations many decades ago.

I agreed to report about these sources under the condition of anonymity. And I am also withholding from this book the identity of Tino's boss and other mob associates involved in his murder, in addition to the names of the other mobsters who ran sex joints in Times Square.

Tino's boss, before his death from a mob hit, was represented by a famous criminal attorney who also represented one of the biggest known organized crime figures in New York.

I wanted to speak with this lawyer about Tino's claims about his boss. The lawyer's daughter responded to me in an email, but said her dad, "now almost 96," was in failing health and couldn't speak to me.

A review of the FBI file and related publicly available archival documents about Tino's late boss remains heavily redacted even though he was murdered in 1986.

The file contains the partial listing of the man's personal phone book. The names and numbers that are not redacted do not show any connection to Trump.

But the man, an alleged mafia capo who also had his hand in other mob-connected businesses at the time and also had control over a Teamsters local, is quoted in one document as discussing "concrete trucks" with an associate and references the then newly constructed Trump Plaza along with another building.

"That's ours," Tino's boss is heard saying, according to the document, adding to his associate that he could help with a "very reduced price on a condominium" at one of the buildings.

Construction started on Trump Plaza in 1982—about the time Trump allegedly was in contact with Tino's boss or an associate about visiting the Times Square sex den. Trump Plaza opened in March 1984.

In a 2016 article for *Politico*, Trump biographer David Cay Johnston discussed Trump's connection with the mob in his business, writing: "But Trump was not clean as a whistle. . . . He'd hired mobbed-up firms to erect Trump Tower and his Trump Plaza apartment building in Manhattan, including buying ostensibly overpriced concrete from a company controlled by mafia chieftains. . . . That story eventually came out in a federal investigation, which also concluded that in a construction industry saturated by mob influence, the Trump Plaza apartment building most likely benefited from connections to racketeering."

Johnston also told me, "Several prominent New York City real estate developers went to the FBI seeking relief, but Trump ran in the opposite direction."

Newsweek also reported on January 10, 2019, that "some of [Roy] Cohn's Mafia clients controlled New York's construction unions, whose blessing Trump needed to complete his projects."

The FBI file of Tino's former boss made several references to the man's operations in distributing pornography.

One document, heavily redacted, also referred to the man's holdings in Times Square, and another document noted an operation that allegedly "provided women for wealthy LCN [La Cosa Nostra] figures coming to the Los Angeles area."

While Tino was too ill to tour the Times Square area with me, the building that may have housed the "VIP Room" in which he claimed he worked had been torn down long ago. Redevelopment has completely extinguished many of these establishments from Times Square. But back when Tino was working there, the area was a cesspool of porn, sex, and violence.

The building most closely resembling Tino's description of where this operation allegedly took place once stood at the corner of Seventh Avenue and Forty-Eighth Street. The corner location would have allowed for a separate entrance around the side where clients would be dropped off so they didn't have to enter through the front door, as Tino noted.

Photos Tino and I examined of the building at the time showed what appeared to be the entrance he had remembered for his VIP clients.

This building housed the Doll Theater, which Cinema Treasures said "flourished in the 1970s and 1980s" and "actually had a live sex show on stage in between features."

Another description from the blog Jeremiah's Vanishing New York was more colorful: "It's nighttime on Times Square. Standing on the northern end of the block, on the corner of 48th and 7th Ave., start off the night with an Orange Julius and a hot dog to charge your batteries. Next, duck into the Doll theater, where the 'Sexsational School for Sex Arts' beckons you above a sign for 'Live XXX Acts.'

Take a seat inside and enjoy the double features interspersed with live sex performances, both onstage and in the audience members' laps."

A third description, from the same blog, this time quoting a writer named Russ Kick, claimed the Doll "was basically a mellow, secure place. Less assault-prone than 8th Avenue's Venus, although Japanese tourists were frequently targets for toilet muggings. . . . The projectionist sold Percodans. The live-sex show teams sold coke and pot."

Above the Doll, at one time, was a joint known as the Satin Ballroom, which featured "dime-a-dance" topless dancing and more.

Before demolition, the white building, built in 1927, had three stories. It had pyramid-capped columns, framing the windows, and ornate trim running along the cornice line. One report noted, "the building was disfigured by years of neglect, garish alterations."

According to the *New York Times*, the Doll was one of two sex-film houses hit by pipe bombs in January 1973. At the Doll, "about 50 patrons had to be routed from the small theater," according to the report, which offered no explanation why the theaters were targeted.

I spoke to an actor who once worked in the Satin Ballroom above the Doll during his youth and asked if he knew what also went on in the other rooms above the theater. "I didn't want to know," he told me.

There were other places in the area where continuous programs of hard-core films were shown, live sex acts performed, and prostitution raged.

"Tri," through my research, was involved in all three: porn films, live sex, and prostitution.

But despite efforts made by me and two private investigators—along with other reporters I spoke to who worked the story—I was unable to find "Tri" or confirm whether she was still alive.

I also conducted interviews with people in the mob-associated porn business specific to the Times Square sex scene in the early 1980s—not one of them knew for a fact what happened to this woman.

Because her circumstances are unknown at the time of this writing and I have been unable to contact her, I am withholding her stage name and also the stage name of a male sex performer she identified as her husband. Their real names are not known to me or to the other people in the industry I spoke with.

With what little information we had connecting the two, we scoured criminal records, court records, marriage records; we even searched for records associated with the old fleabag hotel in Times Square where she and her husband lived for a time—the same hotel where Tino resided during those days a few blocks from the sex den.

But there's no dispute that "Tri" worked in the business at the time and did jobs for people in the mob—people like Tino's boss.

One woman who spoke to people in the business for me about "Tri" was Raven De La Croix, who was called "THE Burlesque Queen of the 80s." She had the lead role in Russ Meyer's 1976 film *Up!* and appeared in the 1980 movie *The Blues Brothers*.

Raven told me she learned from a close friend, a well-known bodyguard to many of the women on the Times Square porn scene back then, that "Tri" "was working in the pocket of the industry for the mob and others" and "was definitely in on the sex parties—she was a thin little thing. She was not the pick of the bunch and did what she could do to hustle."

Raven said two mob families "ran these [sex dens] for men with deep pockets, VIPs," adding: "I wasn't or wouldn't be interested in playing any of that stuff. And lucky for me I was looked after for safety of things I never knew at that time."

Another big name from that era, Samantha Fox, told me she did not interact with "Tri" but knew women like her turned tricks for wealthy men.

"People did those things but I was not part of it," she said.

A third star from that time, who was known as "Seka," called "the Platinum Princess of Porn," wrote in her 2013 memoir, *Inside Seka*, "I'm told a lot of companies involved in our industry have or had mob ties" but her own actions never involved the mob, as far as she knew. "It was a job. I did my thing, I got paid, I went home," she wrote.

The best-known journalist who worked the scene at the time was Josh Alan Friedman, who first reported for Al Goldstein's *Screw* magazine and then penned a 1986 book called *Tales of Times Square*."

"A whore does it for money, for power. A slut does it for free. So don't you dare think of me as a slut," Friedman quoted "Tri" as saying in his book.

Friedman told me he remembered "Tri" well from those days and even wrote about her involving a wild night at the notorious Manhattan swingers club Plato's Retreat (which operated from 1977 to 1985).

Friedman told me: "I had media calls in 2016 from some reporters asking about the 'Donald Trump mistress'—who disappeared. She disappeared well over thirty years ago, a couple of decades. Possibly to drug addiction—that's the story going around."

(In his book, he connected "Tri" to drug use, writing: "A double dose of Quaaludes hits [her] and she starts moaning for a Valium to 'mellow me out.'")

"But she was hot. She told me she was French but who knows? She reminded me of a young Ava Gardner—she had that Old Hollywood look. She stood out among the women. She was a vamp," Friedman told me.

When I mentioned the mobster who was Tino's boss, Friedman confirmed: "Yes [he] and [——] had their hands in a lot of joints at the time.

"Much of Times Square was mobbed up. Back then there were a lot of these places—where the actresses were for sale. There were hundreds of wealthy men. Could have happened at a lot of these locations."

And as far as underage girls being involved?

He said: "Listen, by 1977, there was not a trace of child porn there but that doesn't mean it didn't happen. They could get young girls—they could have been homeless kids."

A former porn film director who worked with "Tri" around the time the alleged events Tino describes took place was Shaun Costello.

"[She] did what I asked her to do," he told me. "It was a really cheap movie, two or three days to shoot. These girls didn't get a lot from films—$100 or $150. So they often turned to other things to make additional money. There were a lot of live sex shows going on at the time, etc.

"Once you had a name you could dance, you could work at the strip clubs. You could work the circuit.

"But she didn't stick around long. She was in and out quickly. And that wasn't her real name. It wouldn't surprise me if she was dead. There was a lot of cocaine in those days. Everyone had a spoon up their nose."

Interestingly, Costello volunteered that he knew Donald Trump. "I've known Donald since high school," he said. "We were the same age. I saw him at parties. I thought he was a rich spoiled kid. Trump was a horny high school kid trying to get laid. But whether he was into this stuff in Times Square I couldn't tell you."

(On Howard Stern's February 6, 2013, show, the shock jock's sidekick Robin Quivers asked Trump, who was calling in, "So, you watching any porn?"

In a transcript of the conversation supplied by Factba.se, Trump's response was: "I've never been totally into it. . . . I have friends who need it, because they think, they get nothing. . . .")

Like some of the others I spoke to, Costello confirmed that Tino's boss "was well known and had connections to these type of sex clubs."

Around the time she allegedly was with Trump, "Tri" also briefly appeared in a documentary made about the porn industry by a Canadian filmmaker, along with a black male porn performer she identified as her husband.

In the film, *Not a Love Story*, "Tri" said to the camera: "I was raised in a sexual atmosphere where my mother was a prostitute and I knew of sex since I've been six years old. This is really nothing for me to be nude in front of people. I feel perfectly comfortable."

She added that it was her preference to perform live sex acts in Times Square with her husband than to turn tricks.

"It was easy from the beginning. In fact, it was easier than being a call girl because I could be with who I choose . . ." she said, wearing a velour track suit, while being filmed backstage at a sex club. "I could come here and I don't make as much money but, you know, I'm with the man that I love."

Unlike in her interview with Josh Alan Friedman, "Tri" this time made a point of insisting, "I'm not raunchy."

She also speculated on the psychology behind men wanting to see her engage in sex acts with her husband on a mattress on a stage.

"The average white businessman who comes in here likes to see [him] with me because it's downgrading me," she said, adding the men would often shout during their show: "Fuck her, hurt her, get it!"

"Tri," who reportedly had a "rose with stem" tattoo on her left shoulder blade, was credited with appearing in a few porn films from 1981 to 1987, but vanished from the industry after that.

For his part, Tino, who I believe is telling the truth after months of investigation, said he's had no contact with "Tri" since those days.

"I tried to convince her that maybe it was time for her to move on," he said. "But then a porno film director who'd seen her live performance decided she'd make a great porno actress. So Tri moved on from the New York City scene and the Fulton Hotel. . . . And I never saw her again."

Even though I could not speak to Tri, the evidence we do have—coupled with the widely reported claims about Trump's fondness for young women, his willingness to offer money for sex, and his fascination with sex workers—leads me to the conclusion that Tino was telling the truth. I attempted to contact Trump multiple times in summer 2019 about these allegations, including sending email and Fedex requests for comment to his White House press staff, as well as placing a call to deputy White House Press Secretary Hogan Gidley, but neither Trump nor his representatives had responded by the given deadline.

———

A few weeks after the article about her affair with Trump ran on The Dirty, Daniels got a phone call from someone at *In Touch* magazine. In May 2011 she sat down with *In Touch* reporter Jordi Lippe-McGraw. "She was just the same way she is now—very matter-of-fact about it," Lippe-McGraw told us. "She wasn't trying to make it into anything more than it was. It wasn't like a love affair they had. In fact, it really kind of seemed like—I guess transaction isn't the right word, but more of kind of an opportunity. Like, 'Hey, I'll sleep with this guy, maybe it will lead me to potentially get on *The Apprentice* or it might just be a good networking opportunity.'"

In Touch also gave Daniels a lie detector test, which she passed. They told her they would be reaching out to Trump for comment, which is standard practice in journalism. What isn't so ordinary is what happened next. Daniels was in Las Vegas and had just parked her car to go to an exercise class that she was running a little late for. Her infant daughter was in her rear-facing car seat on the passenger side of the backseat so Daniels walked around the back of her car to go get her out. As she was trying to unbuckle the baby, a man approached her. "I saw his Converse shoes first," Daniels wrote in *Full Disclosure*. She looked up and saw a "hot guy." He was wearing what appeared to be expensive jeans and a gray hoodie with an asymmetrical zipper. "He looked like a cross between Kevin Bacon, Jon Bon Jovi, and Keith Urban. A sharp, angular face. . . . He had a very kissable mouth. Like if you were talking to him in a bar, you would be like, 'I really just want to touch your lips.'"

Daniels said she figured the man was lost and was getting ready to offer directions when he said, "Beautiful little girl you got there," looking at her daughter. She thanked him and asked him what building he was looking for. He ignored the question, and continued: "It'd really be a shame if something happened to her mom. Forget the story. Leave Mr. Trump alone."

The magazine ended up killing the story because when they called Trump looking for comment, his lawyer Michael Cohen threatened to sue if they ran it, CBS reported. Once news of the affair came out in 2018, *In Touch* dug up the old interview and published it.

———

Trump didn't seem to think much about the affairs he had had during his marriage to Melania until he started running for president. Realizing that his infidelities becoming public knowledge might hurt his campaign, he moved to silence the women, following the Roy Cohn playbook to the letter. Shortly after he won the Republican nomination, a party working on Trump's behalf paid McDougal $150,000 to buy her silence. The *Wall Street Journal* broke the news of McDougal's arrangement just days before the presidential election in November 2016.

McDougal's story wasn't the only one the Trump campaign was working to hide. A month earlier, Trump lawyer Michael Cohen had paid Stormy Daniels, whose real name is Stephanie Clifford, $130,000 as part of an agreement that prohibited her from discussing her affair with Trump. News of that hush money payment was revealed by the *Wall Street Journal* in 2018. Cohen responded to the article by producing a statement signed by Daniels denying she had had a relationship with Trump.

A short time later, Daniels filed a lawsuit against the president alleging that Cohen used "intimidation and coercive tactics" to force her to sign the statement. The complaint also said that the "hush agreement" was invalid because Trump never signed it and that, in any case, Cohen had breached it when he acknowledged its existence in response to the *Wall Street Journal*'s reporting.

When the stories of the affairs broke, Trump, in turns, vigorously denied that he had had relationships with the women, said he didn't know about the payoffs, and said he had nothing to do with the payoffs. The fact is, he had known what was happening every step of the way, an investigation by the *Wall Street Journal* showed, and played a central role in arranging the payments, even getting directly involved in quashing the stories. When he didn't directly have his hands on events, he was briefed on developments.

In April 2018, Trump acknowledged that the payoff to Daniels had happened and Trump lawyer Rudy Giuliani said Trump had reimbursed Cohen the $130,000—though he still insisted the story of the affair was false.

It was classic Roy Cohn—the mentor whose absence Trump felt particularly acutely that year, lamenting "Where's my Roy Cohn?" as the pressure from the expanding investigation into collusion with Russia was mounting. Cohen was the closest thing he had.

"Michael Cohen in a weird way is sort of the Roy Cohn of our time," journalist and Roy Cohn relative David Marcus told us. "Michael Cohen was [Trump's] bag man, his connector. He was actually the one who arranged the payments and things. Now, we don't know everything that Roy did, but there were certainly times when Roy was accused of buying off people, threatening people, silencing people through all kinds of means, either implied violence or money or favors. That's what Trump learned how to do and he did it artfully through [Cohen]."

Cohen later pleaded guilty to campaign finance violations in connection with the payments as well as to a litany of other charges. The twenty-two-page charging document that prosecutors filed in conjunction with his August 2018 guilty plea asserted that Cohen "coordinated with one or more members of the campaign, including through meetings and phone calls, about the fact, nature, and timing of the payments." That unnamed campaign member was Trump, the *Journal* reported—which would make the president an unindicted coconspirator in those crimes. During his court appearance, he said that Trump had directed him to arrange the payments to McDougal and Daniels to prevent them from speaking publicly about their affairs with him.

In testimony before Congress in February 2019, Cohen said that Trump directed the hush money arrangements and, while in office, reimbursed Cohen for the payments "as part of a criminal scheme to violate campaign finance laws." Cohen said that Trump had him lie to Melania about the payments.

What Melania knew and when is the source of endless speculation, and her every look at her husband, her every gesture, is scrutinized. After the news of the payments broke, the *New York Times* reported that she was "blindsided" and "furious" with Trump. For a while afterward, she largely withdrew from the public eye. She canceled a scheduled trip to Davos, Switzerland, with her husband, spending their thirteenth wedding anniversary away from him. She traveled in her own car to the State of the Union speech, instead of riding with Trump.

That was January. By October, during her first solo tour to Africa, she told ABC that gossip about her husband "is not a concern and focus of mine." Still, she acknowledged that weathering that storm had not been easy. "It's not always pleasant, of course, but I know what is right and what is wrong and what is true and not true," she said. When interviewer Tom Llamas asked her if she loved her husband, she answered in the affirmative. "Yes, we are fine," she responded. "It's what media speculate, and it's gossip. It's not always correct stuff. . . . I'm very strong and I know what my priorities are."

When seen together again after her trip, she and Trump appeared to be back on track, even holding hands in public.

Author Laurence Leamer told CNN the two are more connected than some might think. They regularly spend two to three hours over dinner together at the club's outdoor restaurant, he observed. "What married couple spends three hours together alone at dinner?" he said. During Thanksgiving in 2018, "They were holding hands, they were kissing as if nobody else existed, as if their kids and grandkids didn't exist," he said in *People*. "It's like the two of them against the world now."

Part Three

PRESIDENT

TEN

DIVINE TOOL

"Nobody's done more for Christians or evangelicals or,
frankly, religion, than I have."
—DONALD TRUMP, 2018, TO CBN NEWS

In 2012, a private jet touched down at an airfield near Liberty University in Lynchburg, Virginia, carrying what the university's website touted as "its most highly anticipated Convocation speaker" ever. Previous convocation guests had included accomplished political figures such as Senator John McCain and Governor Bobby Jindal, and conservative show-business figures like Ben Stein and Chuck Norris. But none created quite the stir that businessman and *Apprentice* star Donald J. Trump did, who "no doubt drew the largest audience ever," Liberty's press office declared.

The Vines Center, where the event is held regularly throughout the semester, was packed to the rafters with excited undergrads, some of them holding signs proclaiming "We ♥ Donald Trump." After the event, Trump, who said he waived his customary speaking fee "as a gift to the school," penned a note to Liberty head Jerry Falwell Jr.—actual ink on paper, a habit for which he is well known—and an alliance was forged. An emotional one: Falwell later said that

Trump reminded him of his late father, Moral Majority and Liberty University founder Rev. Jerry Falwell.

Trump and the younger Falwell have been members of a mutual admiration club ever since that 2012 visit. At times, the odd-couple nature of the relationship between the evangelical leader and the libidinous Manhattan real estate developer turned president baffles. Falwell, for example, once tweeted a photo of his wife, the then-presidential nominee, and himself in Trump's office. Prominently displayed on the wall behind them was a *Playboy* magazine cover, graced by Trump himself.

Unlikely though the relationship may seem, Falwell was on the vanguard of evangelical leaders who endorsed Trump when he announced in 2015 that he would be pursuing a run for the nation's highest office. Falwell took a lot of heat for his patronage of the thrice-married New Yorker from Liberty's alumni and board members, one of whom stepped down. But Falwell was unapologetic about his backing of the real estate tycoon. "In my opinion, Donald Trump lives a life of loving and helping others as Jesus taught in the great commandment," Falwell said during a 2016 Trump campaign appearance at Liberty.

———

Falwell's full-throated endorsement of Trump gets to the heart of a question that confounded many: Why did white evangelicals come out in droves to vote for a man with such a checkered history with women and fidelity? Why were they willing to support a candidate who so clearly did not share their values?

The truth is, many did not. In endorsing Trump, Falwell had his finger on the pulse of mainstream white evangelicals, but it put him at odds with a good number of other leaders and thinkers in the community, which was and remains divided in its views of the president.

"Trump is a misogynist and philanderer," the Washington, D.C.–based evangelical newspaper *Christian Post* wrote in a February 2016 editorial—the first time the publication had ever taken a position on a political candidate. "He demeans women and minorities. His preferred forms of communication are insults, obscenities and untruths. While Christians have been guilty of all of these, we, unlike Trump, acknowledge our sins, ask for forgiveness and seek restitution with the aid of the Holy Spirit and our community of believers."

As the 2016 Republican primary season progressed, however, grassroots support for Trump among white evangelicals continued to grow (evangelicals of color did not line up behind Trump), outpacing even that for son-of-a-pastor Ted Cruz. Focus on the Family founder James Dobson went so far as to say that he had "heard" that Trump "did accept a relationship with Christ. I know the person who led him to Christ." Trump's inability to sound like a traditional evangelical, Dobson said, was because Trump was still "a baby Christian."

In the end, without evangelicals—more specifically, the white evangelicals who make up the conservative wing of this decentralized faith community—Trump would not have won the presidency. White evangelicals voted for him at a higher rate—81 percent—than they had even for George W. Bush, who garnered 78 percent of their vote in 2004, according to an analysis of exit polls by the Pew Research Center. They are at the core of his base.

———

"The person" so instrumental in Trump's journey of faith, whom Dobson would not name, turned out to be his personal pastor, Paula White. "I can tell you with confidence that I have heard Mr. Trump verbally acknowledge his faith in Jesus Christ for the forgiveness of his sins through prayer, and I absolutely believe he is a Christian who is growing like the rest of us," she told the *Christian Post*. When asked during a telephone interview if she believed Trump's faith is sincere, she replied: "I don't believe it, I know it."

Trump needed the third-party validation, because his track record as a Christian was sketchy. He made rookie mistakes like declining to name his favorite passage of scripture when asked on the campaign trail. At first, he came up blank, then later gave a verse that wasn't in the Bible. On another occasion he referred to "Two Corinthians" instead of "Second Corinthians." And he said that he has never asked God for forgiveness—an act that is at the very heart of becoming an evangelical Christian (and without which, arguably, one is not).

But despite these missteps and the revelations of the *Access Hollywood* tape, for most evangelicals, it seemed, what mattered most was not what Trump did in his own life but what, if elected, he would do for them. And during his 2016 campaign, he signaled to evangelicals that he would do plenty. He talked about his religious upbringing. He started bringing his childhood Bible to campaign rallies and having someone open them with a prayer. He promised to repeal the IRS rule that prohibited churches from endorsing political candidates and to stack the federal courts with pro-life judges. He did interviews with the religious press and created an evangelical advisory board.

———

For many in the community, their support of Trump boiled down to a single reason. "Because of the judges," said Ned Ryun, founder and CEO of American Majority. "That's why you saw eighty-something percent [of evangelicals] break for him in the end. What he was saying at times was making them feel wildly uncomfortable, and then it dawned on them that if Hillary wins, we lose the courts."

But that's not the whole story. A big part of Trump's strong showing among white evangelicals has less to do with him than it does with who his opponent was. In a poll conducted in September 2016 by the Pew Research Center, 76 percent of evangelicals who supported Trump said their dislike of Hillary Clinton was a major reason they did so. It is tough to overstate how deeply the community abhors Clinton. A month before the election, an ABC poll showed that 70 percent of white evangelicals held a negative view of her, and 72 percent of evangelicals said she was not honest or trustworthy. Clinton stands for many of the things that evangelicals feel is wrong with the country today, particularly abortion and feminism, but the antipathy started long before that. Its roots go back to the disparaging "I suppose I could have stayed at home and baked cookies" remark she made when asked about her career during her husband's 1992 presidential campaign. In many ways, Hillary became the embodiment of the culture wars that left evangelicals feeling alienated during Bill Clinton's tenure as president, the personification of progressive secularism.

Hillary was also tarnished by her husband's infidelity—even though she did the "Christian" thing and forgave him and stayed with him. Many of her opponents fault her for attacking the women who claimed to have had relationships with her husband, saying that in doing so, she enabled him. Also at play is the "propensity of evangelical women to blame women for their husbands' infidelity," said Heather Quintero, a math teacher who grew up in the evangelical church but left it two years after Trump was elected. Overtly or implicitly, many evangelicals see Bill's affairs as being at least partly Hillary's fault because she didn't conform to the evangelical ideal of a submissive woman.

Quintero thinks the evangelical response to Hillary spoke volumes about how the church sees women. "I felt like it came down to

. . . You hate women that much, that you are going to vote for this person who is the antithesis of Christianity. . . . There was nothing that [Hillary] could have done that would not have been twisted as a reason not to vote for her," Quintero said. On the other hand, Quintero thinks that pretty much any male Democratic candidate would have been able to beat Trump.

Trump's stance on immigration was also a big selling point for evangelicals; the same ABC poll showed that it was a key factor behind the support of two-thirds of evangelicals surveyed. The current browning of America has left evangelicals worried about America's waning "Christian values" and the loss of their way of life. When asked about projections that the United States would become majority nonwhite by 2043, 52 percent of white evangelical Protestants said the impact of that demographic change would be "mostly negative," according to a survey conducted by the Public Religion Research Institute in July 2018. That was a stark contrast to the 39 percent of white mainline Protestants, 32 percent of Catholics, and 23 percent of religiously unaffiliated Americans who said the same.

Bill Leonard, founding dean and professor emeritus at Wake Forest University's School of Divinity, has written extensively about what he calls the loss of Protestant privilege in America. "I do think there is a concern, implicit or explicit, in the declines demographically among white evangelical Protestants," he said, noting that when Albert Mohler became president of Southern Baptist Theological Seminary in 1993 he began his tenure by encouraging evangelicals to have more children. With dwindling membership and an aging population, white evangelicals are turning to the government for protection. "That's been a reason for their encouragement of Trump."

There is a transactional element to the relationship. "Trump is willing to use the evangelicals as his base, a strong part of his base, and they are willing to use him . . . [B]ecause of the overarching influence of Vice President Pence as an evangelical and a very conservative one, they are willing to use him for that agenda that Pence is navigating with and for them," Leonard said. "They're all using each other."

———

The relationship between Trump and evangelicals has remained strong since he took office. They give him a solid base and he gives them judges and laws. In addition to two conservative Supreme Court justices, as of July 26, 2019, 129 judges whom Trump appointed had been approved by the Senate, including 43 circuit court judges. By way of comparison, 329 federal judges were appointed and approved during President Barack Obama's eight years in office, 55 of whom ascended to the circuit court bench. Trump has successfully reshaped the courts for decades to come. He revived a ban on giving foreign aid to groups that provide abortion counseling. He passed a rule barring clinics that perform abortions or make referrals to abortion providers from receiving federal funds. His Department of Justice established a Religious Liberty Task Force that will enforce a broad interpretation of "religious liberty" in enforcing federal laws. He has tried, but not yet succeeded, to abolish the Johnson Amendment, a provision in the tax code that prohibits tax-exempt organizations, such as churches, from endorsing or opposing political candidates. Even Trump's seemingly small gestures, such as wishing the nation "Merry Christmas," have had a big impact on Christians. "He has really bent to their will," said Ashley Easter, a progressive Christian speaker and author.

And his administration is as populated by evangelicals as any in recent memory. Self-proclaimed believers include Vice President Mike Pence, Secretary of State Mike Pompeo, Secretary of Education

Betsy DeVos, former administrator of the Environmental Protection Agency Scott Pruitt, Trump personal attorney Jay Sekulow, and Secretary of Energy Rick Perry. Many of them speak openly about their faith and make policy decisions accordingly. Paula White said that evangelical access to the Trump White House is "unprecedented."

Trump's continued emphasis on building a border wall appeals to evangelicals, too. In January 2018, a Washington Post–ABC poll found that 75 percent of white evangelicals thought "the federal crackdown on undocumented immigrants" was a positive thing. By comparison, only 25 percent of nonwhite Christians found it positive and only 46 percent of adults overall. They are not much more welcoming to people fleeing war, persecution, or natural disasters. A Pew survey conducted in May 2018 found that 68 percent of white evangelicals said the United States had no responsibility to accept refugees, versus 51 percent of Americans overall. That number is even more striking when looked at in the context of other religious groups: the same survey found that position was held by 50 percent of white mainline Protestants, 45 percent of Catholics, and 28 percent of black Protestants.

Instead of trying to justify Trump's faith, many evangelicals have stopped attempting to portray him as a Christian president and are instead saying he is the tool God has chosen for this moment. Since the campaign there have been rumblings in certain Christian circles that Trump's ascendance was prophesied and that his election was God's plan. That idea got started when a former firefighter named Mark Taylor said he was watching a television interview with Trump in 2011 and heard a voice saying, "The Spirit of God says I've chosen this man, Donald Trump, for such a time as this." The story started making the rounds shortly before the 2016 election—and was eagerly embraced by many—and then exploded in 2018 when students and faculty and Falwell's Liberty

University made it into a film, *The Trump Prophecy,* which was screened in 1,200 theaters around the country. If God put Trump in the White House, then his critics are doing Satan's work, the reasoning goes.

Why women are willing to turn a blind eye to his sexual misconduct is a more complicated question. Quintero thinks it has something to do with church teachings on the role of women, which fundamentally disregard and devalue them. (Though evangelicals would argue that their doctrine of "complementarianism" holds that while the sexes have different roles they have equal worth; a kind of "separate but equal" doctrine for the genders.)

Quintero doesn't buy that. "I think that in the evangelical community, women are seen as less valuable than men," she said. As illustration, she recounted the story of an experience she had while helping to teach a Bible class for some kids. A girl in the class asked why God is assigned a male pronoun if God is a spirit. Quintero told her that God is conventionally referred to as "He" because Jesus called God "Father," but that in the Old Testament there is a lot of imagery that represents God in feminine terms, such as a mother hen sheltering her young. "God isn't male and god isn't female, God is a spirit," Quintero told the girl. The other woman teaching the class with Quintero reported what she had said and Quintero was disinvited from helping with Sunday school after that. "It was worrisome to me, because it was like we are going to ignore any parts of scripture that are affirming of women and overemphasize the male-affirming scripture," Quintero said.

Our conversation with Quintero took place a short time before Easter, when Christians celebrate the death and resurrection of Jesus Christ, and she pointed to the sermons surrounding that occasion as another example. "The quote that I've heard a million times is that Jesus was taken and all of his friends deserted him. That's not true—the women stayed," she said. "But no, all of his friends—the ones that counted. I feel like much of the devaluing of women in the evangelical church and in the church in general has been an effort to maintain status quo and power."

That power is firmly in the hands of men. Women go from being under the authority of their fathers to being under the authority of their husbands, to whom they are to submit in all matters—including, in many households, when it comes to deciding how to vote. "Basically lack of penis equals lack of autonomy," Quintero said. "I have talked to women in the evangelical church in the past whose husbands, for example, were involved in pornography or involved in other things that the evangelical church would consider to be morally wrong. But they have the concept that because their husband was their head of household or their head in the eyes of God, that anything that they did in submitting to him, even if what they were being asked to do is morally wrong, was okay because they were submitting," Quintero said. "On the one hand, I think this is incredibly oppressive. On the other hand, I think many women don't see it that way because there is a lack of personal consequence to any decision."

In this male-dominant world, men are often given allowances that women are not. For example, while the church teaches sexual purity—which means no unpure thoughts, no watching pornography, and no sex before marriage—for members of both sexes, the reality is dramatically different. In truth, pornography is widely used among evangelicals, with 68 percent of churchgoing men and more than 50 percent of pastors saying they used porn on a regular basis, according to a 2016 study by the Barna Group.

While considered a sin, porn use is seen as a problem to be addressed and thus tacitly tolerated—in boys. In girls, it would be seen as deviant, Quintero said. "The evangelical church, as much as they would like to say, 'Oh, no, we expect purity from both boys and

girls,' that's really not—it might be the goal but it's not true in practice," she said. The fact that Trump cheats on his wives, sleeps with
porn stars, and gets away with it all is something that, contrarily,
earns him the admiration of evangelical men, Quintero reckons.
"The annoying thing, I think, is that a lot of evangelical men really
admire him for that," she said. "I think they look at him and they
think, 'If I weren't a Christian, that's who I'd be.'"

Quintero was never a Trump fan, but when the *Access Hollywood* tape was made public, a switch flipped. "It was at that point
that I stopped just being like, okay, I'm not voting for Trump, and
started being vocal about the reasons why," she said. "I think that for
a lot of women, at least for me, it was infuriating. It was like, okay,
I'm done being quiet."

The attitudes revealed by the church's acceptance of Trump and
his treatment of women was a big part of what ultimately pushed
Quintero away. "What really helped me make the decision about leaving the evangelical church was that I recognized that at the end of the
day . . . the patriarchy still rules the church," she said. "In the evangelical church it's not even under the rug, or 'Oh, it's not really like that.'
They would say, 'Yes, and that's the way it's supposed to be.'"

Many young evangelical women are coming to similar conclu-
sions. "I think it's been devastating for many women to know that
their male friends and family support somebody like this and it
really kind of shows how women are viewed and where their worth
is," Easter said. "I've seen an exodus from the evangelical community by people who said, 'I can't identify that way anymore.'"

———

Many of the evangelical women who support Trump choose to focus
not on his shortcomings but instead on the things they like about
him. Deb G., who asked us not to use her full name, works in minis-

try, and some of the people she counsels are women in jail. She tells them that what they did to get there is not who they are. She takes a similar approach to Trump. She was a Trump fan from the moment he threw his hat into the ring. "I liked his frankness," she said. "I thought he was extremely bold. I thought there were some other good contenders, but I did not think that any of them were going to be able to get done what we needed to have done." She believed that Trump would address the issues of abortion, Israel, and immigration.

And it was about time, she said. "For over 40 years, men who talked right, dressed correctly, their backgrounds were 'clean,' they were supposed to be the perfect candidate for the presidency. Evangelicals voted for them because of how they projected and perceived themselves . . . their character and moral standing," she wrote in an email following up on our video call. "They made promise after promise. Some followed through, most did not. Slowly but surely I have watched our country move closer and closer towards communism and socialism."

Trump, on the other hand, has not disappointed her. "I think for the very first time in a long time, and I'm including the Bushes, I really feel like my constitutional rights as a believer, as a Christian, for the first time are really going to be protected," she said.

When asked in what way she felt those rights were at risk, she mentioned the Pledge of Allegiance, which she said was no longer respected or taken seriously when her children were in school "because it's offensive, because God's mentioned in it." She is also concerned that schools don't promote nationalism anymore, and she feels that Trump does that.

She would also like to see her religious freedoms be as protected as anyone else's. "You hear all the time stories of students who are coming into the school system and they're bringing their Bibles and they're told they can't bring their Bibles to school anymore because it might offend somebody. But yet a Muslim can pull out their prayer rug and get on the floor and say their prayers, and I will defend their right to do that," she said.

Whether or not Trump is actually a Christian is not her concern. "That's not my thing to figure out," Deb G. said. "That's God's thing to figure out. That's between Donald and his maker."

Deb G. said she wasn't thrilled when she heard the *Access Hollywood* tape, but also noted that we live in a society where women are routinely objectified, and Trump's comments are a reflection of that culture. But she believes he is not the same man he was when that recording was made. She says that his esteem for women is evident in the women who are in his orbit. "I look at the women who he has around him, his daughters, they're brilliant, they're well educated, they speak well, they have good positions in companies, and not just them but other women. I don't see that part of him anymore," she said. "It may have been there. Obviously it was, but again, people change, I think he's changed . . . I think he's still changing."

––––––

Trump's friendship with Pastor Paula White dates back to 2002 when he called her out of the blue after seeing her preach on television, impressed by the diminutive, golden-haired White's inexhaustible energy and preaching style. When he started hosting *The Apprentice,* Trump invited her to come deliver a prayer at the season finale. When she would go to New York, she would stay in Trump hotels and eventually ended up buying an apartment in one of his buildings. And when he considered a presidential run in 2011, he asked White and some other ministers to pray with him. Afterward, he and White agreed it wasn't the right time for him to enter politics. When he threw his hat in the ring in 2015, she was there as his spiritual counselor. She delivered a prayer at Trump's inauguration.

Pastor White says the man she sees depicted in the press is not the man she has known and spent time with over their eighteen-year friendship. "I have watched him in so many settings and seen absolutely nothing but respect for women," she said in a telephone interview for this book. "I see nothing but honor. I have never heard him speak ill, I've never heard him joke, and I've spent a lot of time." At the same time, White doesn't gloss over the things he has said in public. She brought up the insults he made about Rosie O'Donnell and said "they weren't so nice." She wasn't making excuses for him. "That language to any woman, or to any person, is never okay," she said. But she stressed that over nearly two decades of friendship, she has seen no signs of the man that Trump's accusers describe. "I make this very clear, that's not the man that I've known or seen," she said. The sexist behavior that is so widely reported? "I've never seen it, never experienced it, never watched it," she asserted. "And I have been around him a lot. I've watched him interact with hundreds of women, from social settings to private settings."

Being Trump's personal pastor brings with it a duty of confidentiality, so she is unable to talk about what she has gleaned from their interactions in that capacity. About the *Access Hollywood* tape she was able to say only that he exhibited a "heaviness" when the tape came out, more for familial concerns than political. She, too, said he is a man who has changed over time.

A survivor of sexual abuse herself, White is careful not to discount the women who have come forward with accusations against Trump. "I understand this from the other side. All I can tell you is my experience," she said. "I'm not saying that's not so, I'm not discrediting the people you've talked to. I haven't spoken to them. I'm saying to you, I can tell you, I do live in Trump Park Avenue and whether it is our receptionist or whether it is . . . our janitor, him being as kind and caring and concerning and nice. That was one of the things that was impressive to me; it didn't matter."

When asked about the manner in which Trump talks about women, White says that, in his actions, Trump has been empowering to them. She points to all the women he has put into positions of authority—and to herself as a prime example. "He considers me his pastor," she said, a reference to the widely held belief in evangelical circles that women are prohibited from being ordained ministers and are limited to teaching other women and young children. "You know how many men would not do that?"

ELEVEN

POWER PLAYS

*"No politician in history—and I say this with great
surety—has been treated worse or more unfairly."*
—DONALD TRUMP, 2017, COMMENCEMENT ADDRESS AT
THE U.S. COAST GUARD ACADEMY

"Women are doing great."
—DONALD TRUMP, 2018, TO A JOURNALIST

There is a photograph taken on Monday, January 23, 2017, the first full working day of Donald Trump's presidency, that encapsulates the significance of his presidency for women. He is sitting behind the carved oak Resolute Desk, wearing a dark suit with a sky-blue tie. Surrounding the new president is a coterie of middle-aged white men—including then chief of staff Reince Priebus, trade assistant Peter Navarro, son-in-law Jared Kushner, advisor Stephen Miller, and strategist Steve Bannon. Not a woman is in sight. The occasion of the photograph was Trump, in his famously vertical handwriting, signing an executive order that would bear upon the health of women around the world.

In signing the measure, Trump was fulfilling a campaign promise that matters dearly to evangelicals. As had other Republican administrations before him, he was reviving the Mexico City Policy,

known as the global gag rule, which prohibits foreign nongovern-
mental organizations (NGOs) that receive federal funds from providing abortion services or referrals, even if they use other sources
of money to do so. Trump's order went further, than those of previous Republican presidents, expanding the rule to apply to a broader
pool of recipients of health funding. One watchdog group said the
measure, which would apply to roughly $9 billion of U.S. global
health assistance, could now affect organizations involved in such
wide-ranging activities as supporting clean water and sanitation,
and could affect as many as 225 million women.

"This photo is what patriarchy looks like," one columnist wrote
the following day.

Trump evidently took the action to please his base, among them
evangelicals who want to see the number of abortions performed in
the world reduced, ideally, to zero. The effect, though, is likely to be
the opposite, multiple studies have shown. Data gathered from more
than 250,000 women in twenty nations suggested that the global
gag rule is, in fact, associated with an increase in abortions. It also
leads to lack of access to birth control, more unwanted and high-risk
pregnancies, and maternal illness and mortality.

This measure was not the only move that made women's lives
less safe. Trump officials fought against the expansion of rights for
women, girls, and LGBT people at a United Nations conference in
March 2019, shunning its traditional allies and teaming up instead
with nations with dismal rights records, such as Saudi Arabia and
Malaysia.

In February 2019 the Trump administration announced a measure that would stop providing federal family planning dollars to
organizations in the United States that provide abortion referrals or
that share space with abortion providers. Not only would that take
millions of dollars away from Planned Parenthood, but it would

affect health-care providers that offer an array of services, not only supplying birth control but screening for diabetes, sexually transmitted diseases, and cancer as well. People in low-income areas would be particularly hard hit.

Trump also repealed a rule that held that states and local governments could not use an organization's stance on abortion and abortion counseling as a reason to withhold federal family planning dollars funneled through local authorities, hitting another funding source for Planned Parenthood. And, making birth control even harder to access for young people, the administration is promoting abstinence-only sex education—which studies repeatedly show doesn't work to prevent pregnancy. "The strange thing about this is that people who want to decrease the number of abortions are taking away access to the very services that help prevent them," said Dr. Hal Lawrence, CEO of the American College of Obstetricians and Gynecologists.

Were all these actions really about eliminating abortion? Many of these measures will likely be challenged in court and may never take effect. They can nevertheless motivate their intended audience and buy its loyalty. The moves also emboldened pro-life legislators to take action. A rash of states passed abortion bans of varying degrees of restrictiveness in the first half of 2019. Among them was Alabama, which approved a measure so extreme that even televangelist Pat Robertson criticized it. That proposed law bans nearly all abortions, including in cases of rape and incest, and punishes doctors who perform them with up to ninety-nine years in prison. Other states, including Georgia, Kentucky, Mississippi, Louisiana, and Ohio, passed fetal heartbeat bills, which effectively outlaw abortion as early as at six weeks of pregnancy, and Missouri's governor signed a bill prohibiting abortion after eight weeks of pregnancy. Utah and Arkansas took steps to prohibit terminating a pregnancy after the eighteenth week, the middle of the second trimester. Iowa passed a fetal heartbeat law in 2018 that was struck down by a court. As of May 2019, nineteen states had laws on the books that could be used to restrict access to abortion. None of those laws, though, is enforceable, because they violate *Roe v. Wade,* the 1973 Supreme Court decision that ruled that women have a constitutional right to choose to terminate a pregnancy, and the measures passed recently are sure to be challenged in court.

That was precisely their point. Anti-abortion activists are hoping that there will be enough cases contesting the constitutionality of the new laws to compel the Supreme Court to reconsider *Roe.* For the first time in decades, opponents of abortion believe overturning the ruling is a real possibility, thanks to the two conservative justices Trump appointed to the Supreme Court, Neil Gorsuch and Brett Kavanaugh.

In the meantime, though, the administration is attacking abortion rights through other means, and sometimes egregiously. In November 2018, Office of Refugee Resettlement director Scott Lloyd was ousted from that job after the ACLU filed a lawsuit showing that he had been forcing teenage migrants to carry their pregnancies to term, even after they asked to terminate them. He had gone so far as to build a spreadsheet to track pregnant minors in his care. If a girl asked for abortion counseling, she was directed to a "life affirming" pregnancy resource center. In the autumn of 2017 Lloyd refused to allow a pregnant seventeen-year-old to leave the shelter where she was staying so she could terminate her pregnancy. He also denied the abortion request of a girl who said she had been raped.

Lloyd, who had helped draft a law restricting abortion before he joined the Trump administration, was one of many senior officials brought in to the Department of Health and Human Services who had previously worked as social conservative activists, including for groups opposing gay and abortion rights. Their influence is apparent; in January 2018, the department created the Conscience and Religious Freedom Division to "vigorously and effectively enforce existing laws protecting the rights of conscience and religious freedom" for health-care workers. The division will be tasked with looking into allegations of discrimination against people who refused to perform actions that they feel violate their personal or religious believes. In May 2019, Trump announced an expansion of the so-called conscience rule, broadening the pool of people who could claim conscience exceptions, largely in relation to procedures such as abortion, sterilization, assisted suicide, gender reassignment surgery, and other medical activities. The *New York Times* reported that when it comes to abortion rights "many of the most significant developments today are occurring at the agency level, largely out of public view."

———

Abortion is the marquee issue when it comes to Trump administration policies on women, but there are plenty of others that feminists and women's rights activists point to when discussing what they contend is a war being waged on women. They say that the repeated attempts to repeal the Affordable Care Act, if successful, would hurt women as well. Before the ACA, women had greater barriers to getting affordable insurance because they paid higher premiums than men; they didn't have protections for previously existing conditions, which included pregnancy and domestic violence; and they could be denied coverage for maternal health care and contraceptives. When the Republican-led Congress couldn't get rid of the ACA completely, Trump began whittling away at it, rolling back safeguards to prevent discrimination based on gender identity or against women who have previously had abortions, and issuing rules to allow more employers to deny insurance coverage of birth control on religious or moral grounds.

Early in his tenure, Trump revoked the 2014 Fair Pay and Safe Workplaces order, which, among other things, required wage transparency and barred forced arbitration clauses that made it harder for women to sue for sexual harassment. He also proposed funding cuts for food stamps; the Special Supplemental Nutrition Program for Women, Infants, and Children (WIC), which provides food assistance, baby formula, nutrition education, breastfeeding support, and access to health care and social services for low-income women who are pregnant or breastfeeding and children under the age of five; and after-school and summer programs that enable working mothers to hold down jobs. Additionally, key positions in the administration dealing with programs that help women have been left vacant, such as the ambassador at large for global women's issues in the State Department. He also disbanded the Council on Women and Girls in the White House.

"Their rhetoric is one thing, but the reality of their policies has made it incredibly clear that this president doesn't want to help women with families, doesn't want to invest in women, doesn't want to empower women, and really shows how even when they try to do it their policy actions always fall short," said Shilpa Phadke, vice president of the Women's Initiative at the Center for American Progress.

The future of the Violence Against Women Act is also in question.

"I think he has shown that he is in pretty much opposition to what we would call the sexual politics issues of women's rights," said Charlotte Bunch, distinguished professor of gender and women's studies at Rutgers University. "Of course, reproductive rights is the most obvious and the global gag rule alerted everybody to that immediately after he was inaugurated, but I think what has been less understood is the way in which his policies seek to undermine the legislation and changes in attitudes around violence against women more broadly, and particularly around sexual harassment."

"I think, very clearly, [Trump] has an administration that is quite singularly focused on enforcing white Christian hetero patriarchy in the United States," said Soraya Chemaly, a journalist and the author of *Rage Becomes Her: The Power of Women's Anger.* "Whatever the policies are, it's almost a straight line to accomplishing those objectives and maintaining that dominance."

A good number of Americans consider that a good thing. Women who support Trump see his presidency as a net positive for them. They cite the Child Tax Credit and the economy, saying unemployment for women is at an all-time low. (While the overall unemployment level has been steadily declining since 2010, decreases for men have been more dramatic than they have for women.) Republicans also point to a bill that Trump signed to encourage the National Science Foundation to recruit more women and support female entrepreneurs, and to another bill he signed directing NASA to encourage women to pursue careers in the aerospace industry.

Many hoped that presidential daughter and advisor Ivanka would be a softening influence on her father and would promote the interests of women. In her role at the White House, she promised to address matters such as paid family and medical leave, pay parity, and child care, among others. Advocates say that there is little to show for her efforts and that her initiatives are "half measures, total shams, steal from other programs that paid for paid leave," Phadke said. "Really, any serious person would think they are wolves in sheep's clothing." In February 2019, Ivanka announced the Women's Global Development and Prosperity Initiative, which will eventually give up to $300 million to help women in the developing world make economic gains. Her father's policies, however, and specifically the global gag rule, directly undercut her efforts. A study conducted across 97 countries found that each additional child a woman has between the ages of 20 and 44—the prime working years—reduces her likelihood of participating in the workforce by 5 to 10 percentage points. Even when effective, economic empowerment programs help only a small demographic. "Mostly they are for women who are individual starters, so it is helpful but it doesn't systemically challenge any of the problems women have," Bunch said.

———

In addition to policy positions that many see as detrimental to the health and well-being of women, Trump's critics point to another disturbing element of his presidency: verbal attacks on women he dislikes. Trump had long been willing to insult women in public; Rosie O'Donnell was "a fat pig," Bette Midler "disgusting," and Arianna Huffington a "dog."

Trump's lack of respect for women was on display early on in the Republican presidential primary season. "Look at that face! Would anyone vote for that?" Trump queried a reporter from *Rolling Stone* when primary opponent Carly Fiorina appeared on television. "Can you imagine that, the face of our next president? I mean, she's a woman, and I'm not s'posedta say bad things, but really, folks, come on. Are we serious?"

When Fox News host Megyn Kelly asked Trump during a presidential debate about the insults he had used against women, he lashed out against her, too, later telling CNN, "You could see there was blood coming out of her eyes, blood coming out of her wherever."

Occupying the Oval Office hasn't rendered his commentary about women any more presidential. He referred to Stormy Daniels as "horseface" and to former White House staffer Omarosa Manigault Newman as a "crazed, crying lowlife" and a "dog." In July 2019 he tweeted that the "squad" of four progressive freshman congress-women, Alexandria Ocasio-Cortez, Rashida Tlaib, Ayanna Pressley, and Ilhan Omar, could "go back and help fix the totally broken and crime-infested places from which they came" (among them, only Omar was not born in the United States). Even when he's trying to be complimentary, his sexism can get in the way. He made headlines in Paris in July 2017 with an awkward faux pas by telling French first lady Brigitte Macron that she was in "such good shape, beautiful."

As president, Trump has also repeatedly stood by men who are accused of sexual abuse and domestic violence. He has treated women's accusations with skepticism or outright disbelief while accepting men's denials on the basis of their word. When Alabama Republican Senate candidate Roy Moore was abandoned by senior members of his own party, Trump stood by him. Multiple women alleged that Moore had made sexual advances toward them while they were in their teens and he was in his thirties, one of whom said he sexually molested her when she was fourteen and another of whom said he sexually assaulted her when she was sixteen. Senate majority leader Mitch McConnell called on Moore to withdraw from the special election, but Trump continued to defend him. "He totally denies it," Trump said. "He says it didn't happen. You have to listen to him, also."

Trump went beyond just lending a supportive word to men accused of abuse—he brought them into his administration. Advisor Steve Bannon was charged with domestic violence in February 1996 and Secretary of Labor nominee Andy Puzder, who later withdrew his nomination, was accused of abuse by his then wife in 1986; police were called to their house on two occasions. White House speechwriter David Sorensen resigned after his ex-wife said he had been emotionally and physically abusive during their short-lived marriage. She alleged he had run over her foot with a car, snuffed out a cigarette on her hand, and thrown her against a wall. During a boat outing he grabbed her by her hair in a manner so menacing that she feared for her life, she said. She told the FBI about his behavior during their background check of him, but had not previously reported it to the police because he had ties to law enforcement, she said. She provided the *Washington Post* with evidence corroborating her allegations, which Sorensen has denied.

Sorensen's departure came only two days after Trump staff secretary Rob Porter was asked to submit his resignation after his two ex-wives each said he had been physically violent with them and that his mistreatment was the reason they left him. A third woman, a former girlfriend, said he had abused her as well. His ex-wives told the FBI about their allegations during his security clearance investigation, and the bureau relayed that information to the White House. Administration officials didn't take any action. It was only after a photograph of his first wife with a black eye was made public that he was asked to tender his resignation. She said she got the injury when he punched her in the face. Porter said it had been an "accident" and had happened as the two were arguing over a vase in their hotel room during a vacation.

Even after Porter resigned, Trump continued to defend him. "Now he also, as you probably know, says he's innocent and I think you have to remember that," Trump said in the Oval Office. The same day, he tweeted: "Peoples [*sic*] lives are being shattered and destroyed by a mere allegation. Some are true and some are false. Some are old and some are new. There is no recovery for someone falsely accused—life and career are gone. Is there no such thing any longer as Due Process?"

Trump did not publicly show any sympathy for the alleged victims of the men working for him.

Two months after Porter resigned, the Justice Department quietly changed the definition of domestic violence to encompass only physical harm that would classify as a felony or misdemeanor. Other forms of abuse—such as psychological—no longer qualify. "We have literally gone back to the seventies," said Holly Taylor-Dunn, a senior lecturer at the University of Worcester who is an expert on domestic abuse. "Changing the definition to take it back to being about physical harm completely undermines what domestic abuse is about."

They also made changes on the university level. Secretary of Education Betsy DeVos proposed regulations to weaken the enforcement of Title IX protections against sexual assault and sexual harassment in schools. Women's rights groups said the proposed changes would make it more difficult to prosecute alleged assaults and would discourage students from reporting incidents of sexual misconduct.

———

On October 6, 2018, the Senate voted on the Supreme Court nomination of Brett Kavanaugh as a riveted nation watched live on their televisions. He was approved 50–48, essentially along party lines, in one of the slimmest margins in U.S. history. As the result was announced, women from the galleries above the Senate floor shouted "Shame!"

The outcome was no surprise for anyone who had been watching the weeks-long soap opera of his nomination, but it was a moment of harsh realization for many women in America nonetheless. It forced them to confront a bitter truth: despite all the gains they thought they had made since the 1960s and 1970s, systematically little had changed.

The drama began with Kavanaugh's nomination to the Supreme Court in July, Trump's second. It was a bitter pill for Democrats, who had seen Obama's Supreme Court nomination scuttled by Republican maneuvering in the Senate. Democrats were in the minority in the Senate, leaving his appointment looking like a sure thing. And then a ray of hope appeared, in the form of a Stanford professor named Christine Blasey Ford, who said that Kavanaugh had tried to sexually assault her decades earlier when they were both in high school. To Democrats, Blasey (the surname she uses professionally) looked like the perfect accuser. Soft-spoken and vulnerable and at the same time strong, poised, and accomplished, Blasey is a psychologist, someone who could not only describe her experience but could explain the science behind why some of the details of that night were seared on her brain while others were beyond her recall. The neurotransmitter epinephrine "codes memories into the hippocampus, and so the trauma-related experience is locked there, whereas other details kind of drift," she would later tell senators.

For Republican women, though, and particularly white evan-gelical women, she was something else entirely. She was an edu-cated, professional woman; the personification of the liberal coastal elites. The Catholic Kavanaugh, despite his prep school and Ivy League credentials, was seen as having the right values. They were pitch-perfect proxies for the culture battle raging in America.

In the week before Blasey's testimony, Trump tweeted that he had "no doubt" that if the attack had been "as bad as she said," charges would have been "immediately filed." His tweet sparked outrage and hundreds of thousands of counter-tweets from women (and some men) using the hashtag #WhyIDidntReport and explain-ing the reasons they didn't tell loved ones or authorities about sexual assaults they had suffered. But Trump's message clearly resonated with a large part of the population—including many women.

The two faced off—not directly, but in a day of dueling testimo-nies in front of the Senate Judiciary Committee, each compelling in its own way. Blasey delivered a composed and riveting account of the pain that the incident caused her as a teenager and in the ensuing years. She was "terrified" to be there, she told the committee, but was telling her story not because she wanted to but because she believed it was her civic duty. Her testimony was thoughtful and sobering, and reporters in the room said they could hear crying and see tears on the faces of women throughout the room. Women watching on television or listening on the radio had similar responses. Twitter was filled with missives about weeping women standing around in clusters, women wearing headphones in tears on the subway, and many, many women tweeted that they were crying as she spoke. Even Trump said he found her to be a "credible witness" the day after her testimony and that she looked like "a very fine woman."

Then it was Kavanaugh's turn, and the mood shifted dramatically. He came out swinging, angry and indignant. He expressed outrage that he had been put in a position where he had to defend himself and choked back tears when talking about his children. He said he was the victim of a conspiracy against him drummed up by left-wing groups on behalf of the Clintons. And he was utterly convincing to those who had believed him in the first place.

Women were split on whom they believed, and that cleavage fell right along party lines (a Marist poll showed that 74 percent of Democratic women believed Blasey, while 73 percent of Republican women believed Kavanaugh), revealing a wider unease among many with where #MeToo, which had blown up exactly a year earlier, had taken society. Discomfort with evolving gender roles was one of the reasons that white women without college degrees had resoundingly supported Trump over Clinton; this was yet another manifestation of that dynamic. Trump had tapped in to a feeling that white men— and, by extension, the women beside them—have been pushed down the ladder not only as a result of of globalization and increased ethnic diversity but also due to the ascendancy of women. These women sympathized with Kavanaugh's plaint that a false accusation was turning his life upside down and worried that the careers of the men they loved and, by extension, their own lives, could be ruined by any woman who pointed a finger.

These Americans saw Trump's leaked "grab 'em by the pussy" tape as exactly what he said it was: locker-room talk. These men and women believe that boys will be boys and women need to loosen up and not take it all so seriously. As one Montana mom, standing next to her two teenage daughters, told MSNBC in the wake of the Kavanaugh accusations, "groping is no big deal." In other words, it's not the men who are wrong in such cases of sexual misconduct. It's the women, for overreacting.

Trump threw gasoline on the raging debate when he told reporters on the South Lawn of the White House that it was "a very scary time for young men in America." He seemed to be talking about himself as much as anyone. "You could be somebody that was perfect your entire life and somebody could accuse you of something," he said. Asked if he had a message for young women in the country, he responded: "Women are doing great." At a rally later that night, he openly mocked Blasey, to the cheers and jeers of the crowd.

The accused-as-victim trope is one Trump resorts to regularly, including when it comes to himself. "Every woman lied when they came forward to hurt my campaign. Total fabrication. The events never happened," he said at a campaign rally in 2016. And he went on to fan the flames of fear. "If they can fight somebody like me who has unlimited resources to fight back, just look at what they can do to you."

And he had brought it up the day before Blasey and Kavanaugh gave their testimonies, setting the stage. "I could have you chosen for a position. And somebody could say things," he said to a reporter in response to a question about the accusations against Kavanaugh. "And it's happened to me, many times, where false statements are made and, honestly, nobody knows who to believe."

Anyone could become the victim of a false accusation, he went on to say. "I could pick another Supreme Court judge, justice. I could pick another one, another one, another one. This could go on forever. Somebody could come and say thirty years ago, twenty-five years ago, ten years ago, five years ago he did a horrible thing to me. He did this, he did that, he did this, he did that. And honestly, it's a very dangerous period in our country . . . being perpetrated by some very evil people, some of whom are Democrats, I must say," Trump told the assembled reporters. "It's a con game at the highest level."

When asked if the allegations of sexual impropriety that had been leveled against him influenced his perception of Kavanaugh's accusers, he replied "Absolutely. I've had a lot of false charges made against me, really false charges."

Older white women have grown more convinced that men are vulnerable to malicious accusations over time. In November 2017, 8 percent of Republican women over the age of sixty-five said that a false accusation is worse than an unreported assault; by January 2019 that number had risen to 42 percent, according to two polls conducted by YouGov for the *Economist*. This same cohort was also most likely to say that a man should not lose his job over having harassed a woman twenty years earlier, and that a woman complaining about harassment causes problems.

Progressive women were doubling down on their own point of view. The Kavanaugh hearings revealed to them that the levers of power in America remain firmly in the hands of men, and those men will band together if their dominance is challenged. Women had been led to believe that one of the great barriers to stopping sexual harassment was the culture of silence, the reluctance of women to come forward and be heard. But Blasey came forward. She got her hearing. She was even believed by many. And it made no difference. She may have been given a more welcoming reception than was Anita Hill a quarter century before her, but the outcome was the same: men in power voted to dismiss the accusations of a credible woman and support an alleged offender.

The progress women had made, the strides toward equality—a journey no one thought complete but that seemed to be well under way—hadn't gotten them nearly as far as they had thought. Women had better educational opportunities, better jobs, better pay, and more help around the house from their spouses than they had a generation earlier, but the power structure was still solidly male. "Many women felt insulted and aware that patriarchy can still win and does still win," Bunch said.

———

In the run-up to the Kavanaugh nomination, women had endured more than a year of grueling revelations of sexual harassment and worse at the hands of powerful men. It started in July 2016 when Gretchen Carlson filed a harassment suit against Fox News head Roger Ailes, prompting other women to come forward as well. Next came allegations against Uber CEO Travis Kalanick and Fox News anchor Bill O'Reilly. And then the dam broke, with a flood of accusations against Harvey Weinstein, who had been quietly terrorizing Hollywood women since the late 1970s, according to the allegations. Amazon Studios' Roy Price was the next to be accused before Alyssa Milano issued a call on Twitter. "If you've been sexually harassed or assaulted, write 'me too' as a reply to this tweet," she wrote, reviving a phrase that had been coined by activist Tarana Burke more than a decade earlier. The #MeToo hashtag went global, and allegedly abusive men began falling like dominos. These included USA gymnastics doctor Larry Nassar, Vox Media's Lockhart Steele, restaurateur John Besh, director James Toback, fashion photographer Terry Richardson, magazine publisher Knight Landesman, journalist Mark Halperin, actor Kevin Spacey, comedian Louis C.K., Senator Al Franken, NBC's Matt Lauer, chef Mario Batali, journalist Charlie Rose, and CBS CEO Les Moonves. In all, more than two hundred celebrities, CEOs, and politicians were accused of sexual impropriety, and many of them had used their positions of power to intimidate and silence the women they had abused.

Trump set the stage for much of this. Women were furious over his crude and sexist boasts in the *Access Hollywood* tape and indignant that his accusers were dismissed as quickly as they emerged. "Trump's election catalyzed that because he was such a blunt-force tool of misogyny," Chemaly said. "He was so careless and obvious that even the most erstwhile person could not look away from it."

―――――

On May 17, 2018, Gina Haspel stepped onto a stage in Langley, Virginia, and into history. Placing her hand on a Bible held by outgoing CIA head Mike Pompeo, who was leaving to become Trump's secretary of state, and repeating after Vice President Mike Pence as he read her the oath of office, Trump standing between them with a scrutinizing gaze, she became the first ever female director of the Central Intelligence Agency. Trump looked solemn and proud.

Despite the hostility with which many activists and pundits say the Trump administration treats women, conservatives point to women like Haspel as proof that Trump is, in fact, their champion. He has appointed women to key positions—though in numbers far lower than Presidents Obama and Clinton and roughly equal to those of his Republican predecessors, who, as Bunch points out, governed in a different era and climate.

These women, though, are the shining examples that distract from the deep gender imbalance among Trump appointees across the administration. A detailed analysis by the *Atlantic* found that there was no agency in which Trump appointees reached gender parity and in most were well below; Obama, on the other hand, appointed more women than men to three agencies and came close to parity in the majority of others. "He does use women symbolically and not substantively," Chemaly said of Trump. "The women in his cabinet are at lower-level positions and pretty silent. They are not particularly feminist in any of their policy pursuits" and they are disproportionately white, she notes.

Of the Trump distractors, the most effective is his daughter Ivanka, whose poise and visible belief that she belongs at the table are testimony to a father who believes in her worth and ability. There are few of any persuasion who would argue that Trump does not have an extremely high opinion of Ivanka and a deep respect for her. But that doesn't mean he isn't sexist, Chemaly said.

"He is the classic benevolent sexist," she said, explaining that benevolent sexism, a well-known theory in social psychology, is a reflection of separate sphere theories, such as complementarianism, which hold that men and women serve different roles. "As long as a woman understands what that role is and performs that role and looks like she's performing that role then, a benevolent sexist can also, if he is a man, perform his role, which is to be the broad-shouldered protector and to provide money and to be the father and to be that kind of idealized masculine person."

Such a view of gender relations colors how one interprets interactions between men and women. "Benevolent sexists are demonstrably more likely to doubt women if they talk about their experiences of sexual harassment or rape, more likely to be harassers and rapists," she said. A hostile sexist—which Trump can be at times, as well, is "more likely to stereotype women as liars or manipulators," she said. "The thing with a benevolent sexist is they can say things like, 'But I love women.' It's pedestal sexism; it's putting women on a pedestal and treating them as though they're purer and have more moral clarity."

Benevolent sexism isn't solely the domain of men. While Ivanka's identity is tied up in her business acumen, she is careful not to stress that part of her life in her tightly controlled public image. The photos on her Instagram account, for example, that are not of her carrying out her father's work are pictures of her with her husband—performing the role of wife—or her with her children, or of just her children—stressing her role as mother. There are extremely few pictures of her alone.

Ivanka, for all her accomplishments, is a glowing illustration of the way the separate sphere theory functions in the real world. Ivanka puts forth a "fake feminism and [an] idealization of the effortless perfection of this kind of white woman who just drifts through her existence and detaches from the really, really ugly aspects of how she maintains her status and identity," Chemaly said. "She does that within the framework of what makes a good woman. A good woman is a good mother first and foremost. A good woman stands by her man. A good woman is not too loud and is pretty. She has this feminine ideal."

TWELVE

SHE CHANGE

"Exactly one century after Congress passed the constitutional amendment giving women the right to vote, we also have more women serving in Congress than at any time before."
—Donald Trump, 2019, State of the Union address

"If Congress refuses to listen to and grant what women ask, there is but one course left then to pursue. What is there left for women to do but to become the mothers of the future government?"
—Suffragist Victoria Woodhull

The PBS broadcast of Trump's second State of the Union address in February 2019 looked routine enough in the beginning. Trump was in his regulation blue suit and red tie, standing before a backdrop of a massive American flag. Vice President Mike Pence sat behind him, flanking him to his right; blue suit, blue tie. Speaker of the House Nancy Pelosi took the left flank; cream suit, white T-shirt, statement necklace. The camera panned over the assembled officials, starting on the Republican side of the aisle. It was the usual sea of navy and black suits. Once the camera crossed the center walkway, though, the scene changed, revealing a mass of women dressed in white, close to one hundred of them, paying sartorial homage to the women who fought a century earlier to win their right to vote. They were the Democratic female senators and representatives, the fruit of 2018's Year of the Woman, which returned the most female Congress in history, in which 127 women hold seats. Without Trump they might never have been elected.

Trump's 2016 victory galvanized women in America. While conservative women may have been jubilant at his win, progressive women were utterly dumbfounded. The idea that someone who said the things Trump said about women could beat Hillary Clinton, the first female candidate to win the nomination of a major party, was beyond the realm of possibility in their minds. When the impossible happened, women on the left realized that many things they had taken for granted still needed to be fought for.

"The forces he has unleashed, the women, particularly young women but also middle-aged women who thought that we had won, who thought that basically women's issues and the women's movement was on a course upward have been awakened," said Rutgers professor Charlotte Bunch.

Women ran for office in never-before-seen numbers in 2018, for everything from Congress to governorships to state legislatures: 53 women ran in either a Democratic or Republican primary for Senate, 23 of whom competed in the general election; 476 women ran in a primary for a seat in the House of Representatives and 233 made it through to the general election; 61 women filed for gubernatorial primary races and 16 competed for seats, as did 66 women for lieutenant governor, out of whom 28 passed through to the general election; and 122 women ran for other statewide seats and 86 made it through the primaries, according to the Center for American Women and Politics (CAWP). And they were diverse—a CAWP analysis showed that among Democrats, women of color are proportionately represented. A majority of the women running were Democrats.

A record number of them won. Women were instrumental in the Democratic take-back of the House of Representatives, winning more than 60 percent of the seats that had flipped. There are now 127 women serving in Congress, representing 23.7 percent of seats, more than at any time in history. Among those are the nation's first Muslim and Native American congresswomen. A lot of that was a reaction to Trump; the midterm election is always a referendum on the sitting president, but a higher percentage of voters said that the sitting president would be a factor in their 2018 voting decision than at any time since 1982.

A similar trend played out on the state level; 86 women hold statewide elected offices, including 9 governors and 15 lieutenant governors. In state legislatures, 2,127 women hold seats. South Dakota elected its first female governor, as did Guam.

Nevada elected the nation's first-ever majority female legislature in the 2018 midterm election, with women holding 23 seats in the Assembly and 10 in the Senate for a combined 52 percent. The newly elected officials there are younger and increasingly diverse.

Just a few months into the new term, the impact these Nevada women were having was apparent. When a male Republican defended a law that required doctors to ask women seeking abortions about their marital status, newly elected Democrat Yvanna Cancela retorted that men are not asked about their marital status when getting vasectomies. "The packed hearing room fell silent," the *Washington Post* wrote. "Bills prioritizing women's health and safety have soared to the top of the agenda. Mounting reports of sexual harassment have led one male lawmaker to resign. And policy debates long dominated by men, including prison reform and gun safety, are yielding to female voices," the *Post* reported.

When the *Post* article ran in mid-May 2019, more than seventeen bills were pending that dealt with sexual assault, sex trafficking, and sexual misconduct. There were also bills banning child marriage and looking at the causes of maternal mortality on the docket. Nevada Assembly Majority Leader Teresa Benitez-Thompson told the *Post* that none of those bills "would have seen the light of day" just a few years earlier. Case in point: in 2015 legislative leaders refused to schedule a hearing on a bill to promote pay equity for women.

One of the women who heeded the call to run for office—women historically have needed to be asked to run, multiple times, although that changed in 2018—was Rachel Crooks, the woman who said Trump kissed her in Trump Tower in 2006. She made a bid for the statehouse seat representing Ohio's 88th district, which Trump had carried by nearly 26 points over Hillary in 2016. Perhaps unsurprisingly for a woman accusing Trump in a district in which he enjoyed considerable popularity, she lost. She's able to see the bigger picture, though. "The silver lining, if we have to get a positive from him running, it certainly is that he motivated a lot to get involved in politics and to say this isn't okay," she said.

————

The day after Trump's election, Debbie Walsh and some colleagues sat around a large wooden conference table on the second floor of Wood Lawn Mansion, the graceful, colonnaded home of Rutgers University's Eagleton Institute of Politics, which was established in 1956 with a bequest from suffragist Florence Peshine Eagleton. Walsh is the director of the Center for American Women and Politics (CAWP), which falls under the auspices of Eagleton, and she and some of her CAWP colleagues were trying to make sense of Trump's surprise victory.

One of the things they were trying to figure out was what the result would mean for the nonpartisan campaign training program for women that CAWP runs every March. "We thought now no one is going to come because they're going to be so blown away by this," she said. They couldn't have been more wrong. "Literally, that day, while we were sitting here, people started registering," she said. "The day after the election."

Normally, CAWP begins advertising for the program in October and registrations roll in a few month later. In any given year, roughly three or four people have registered and paid their money by December, and about 150 people end up participating in the program. Not this year. By the end of December 2016, more than one hundred people had enrolled and paid. By January, CAWP was scouting bigger venues. Roughly three hundred people attended the program in March, and others had to be turned away for lack of space.

"It was Hillary's loss, but I think it was just as much this utter disbelief that the American public would go down this path, and a wake-up about the role of women, the value placed on women or the lack thereof, and a need, almost like a visceral need," Walsh said. "What they wanted to figure out was how can I have a voice? I've got to fight back against this, I have to have a voice. This can't stand."

Melanie Ramil, executive director of Emerge California, which trains Democratic women to run for office, said that not only did her organization see a huge uptick in the number of women interested in their program in 2016, but they were fielding inquiries from women who hadn't previously been politically active. "They've never knocked on a door, never volunteered on a campaign, they've never called a fellow voter on the phone," she said.

———

Running for office wasn't the only means through which women started working to make their voices heard in the public arena. Women who had opposed Trump came together in the days and weeks after the election, both to commiserate and to take collective action. They realized that many of the battles they thought had been won by their mothers and grandmothers—such as easy access to birth control and abortion and protection against discrimination and sexual abuse—were, in fact, unfinished. Trump's election and, even more so, his presidency, were a clarion call heard by women throughout the nation.

Kate Schatz and her friend Leslie Van Every had started Solidarity Sundays in Northern California's Bay Area in January 2016 to try to make activism feel more accessible to people. "We felt that we knew a lot of women who were really upset about things in the world," said Schatz, who was already a veteran activist. "We knew the election was going to be coming in November and we wanted to get people, women in particular, ready." They held monthly meetings that were regularly attended by about fifty people.

And then the election happened.

Three days after Trump won the presidency, Schatz put a notice on Facebook saying she was calling an emergency meeting at her house to "cry and brainstorm," she said. About one hundred people showed up. The Solidarity Sundays Facebook group, which had several hundred members before the election, mushroomed to nearly 10,000 followers within a week of Trump's victory and roughly 95 percent of the new members were women. Local chapters of the group began popping up throughout the country. By January 2017 there were about fifty; today there are more than one hundred. More than two years later, they continue to be active. Schatz and her partners send out a monthly missive to all the chapters in which they chose a theme for the month—say, the environment—and propose actions, such as writing letters or making phone calls with suggested targets (local EPA offices, elected officials, etc.). They also give "homework" consisting of recommended articles, speeches, podcasts, television shows, and other educational materials.

Other groups were just getting organized. "The week after the election our council member, Brad Lander, and the local rabbi called a community meeting to commiserate and be like, 'What the fuck just happened and what do we do,'" said Amy Bettys, who lives across the country in Brooklyn, New York. About 1,200 men and women showed up to the meeting, and they broke up into groups around issues they wanted to work on. Bettys veered toward women's health and reproductive rights and is now the cochair of WHARR (Women's Health and Reproductive Rights), one of several political action committees that came out of that meeting. There were roughly 50 people in her group that night, almost none of whom had been politically active before, and many of them have continued to be involved. About five hundred people have signed up for WHARR's weekly digest of issues and actions that can be taken at home.

Thanks to organizations like these, women are now able to be mobilized at a moment's notice. The Alabama Senate approved its near-total abortion ban on May 14, 2019. Exactly a week later more than five hundred #StopTheBans protests took place at statehouses, on Main Streets, and in town squares across the country, as well as on the steps of the Supreme Court.

Women's activism is taking varying forms. In January 2019, a team of women produced and performed *The Pussy Grabber Plays* at Joe's Pub in lower Manhattan to tell the stories of seven of the Trump accusers who had come forward during the presidential campaign. The vignettes describe the women's decisions to go public with their allegations and chronicle the backlash that confronted them once they had.

Cocreators Sharyn Rothstein and Kate Pine conceived of the project because they thought the women had been given short shrift in the media. "We felt like they'd been reduced to a number and their bravery had just been completely forgotten or pushed aside,"

Rothstein said. "And so, knowing that what theater does best is to give deep context, create empathy, spark discussion, and really contextualize a human beyond just a sound bite to really tell their story, we had this idea that we could match some of the best female playwrights we knew with some of these women to really fully explore their story and amplify their voice."

As they woke up and stepped up in their different ways in reaction to Trump, white women realized they had some soul-searching to do. "A lot of feminists are challenging—specifically challenging white women who have more resources, who have more proximity to power—are challenging them to consider why it is that they are only now feeling outrage," Chemaly said. "And that's legitimate when you think of mass incarceration or the treatment of black children in schools and you think of all of these issues that black women have to encounter as a function of racism, and why it is that those issues were not centralized in funded movements."

Both Chemaly and Schatz warn, as did nearly every other feminist or activist we spoke with, that to talk about women's reaction to Trump without considering race is to have only half the conversation. White women and women of color have deeply divergent experiences in the United States and therefore see Trump's presidency through very different lenses. Immigrants, Muslims, poor women, and women of color have not had the same sense of security as white women living above the poverty line have had, and while white progressives were shocked at the racist strain in America, Trump's campaign revealed that had always been apparent to black people. "For progressive white women, Trump has had a profound effect on waking them up, challenging them deeply on many, many levels and, yes, activating many who were not previously activated," Schatz said. "All of this stuff that we're now talking about all the time is stuff that those communities have been talking about forever; it just hasn't been on the forefront for women who are living in comfort and privilege."

Walsh echoed that. "If you talk to black women in particular, they will say they were not surprised by the election of Donald Trump. White women were naive to think there was no racism and there was no sexism," she said. What's more, black women were already active and mobilized. White women are just catching up.

———

If they had been able to live in privileged bubbles for most of their lives, progressive white women got a glimpse of what it feels like to realize the deck is stacked against you during Brett Kavanaugh's Supreme Court confirmation process. After all the demonstrations and the face-offs in Congress and the outpouring of emotion on the part of women who had been abused and a delay in the vote for an abridged FBI investigation into the allegations against him, he was confirmed anyway.

"The Kavanaugh hearings have been one of the most emotionally devastating things I've seen for women in a very long time," Schatz said. Around the time of the hearings, Schatz extended an invitation on social media, welcoming anyone who felt the need to come over and release some of their anger on her punching bag. "My garage was filled with women for several days who just kept coming by," she said. There was a "choose your angry song" theme—Bikini Kill, Sleater-Kinney, and Beyoncé were popular choices among her peers and Katy Perry among her daughter's—and they blasted music, swigged tequila, and donned boxing gloves. "Everybody had a very cathartic therapy session with the punching bag," she said. Schatz urged women to direct their feelings into political action, too. "All that anger and rage that you felt about this hearing, now channel that into getting people elected," she urged. Women across the country seem to have heeded her call.

Can the Democrats channel the same energy that propelled unprecedented numbers of women into elected office in 2018 again in 2020? Ramil suggested they will be even more energized due, in part, to the restrictive abortion laws being passed. "I think we will see that sense of urgency and that continued desire to get engaged from people who had never thought of office before," she said. Ramil anticipates receiving applications from a younger and more diverse group of women who want to run for office.

Emily's List has been bombarded. During the 2016 election cycle they were contacted by 920 women, said Miriam Cash, deputy press secretary for the organization, which helps elect pro-choice Democrats to office. Since then, they have heard from more than 46,000 women who are interested in becoming political candidates. "While not all of these women will be running for office in 2020, they will become a valuable pipeline of women running up and down the ballot this cycle and for many years to come," she wrote in an email.

The 2020 elections are shaping up to be, at least in part, a plebiscite on the place of women in America. For starters, there are all the female candidates—as of May 2019 an unprecedented five current lawmakers had declared they would compete for the Democratic presidential nomination. Then there are the staff members; women hold the majority of senior positions in the campaigns of top Democratic presidential hopefuls, and a quarter of them identify as women of color. And many of the candidates are stressing women's issues and strenuously promising to protect abortion rights.

While a loyal core of Republican women continue to back Trump robustly, it may not be sufficiently manifold to get him over the finish line in 2020. The gender gap always favors Democrats, and college-educated women in the suburbs look to be a lost cause for him. Trump is spending millions of dollars in advertising to specifically target women over fifty-five.

But even as he is trying to win over women who might vote for him, he will be fighting another: Summer Zervos. She's the former *Apprentice* candidate who accused Trump of sexually assaulting her in 2007 and then sued him for defamation when in 2016 he called her—along with all of his other accusers—a liar. "Mr. Trump's false, defamatory statements about Ms. Zervos—that, among other things, she made up her descriptions of Mr. Trump's misconduct as a hoax, and that she is creating a 'phony' story just so that she can be famous—have been deeply detrimental to Ms. Zervos's reputation, honor and dignity," the lawsuit contends.

Trump lawyers have tried to get the case shut down or postponed but have not yet been successful, and Zervos's lawyers may well obtain information through the discovery process that could be damaging to Trump. "I think it's fair to say, without going into detail, that discovery is going very well and we've obviously now repeatedly beaten back the motions to dismiss, so we feel very positive about it," Zervos's lawyer Mariann Wang told us.

Trump seems to have at least momentarily escaped having to defend himself against a gender and race discrimination suit filed by former campaign staffer Alva Johnson—who accused the president of kissing her—that alleged that women on the campaign were paid nearly 20 percent less than their male counterparts. Johnson had been hoping to have the lawsuit, which was filed in a federal court in Florida, recognized as a collective action suit, but a judge dismissed it. Still, the judge left open the possibility that the suit could be refiled.

Regardless of the outcome of the Zervos case, progressive women will be fighting not just to defeat Trump at the polls but to upend the system and the attitudes that allowed him to get elected in the first place. "There are so many things that are fundamentally wrong in society that have been unjust for so long now and never corrected systematically that I think there's so much work to be done regardless of who's president. And even if we are getting great elected officials we want to hold them accountable," said Bettys, the Brooklyn activist. "You can only do that if you're paying attention and involved. That was our big lesson of 2016."

The older generation of feminists is hoping that lesson will stick, and that younger women will now carry their torch. Bunch, who earned her activist bona fides in the 1960s, was at a dinner party with some other feminists shortly before she spoke with us. They had been debating whether Trump's presidency has been so detrimental to women that it will take decades to undo the damage, or if the energies he has ignited are strong enough to overpower his policies. "I keep emphasizing the combination of older women and younger women. Even though they aren't always doing the same things, it's the activation of that whole spectrum that I think will bring the change," she said. "We don't know what will happen. I can't say for sure. But I've certainly seen change happen many times in my life here and in other countries. I think the conditions are there for us to move some things very important over the next five to ten years. And I hope that's what it leads to. And that's what I want to make happen."

STORMY IN LEXINGTON

"I'm fine with women coming up to me and saying,
'You've inspired me.' That's great. But I'm quick to point
out that's not my story. I suck dick for a living."
—Stormy Daniels to Mitchell Sunderland in *Penthouse*, May/June 2018

"The women I see on the road have a lot of anger . . . they're angry
at Trump, who seems to be a stand-in for every man who's ever bullied
them. . . . 'You have to get him,' they say. 'Get that orange turd.'"
—Stormy writing in her 2018 book, *Full Disclosure*

BARRY LEVINE, Lexington, Kentucky: *May 4, 2019*

Stormy Daniels's tour bus was late.

On this Saturday night, she was due to perform two shows, the first scheduled to begin at midnight at Deja Vu Showgirls, an "18 & Over Full Nude" strip club in Lexington, Kentucky.

At the end of my reporting journey for this book, I decided to come here for a kind of *summing up*. There was no better person to do that with, I thought, than Stormy Daniels. After all, it was her "hush money" scandal a little more than a year ago that really served as the catalyst for this book. And like all the women accusers who had come forward during the campaign, Daniels's credibility had been viciously attacked by Trump and his team.

While her sexual encounter with the president may have been consensual, the efforts to cover up their affair, as well as Trump's dalliance with Karen McDougal, were conducted purposely to hide his actions from voters. For me, "Stormygate" defined Trump's true character after decades of womanizing, misogyny, and the rest. Daniels's scandal brought it all to a head, you could say—or in her own words, to "a huge mushroom head."

Her press guy, whom I only knew as "Denver," told me to check in with him when I arrived in town. He had first said I should arrive at the club at 10:30 p.m. Then, he later texted me to make that 11:30.

It had been a strange day—and would turn into an even stranger night.

I had thought about making the drive to Louisville to see the Kentucky Derby, but with the rain, I decided to stay put and watch the race on a big-screen TV at a downtown Lexington restaurant. For the first time in its 145-year history, the winning horse was disqualified and a 65-to-1 long shot was awarded the roses.

The people around me freaked out, screaming at the giant TV.

As I passed the hours between the surprise ending at the Derby and my appointment at the strip club, I was also thinking about Trump's onetime fixer Michael Cohen, who back in New York was dealing with his own surprise ending. It was his last Saturday night of freedom before having to report to jail on Monday to begin serving a three-year federal prison sentence.

In addition to tax evasion and other crimes, he had pleaded guilty to campaign finance violations for arranging the "hush money" payments to Daniels and McDougal, and had admitted in court that the payments were "for the principal purpose of influencing the election."

In a brief phone call with me last January, Cohen sounded totally distraught, but in his prepared statement before testifying in front of the House Oversight Committee, he was calm and matter-of-fact.

"He [Trump] asked me to pay off an adult film star with whom he had an affair, and to lie to his wife about it, which I did," Cohen said. "Lying to the first lady is one of my biggest regrets. She is a kind, good person. I respect her greatly. And she did not deserve that."

I wondered on this night if Michael Cohen had thought at all about Stormy Daniels and whether he owed her an apology, too?

———

Deja Vu was located next to a Greyhound bus station and across the street from a Walmart. I made sure I was there at 11 p.m.

The rain was really starting to pound as a steady stream of patrons, including a good number of women, jostled to get in. The place was filling up for Stormy, the latest stop on what she called her "Make America Horny Again" tour.

Whether he was joking or not, the young security guy at the door waved a metal detector at the incoming, repeating, "Any metal in your pockets, bombs, knives, or guns?"

At 11:06 p.m., a new text arrived from Denver. It was not good news.

"Hey Barry," he wrote, *"Our bus broke down a ways from the club. Doing a roadside repair at the moment but just letting you know we will be a bit late. As soon as we get there would be great to get you on the bus to do your interview if you can be ready. My apologies for the time switcharoo."*

E.J., the club manager, had obviously received a similar message. Fearful the bus wouldn't get repaired, he began furiously cleaning out a Town & Country van parked out front to use as a rescue vehicle. A few minutes later, he peeled out of the parking lot to find Stormy's stranded bus.

Midnight came and went. The rain came down harder, and the crowd grew larger. Besides knives and guns, the security kid and I were now on the lookout for the van or bus.

E.J., sweating bullets, returned and reported that the bus—now repaired—was finally on its way.

After its arrival, Denver greeted me and apologized profusely for the delay. He was a young guy who proudly told me he had a master's degree from New York's Columbia University journalism school. Soon he walked me onto the bus and sat me down at a little banquette table after introducing me to Stormy's security guards.

It seemed like a rock star was about to emerge from the back of the bus, and she didn't disappoint.

"Hi, I'm Stormy," she said, shaking my hand.

Despite the swelling crowd inside the club, and being way behind schedule, she appeared cool and calm and said she was happy to answer my questions.

She had not yet changed into her stage attire and, in regular street clothes, Daniels looked far more like the hardworking single mom she is and less like the porn star who identified Trump's junk from "a mushroom lineup" on *Jimmy Kimmel*.

Sitting across from me at the banquette, Daniels was candid in her responses to my questions. Here's the text of our short conversation:

LEVINE: In your book *Full Disclosure*, you describe the women who turn out at these appearances as "angry"; who want you to "get him." Will they carry this anger into the 2020 election?

DANIELS: Yes, and I don't say that because I think so. I say that because they've all told me so. It's very presumptuous to assume what people are going to do or not do, but unless they're all lying, then the short answer is yes.

LEVINE: Are you going to continue to do what you're doing right up until the election?

DANIELS: Well, this is my job. You know, that was a big misconception that this was new for me. I mean, I've been stripping since I was seventeen, and feature dancing since I was twenty-one. Nothing about my job has changed except the frequency.

LEVINE: What's your take on the election right now?

DANIELS: Not yet, no . . . if I had a better sixth sense I would have done much better in the Kentucky Derby today. (Laughs)

LEVINE: You write in your book that before the sexual encounter in Lake Tahoe, Trump came out wearing black silk pajamas. Do you think he's a wannabe Hugh Hefner, still living out his *Playboy* fantasies?

DANIELS: I think any guy wants to be . . . Fuck, I want to be Hugh Hefner! I think everybody wants to be Hugh Hefner. I guess, you know, the biggest difference is Hugh always asked before he grabbed somebody by the pussy.

Yeah, he [Trump] definitely is more predatory. But he probably in his mind, that's probably what he wanted to be. But like I said, who doesn't want to be Hugh Hefner. I want to be Hugh Hefner!

LEVINE: Trump called you a liar and tweeted about the man who threatened you. He said it was "a sketch years later about a nonexistent man . . . a total con job." Does it still bother you that this man has not been officially identified?

DANIELS: Of course, for the main reason that he's still out there.

LEVINE: Since your book and the worldwide publicity, has anybody provided you with new information as to who this person really is?

DANIELS: Several people have sent leads and photos. To my knowledge, none of the ones that were investigated checked out. We thought we had a really solid lead at one point. And I was almost also very sure that it could possibly be him.

I mean, ninety-nine percent of the time people send me stuff and I'm like, 'no.' I thought we had a really solid one and I guess for whatever reason they decided that it wasn't him. But I never got to confront him myself.

LEVINE: Does it still keep you up at night?

DANIELS: Not so much. I don't think about it very often. But it bothers me that they haven't caught him because, like I said, he could be sitting in the club right now for all I know. And most importantly, the second he's caught I'll be demanding a very large public apology—not that I'll get it!

LEVINE: But that type of pugilistic comment from Trump, does it just rub salt in the wound?

DANIELS: He can call me anything he wants, but I'm not a liar. As I think it's been proven over and over this year except for so far that one thing.

LEVINE: So it didn't bother you when he called you "horseface"?

DANIELS: (Laughing) No, I've never laughed so hard in my life! Mostly because I remember turning around to my friend in the backseat and going, "Uh-huh, shots fired. Now I get to tweet back." And I'm pretty sure mine was ten times better.

(Stormy had tweeted: ". . . He has demonstrated his incompetence, hatred of women and lack of self control on Twitter AGAIN! And perhaps a penchant for bestiality. Game on, Tiny.")

Besides, a 'horseface' . . . I don't look like a horse. You can come up with something *way* better. It's actually—he should have done better! Come on! And I have nine horses. I think they're awesome. I took it as a compliment.

LEVINE: It's ironic we're talking on the day of the Kentucky Derby. Did you go?

DANIELS: Yeah, we were there. Yeah, I lost.

LEVINE: Michael Cohen has lost, too. He's going to jail on Monday. In fact, tonight's like his last Saturday night of freedom. Do you take any satisfaction in that he's going to do time?

DANIELS: Yes, I think so. I mean, but I still feel probably a little misplaced guilt for his wife and children. But yeah, of course. Especially since he was so adamant that they were going to lock me up and all that stuff. And clearly, it's exactly opposite of what he said was going to happen.

LEVINE: Whether it happens or not, when Trump's out of office he could be indicted. Would you like to see that?

DANIELS: Of course. And it's not even just about Donald Trump per se. It's that I don't think anybody should be above the law whether it's the president or not. And if he continues to get away with the things he's gotten away with, what is someone else going to come along and do?

LEVINE: I went to the Beverly Hills Hotel recently to see the bungalows where he met you and also allegedly met Karen McDougal and Summer Zervos. Have either of these women contacted you to compare notes?

DANIELS: No, nope.

LEVINE: Would you ever want to meet them in person?

DANIELS: I don't know. I don't have a particular interest or need to. But I wouldn't say no if they invited me. Especially if they were paying! (Laughs) Not for me, I meant for dinner! (Laughs again) As long as they were buying or had good snacks!

LEVINE: Did it bother you that Trump was also sneaking around with Karen when he was seeing you?

DANIELS: I didn't know anything about it at the time. And I wouldn't have cared.

LEVINE: Karen apologized to Melania in her CNN interview with Anderson Cooper. Is there anything you want to say to Melania—whether personally or publicly?

DANIELS: No. I'll apologize to her when she apologizes to the country. I'm going to get in trouble for that one, aren't I?

LEVINE: I've heard stories about him and other adult film stars.

DANIELS: The only one I know of is that lying bitch Jessica Drake, who made up a story and tried to steal mine. But I think that's been pretty adequately disproven the second I came forward. Of course, she vanished because she knew she was in trouble. (Drake has stood by her allegations.)

LEVINE: Alana Evans said she was told directly by a few other porn stars about Trump.

DANIELS: She's never said that to me.

LEVINE: While it's clear you didn't find him a good sexual partner or even, for that matter, a good kisser, there are women who have said they have. Can you understand Trump's appeal to these other women?

DANIELS: Not to me. But I'm sure some were very swayed by his pocketbook—or alleged pocketbook. (Laughs)

LEVINE: Do you think in retrospect, when you look back on your life, meeting Donald Trump and the relationship or whatever it was—has this been a good thing for Stormy Daniels or a bad thing for Stormy Daniels?

DANIELS: It's been the worst thing that's ever happened to me! (Laughs) No, overall, one hundred percent terrible!

LEVINE: Even with all these new fans—they tell me you have the largest crowd ever at this place waiting for you to perform tonight?

DANIELS: None of my friends or family are in there. They're all gone.

On that note, it was time for her to go. But those words struck me.

She had drawn the largest *60 Minutes* audience in more than a decade; her name was the top search term of 2018 on Pornhub, which counts 100 million daily visits; she had done *Saturday Night Live* and had taken her place in pop culture history; she had even been name-checked by Kanye West on his album *Ye*.

But was this person sitting across from me just a girl away from home who missed her family like we all do when we're on the road? For me, I felt she had "summed it all up" nicely in her own Stormy way.

I said my goodbyes and left the tour bus so Stormy could change into her work clothes.

Inside Deja Vu, there was a standing room only crowd and I took a spot in the back.

With the crowd chanting *"Stormy, Stormy!"*—including the local dancers—she suddenly appeared on the small stage. It was 1:17 a.m.

The back of the stage has vertical mirrored panels and there were three dancing poles. The neon lights bathed her and suddenly some guys sitting ringside were raining dollars down on her.

She was wearing what's been previously described as her "Little Red Riding Hood" outfit. But it didn't stay on for long. She quickly discarded it as she danced to the Whitesnake song "Still of the Night."

By 1:23, with the crowd hooting and hollering, Stormy had stripped down to her garter belt and G-string. She then sprawled out on a small gray blanket.

Duran Duran's "Hungry Like the Wolf" played, and she gave the crowd what they had come for.

After returning to her tour bus for a break, Stormy was back for her second performance, which began at 3:19 a.m. (the place, they told me, was actually open until 5).

This time she entered the room from the rear, wearing a sparkly silver gown. She also showed off a white fur-like wrap.

On her way to the stage, she stopped to play around with some audience members, giving equal time to both men and women with what she calls her "thunder and lightning."

Journalist Amanda Whiting, writing in the *Washingtonian*, had previously described this experience: "feeling Stormy Daniels's breasts against your cheek is like diving head first into a velveteen ball pit."

Once back onstage, Stormy performed her routine to songs including "Material Girl," "Diamonds Are a Girl's Best Friend," and "Big Spender."

A young tattooed dancer in earshot of me said: "You go, girl. I fucking love you!"

Soon it was over and I caught my last glimpse of Daniels. She disappeared into the smoky haze with bodyguards both in front of and behind her. Someone else from her entourage trailed them carrying the bucket of her cash tips.

As I drove back to my hotel in the nearly deserted streets of Lexington, I couldn't help but think of the headline to a story I had read earlier in the day on the plane. *Rolling Stone* had published it on March 9, 2018.

The headline read: "One Night with Stormy Daniels, the Hero America Needs."

ACKNOWLEDGMENTS

Our thanks first go out to the many courageous women who gave us their time and their trust in allowing us to share their stories. We owe them our sincere gratitude. Without them this book could not have been written.

We owe a great debt to those who spoke to us on the condition of anonymity. Their input was invaluable.

We are grateful to the many people at Hachette who helped shepherd this book into existence. We are deeply indebted to Mauro DiPreta, who first embraced this book and encouraged us to see the larger picture. We thank him for his commitment.

Mauro handed us off into the able hands of our editor, Paul Whitlatch, who skillfully brought the manuscript to life and helped us navigate an ever-changing landscape. Thanks also to Sarah Falter and Michael Barrs for crafting an incredible plan to get the word out about this project and to Mollie Weisenfeld, who aided us at every step along the way.

We are also grateful to our legal team—Carol Ross, Andrew Goldberg, and Jack Browning—for their thorough reading of the material and their wise counsel.

We must acknowledge the tremendous contribution of Whitney Clegg and Lucy Osborne in the reporting of this book. Not only did they bring a superior level of investigative journalism, but they helped make this into a team effort, for which we are grateful. Samantha Panagrosso was also instrumental in the reporting from the very beginning, and a supportive friend.

This project couldn't have been accomplished without the input of Mike Mancuso, who researched tirelessly over many months, nor without the expert reporting and research of Palm Beach journalist Jose Lambiet. We also offer our gratitude to the journalists who generously shared their insights on Trump with us, including David Cay Johnston, John Connolly, Peter Manso, Michael Gross, A. J. Benza, George Rush, Ben Widdicombe, George Wayne, and Michael Daly.

A tremendous gallery of photos, many of them rare images, were brought together for this book. For this we owe our sincere thanks to Jodi Peckman and Meghan Benson. In addition, we want to thank Jolie Novak and Candace Trunzo at DailyMail.com for allowing us to publish some of their amazing "treasure trove" of Trump family pictures. Russell Turiak also graciously opened his picture files to us.

The authors individually wish to thank the following:

BARRY LEVINE

Two special women who trusted me to tell their stories for the first time are Karen Johnson and Maureen Gallagher. I thank them both.

In addition, I want to personally thank Alana Evans, Katherine Walker, and Heather Braden for speaking to me on my trip to the West Coast—and I wish to thank Stormy Daniels for speaking candidly to me in Lexington, Kentucky, one late night.

This book wouldn't have had a chance had it not been for Lisa Leshne taking this on as my book agent. She believed in this project from the very outset and guided me through this difficult journey. I can't thank her enough.

In addition, I have to give thanks to two veteran book editors who graciously worked with me in the first days and helped me see a substance to my original ideas and thoughts—Julie Mosow and Stephen King's first editor, Bill Thompson. My sincere thanks to you both!

I've had many mentors over the course of my career in print and television, but none like Steve Dunleavy. He sadly passed away at the end of my book journey. His friendship, guidance, and encouragement I have valued immensely dating back to the early 1990s.

I would personally like to thank my family for their support and love, especially Terry, Steve, and Jerry.

Friends who offered moral support include Alan Gasmer, Peter Khoury, Santina Leuci, Phil Messing, Alexander Hitchen, Glenn Horowitz, Jerry Burke, Irv Slifkin, Dan Schock, Michael Dub and Charles Ernst—and additionally, "Big Al" Kelner and Annette Housey, two dear friends who go way back with me to the very beginning (the 1970s) and saw me start on my reporting path (and even better, both knew and loved my mom). There is also Dick Siegel, a great writer and a dear pal who was taken from us way too soon. I will always have a dirty martini waiting for him at the place we still call the Lion's Head.

MONIQUE EL-FAIZY

Thanks to Deborah Copaken and Lisa Leshne for starting me down this path, and to Rachel Sussman for her tireless encouragement, guidance, and support. I owe an immense debt of gratitude to the many friends in Paris, New York, and elsewhere who helped shape my thinking, and whose constant texts, emojis, emails, and phone calls kept me going. I truly would not have reached the finish line without all of you.

I am profoundly thankful to Susannah Shipman, who, in addition to being a steadfast friend, has for years provided me with a home away from home. The Reyl family and Nina Lorez Collins also generously opened their houses to me and supplied both encouragement and relief. Thanks, too, to Ton Lowies for giving me a quiet place to write, and to both my parents for their understanding and support.

No one has done more than my husband and sons. While I missed countless basketball games, plays, dinners, and movie nights, they uncomplainingly picked up the slack that I had left at home, shouldering more than their fair shares of the duties of daily life. I am incredibly lucky to have two of the most empathetic and kind young men I know as my sons. I am grateful to Theo for his insightful feedback on the manuscript and his sympathetic ear during the most trying of moments, and to Xander for being ever imperturbable when I was not and for his ability to always make me laugh.

I am enormously grateful to my husband, Firas, who kept everything going during my daily absences in the house and extended writing trips. His belief in the importance of this project and his encouragement of me are a big part of why this book exists today.

TIMELINE

June 14, 1946

Donald John Trump born in Queens, NY

1964

Trump voted "Ladies' Man" in the New York Military Academy yearbook

1968

Trump graduates from the Wharton School of Business at the University of Pennsylvania in Philadelphia and officially joins his father's real estate business

1971

Trump takes control of the family company and renames it the Trump Organization

April 7, 1977

Trump marries Ivana Zelníčková in New York

December 31, 1977

Donald Trump Jr. born

September 26, 1981

Trump's brother, Fred Trump Jr., dies at the age of forty-three

October 30, 1981

Ivanka Trump born

1983

Trump Tower on Fifth Avenue opens

January 6, 1984

Eric Trump born

November 1987

Trump's book *The Art of the Deal* published

1989

In 1991, Ivana made a sworn declaration in divorce proceedings that she was "raped" by Trump two years earlier

December 1989

In Trump's presence, in Aspen, Colorado, Ivana confronts Marla Maples

1990

Trump dropped from Forbes 400 list of richest billionaires

1991

Trump's Taj Majal Casino in Atlantic City files for bankruptcy

1992

Trump and Ivana finalize divorce

January 24, 1993

In a 1997 lawsuit, Jill Harth accuses Trump of sexual misconduct at Mar-a-Lago around this date

April 1993

Trump confirms out-of-wedlock pregnancy with Marla Maples

October 13, 1993

Tiffany Trump born

December 20, 1993

Trump marries Marla Maples in New York

1996

Trump buys Miss Universe Organization, including Miss USA and Miss Teen USA

1997

Trump and Marla file for divorce

1999

Trump Model Management founded

June 25, 1999

Trump's father, Fred Trump, dies at ninety-three

August 7, 2000

Trump's mother, Mary MacLeod Trump, dies at eighty-eight

January 8, 2004

The Apprentice premieres on NBC

January 22, 2005

Trump marries Melania Knauss in Palm Beach, Florida

September 2005

The "Grab 'em by the pussy" tape is recorded

March 20, 2006

Barron Trump born

July 2006

Alleged sexual encounter between Trump and Stormy Daniels in Lake Tahoe

2006

Karen McDougal claims 10-month sexual affair with Trump begins this year

2007

In a 2017 lawsuit, Summer Zervos accuses Trump of sexual misconduct this year

April 2011

Trump attends White House Correspondents' Association dinner in which President Obama jokes about him in his speech

2012

Trump offers to donate $5 million to charity if Obama makes public his college records and passport application records

June 16, 2015

Trump announces he's running for president at Trump Tower in New York

August 2016

McDougal agrees to a $150,000 "hush money" deal to prevent her from going public before the election

August 24, 2016

In a 2018 lawsuit, Alva Johnson says she's the victim of sexual misconduct by Trump at a campaign event in Florida on this date

October 7, 2016

The *Washington Post* publishes the "Grab 'em by the pussy" tape

October 2016

Daniels signs contract to be paid $130,000 in "hush money" to prevent her from going public before the election

November 4, 2016

The *Wall Street Journal* reports McDougal's "hush money" deal

November 8, 2016

Trump defeats Democratic candidate Hillary Clinton in the presidential election

January 20, 2017

Trump sworn in as forty-fifth president of the United States

December 11, 2017

At a press conference, three women who accused Trump of sexual misconduct demand a congressional investigation to hold Trump accountable

January 12, 2018

The *Wall Street Journal* reports the $130,000 "hush money" payment made to Daniels

March 22, 2018

CNN airs McDougal interview with Anderson Cooper

March 25, 2018

CBS airs Daniels's *60 Minutes* interview with Cooper

April 5, 2018

Aboard Air Force One, Trump tells reporters he didn't know about "hush money" payment to Daniels

August 21, 2018

Trump lawyer Michael Cohen pleads guilty to eight charges, including illegal campaign contributions; says they were done at Trump's "direction" to silence Daniels and McDougal before election

August 22, 2018

Trump tells *Fox & Friends* cable TV show the money "came from me" to pay Daniels and McDougal—not his campaign, so the payments were not illegal

December 7, 2018

Federal prosecutors say for first time Cohen acted at direction of Trump when Cohen committed election-related crimes to silence Daniels and McDougal; prosecutors refer to Trump as "Individual-1"

February 27, 2019

At congressional hearing, Cohen reveals $35,000 personal check from Trump as part of Daniels's "hush money" reimbursement

May 22, 2019

"I don't do cover-ups," Trump says at press conference

To explore further legal documentation about these cases, please visit AllThePresidentsWomenBook.com.

APPENDIX

ALL THE PRESIDENT'S WOMEN A TO Z

In an effort to provide the reader with the most complete accounting of Donald Trump's history with women, this appendix provides additional information on women included in the book, as well as women who are not included in the narrative but are no less important to the understanding of Trump's lifelong interactions with women.

ACCUSATIONS OF INAPPROPRIATE BEHAVIOR (AND TRUMP RESPONSES)

a). alleged incidents involving sexual contact:

1. Kristin Anderson

Anderson told the *Washington Post* that Trump slid his fingers up her skirt and touched her vagina through her underwear while seated next to him at a Manhattan nightspot in the 1990s. A friend corroborated Anderson's account, saying she was told about the incident a few days later. A New York photographer also remembered hearing the story from Anderson in 2007. In comments emailed for this book, Anderson said she hoped the reader would consider the effects of sexual assault and predatory behavior. She wrote us regarding her accusations against Trump: "I knew there would be retaliation when I spoke up. I spoke up for myself for one reason alone. Self-truth. If I was to remain silent about this 'grab' I may never come clean about all the other abuses I have suffered through and then I would have to bear them all inside me. With this revelation, I was able to crack open the secret, dark box of abuse within myself and begin to heal myself."

> *TRUMP RESPONSE—At a rally in Greensboro, North Carolina, Trump said Anderson's accusations were false because he*

would never have been in a nightclub alone. Trump's campaign
spokesperson, Hope Hicks, said: "Mr. Trump strongly denies this
phony allegation by someone looking to get some free publicity. It is
totally ridiculous."

2. "anonymous teenager (Times Square)"
In an allegation reported in this book for the first time, a former mob
associate, John Tino, claimed he witnessed live via a closed-circuit, sur-
veillance tape television monitor a sexual encounter involving Trump,
a porn actress, and possibly an underage girl, who told the porn actress
she was a teenager. The alleged incident took place in the early 1980s
inside a private Times Square brothel.

3. "anonymous woman (boardroom)"
In 2016, CNN anchor Erin Burnett reported the account of a female
friend who said an incident occurred in 2010, during a meeting in a
boardroom of Trump Tower. Burnett said the woman told her: "Trump
took TicTacs, suggested I take them also. He then leaned in, catching
me off guard, and kissed me almost on the lips. I was really freaked out.
After, Trump asked me to come into his office alone. . . . Once in his
office he kept telling me how special I am and gave me his cell, asked me
to call him. I ran the hell out of there."

> **TRUMP RESPONSE**—*CNN requested comment from Trump but*
> *he did not respond. The* Guardian *also requested comment about*
> *the allegations, but there was no response from Trump.*

4. "attractive interior designer"
A former *Apprentice* sound engineer, identified as Erik Whitestone,
revealed an alleged sexual encounter to author Michael Wolff for his
book *Siege: Trump Under Fire*, published in June 2019. According to
Whitestone, in Chicago, "an attractive interior designer who was pitch-
ing Trump on a project, hitched a ride on Trump's plane." Wolff quoted
Whitestone as saying: "He led her into the bedroom with a mirrored
ceiling. . . . She comes out, half an hour later, dress ripped off, staggering
out, she sits in the seat . . . and then he comes out with his tie off, shirt
untucked, and says, 'Fellas . . . just got laid.'" Whitestone also alleged
to Wolff that he would be asked to fetch women for Trump from the
Trump Tower lobby—often Eastern European tourists. Trump would

tell him: "Erik, go get her, and bring her up." Whitestone added, "He'd hug them and grope them and send them on their way."

> *TRUMP RESPONSE—The White House was quick to dump on Siege, with spokesman Hogan Gidley saying: "This latest book is just another attempt by Wolff to line his own pockets by pushing lies and pure fantasy aimed at attacking the president."*

5. Rachel Crooks

Her unwanted kissing encounter with Trump occurred in Trump Tower in 2005, when she was a twenty-two-year-old receptionist working in the building. She immediately called her sister, who asked, "Are you sure he didn't just miss trying to kiss you on the cheek?" Crooks replied, "No, he kissed me on the mouth. That is not normal." Crooks's account was corroborated by her sister and also Crooks's then boyfriend, who said she "started hysterically crying" when she told him.

> *TRUMP RESPONSE—In an interview with the New York Times in October 2016, Trump denied Crooks's claims and said, "None of this ever took place." He also threatened to sue the Times if it reported the allegations. In February 2018, Trump tweeted regarding Crooks: "A woman I don't know and, to the best of my knowledge, never met, is on the FRONT PAGE of the Fake News Washington Post saying I kissed her (for two minutes yet) in the lobby of Trump Tower 12 years ago. Never happened! Who would do this in a public space with live security . . ."*

6. Jessica Drake

The porn star met Trump at the 2006 golf tournament in Lake Tahoe, which was also attended by Stormy Daniels. Drake claimed Trump grabbed her and kissed her in a nonconsensual way. She further alleged Trump propositioned her but she turned down an offer of ten thousand dollars. Drake said: ". . . I may be called a liar or an opportunist, but I will risk that in order to stand in solidarity with women who share similar accounts. . . ."

> *TRUMP RESPONSE—To a New Hampshire radio station, Trump called the accusations "total fiction," adding: "One said, 'He grabbed me on the arm.' And she's a porn star. You know, this one that came out recently, 'He grabbed me and he grabbed me on the*

arm.' Oh, I'm sure she's never been grabbed before." Trump also called the accusations "false and ridiculous."

7. Jill Harth

In her lawsuit against Trump, she accused him of attempted rape after he invited her to Mar-a-Lago to discuss a business deal and then claimed he attacked her in Ivanka's bedroom, where he kissed and groped her. Harth declined repeated requests to comment for this book.

> *TRUMP RESPONSE—In 1997, Trump told Palm Beach reporter Wayne Grover: "The truth is that Jill Harth is obsessed with me— and would do everything she could to get in my pants. Her claims are extortion, pure and simple. If I sexually attacked this woman in 1993, why didn't they sue me then? This is ridiculous. Harth kept pursuing me. She even moved from Florida to New York to try to get me. But I wasn't interested." During the 2016 campaign, Trump's spokesperson, Hope Hicks, said: "Mr. Trump denies each and every statement made by Ms. Harth." In addition, the Trump campaign provided emails that claimed to show Harth requesting a job and giving support to his candidacy.*

8. Cathy Heller

Dining at a Mother's Day brunch at Mar-a-Lago, she was left "angry and shaken" after Trump grabbed her and tried to kiss her. A relative, who was present, corroborated the incident and said Heller was immediately shocked at what happened. Heller believed the incident occurred in 1997 and first spoke about it to the *Guardian*.

> *TRUMP RESPONSE—Heller's accusations were denied by a Trump spokesperson: "There is no way that something like this would have happened in a public place on Mother's Day at Mr. Trump's resort. It would have been the talk of Palm Beach for the past two decades . . . bogus claim."*

9. Juliet Huddy

A former Fox News anchor, she said on a podcast in December 2017— *Mornin'!!! with Bill Schulz*—that Trump kissed her on the lips without her consent following a Trump Tower meeting in 2005.

> *TRUMP RESPONSE—Huddy's accusation was denied by the White House. But Huddy said Trump himself made light of the*

incident. Huddy said: "He said, to the audience and producers,
not on camera, 'I tried hitting on her but she blew me off.' He was
laughing. At the time I was not offended by it. . . ."

10. Alva Johnson

The event planner and human relations consultant from Alabama was
the first woman to claim Trump victimized her on the campaign trail
when he was running for president. According to her lawsuit, which
was first reported by the *Washington Post* in February 2019, Trump
forcibly kissed Johnson without her consent on August 24, 2016, when
he was leaving a recreational vehicle during a campaign stop in Tampa,
Fla. In June 2019, *Politico* reported a federal judge, William Jung, a
Trump appointee, dismissed the suit but said he would allow Johnson
to file a revised complaint.

> *TRUMP RESPONSE—White House press secretary Sarah Sanders*
> *said: "This never happened and is directly contradicted by multiple*
> *highly credible eyewitness accounts." In July 2019 Trump's lawyers*
> *released a fifteen-second videotape of the incident in an effort to*
> *show Trump intentionally kissed her cheek.*

11. Karen Johnson

In an interview for this book, the married Johnson alleged Trump
groped and kissed her at a New Year's Eve party at Mar-a-Lago in the
early 2000s. Johnson's story was corroborated by a male friend, who
said in an interview for this book that she confessed the details to him
years ago. Johnson said she wanted this book's readers to know: "He's
a fucking stalker. He'll stalk you like prey—that's what he did to me
because I was at Mar-a-Lago many times. Come on, he's a very calculated man. He knows exactly what he's doing. He knows he can get
away with it because no one's ever put the screws to him."

12. "Katie Johnson"

In a lawsuit she has since dropped, "Johnson" claimed that when she
was a thirteen-year-old, Trump raped her, took her virginity, and
forced her into role-play sex. In addition, she alleged Trump and Jeffrey Epstein treated her as a "sex slave." Included in the lawsuit were
also allegations involving a twelve-year-old girl called "Maria." In a
declaration of support from a woman identified as "Tiffany," it stated:

"I personally witnessed the one occasion where Mr. Trump forced the Plaintiff ('Johnson') and the 12-year-old female named Maria to perform oral sex on Mr. Trump and witnessed his physical abuse of both minors when they finished the act. . . . I personally witnessed Defendant Trump telling the Plaintiff ('Johnson') that she shouldn't ever say anything if she didn't want to disappear like the 12-year-old female Maria, and that he was capable of having her whole family killed."

> *TRUMP RESPONSE—When the lawsuit filed by the anonymous plaintiff surfaced during the 2016 campaign, Trump's legal team branded the allegations "disgusting at the highest level" and a "hoax," adding they were clearly framed to "solicit media attention or, perhaps . . . simply politically motivated."*

13. Ninni Laaksonen

At a taping of *The Late Show with David Letterman*, the 2006 Miss Finland said she was groped by Trump. She later said she was told Trump liked her because she "looked like Melania when she was younger."

> *TRUMP RESPONSE—Like other accusations, the Trump campaign denied the allegation but Trump has not commented directly.*

14. Jessica Leeds

"He was like an octopus. His hands were everywhere." This 2016 accuser claimed Trump attacked her on a flight in the late 1970s, putting his hand up her skirt. Leeds told four people about the incident, who confirmed her account to the *New York Times*. She additionally confirmed her story in an interview for this book.

> *TRUMP RESPONSE—During a campaign rally in October 2016, Trump said: "People that are willing to say, 'Oh, I was with Donald Trump in 1980, I was sitting with him on an airplane, and he went after me.' Believe me, she would not be my first choice." The Trump campaign also produced a British man, who claimed to have sat near the two on the plane, who said, "She was the one being flirtatious." Trump also responded: "None of this ever took place."*

15. Melinda McGillivray

Working as a twenty-three-year-old assistant to a photographer on a shoot at Mar-a-Lago, she claimed Trump groped her in 2003. According to the *Washington Post*, the photog, Ken Davidoff, corroborated her account and said he vividly remembered her pulling him aside after the incident and telling him, "Donald Trump just grabbed my ass!"

> *TRUMP RESPONSE—While Trump did not respond for comment directly on McGillivray's accusations when first reported by the* Washington Post, *White House press secretary Sarah Sanders later said: "The timing and absurdity of these false claims speaks volumes and the publicity tour that has begun only further confirms the political motives behind them."*

16. Cassandra Searles

The 2013 Miss USA pageant contestant from the state of Washington said on Facebook that Trump had groped her. "He continually grabbed my ass and invited me to his hotel room," she wrote.

> *TRUMP RESPONSE—Trump has not directly responded to Searles's accusations.*

17. Jennifer Murphy

A contestant on the fourth season of *The Apprentice*—who had previously competed in the 2004 Miss USA pageant from Oregon—she claimed Trump kissed her on the lips as she was leaving a job interview shortly after he had married Melania. She told the women's magazine *Grazia:* "I think maybe in his mind he may have thought of me and maybe fantasized, or romantically, but I didn't feel at the end of the day he would take action. I would hope that he would be true to his marriage, and I was also engaged at the time." Despite that, Murphy told CNN she voted for Trump for president and created a Katy Perry parody video in which she sang, "I was kissed by Trump and I liked it."

> *TRUMP RESPONSE—Trump has not commented directly about Murphy.*

18. Natasha Stoynoff

The *People* magazine journalist joined the list of accusers when she wrote of a 2005 encounter in October 2016, saying she met with Trump and Melania for a one-year anniversary piece. While giving them a tour of Mar-a-Lago, Trump allegedly forcibly kissed her after pushing her against a wall. At least five people corroborated Stoynoff's account, including Marina Grasic, a friend, who said Stoynoff called her the day after the alleged incident and told her what happened. A reporter for *People*, Liz McNeil, was told about the incident when Stoynoff returned from the assignment. "She was very upset and told me how he shoved her against a wall," McNeil said.

> *TRUMP RESPONSE—In denying Stoynoff's allegations, Trump tweeted: "Why didn't the writer of the twelve-year-old article in* People *magazine mention the 'incident' in her story. Because it did not happen!" A spokeswoman for Trump also denied the allegations: "This never happened. There is no merit or veracity to this fabricated story."*

19. Temple Taggart

Admitting she was very naive and "21 going on 16," the accuser said she received an unwanted kiss from Trump when the Miss Utah was competing in the 1997 Miss USA pageant. And when she traveled to New York to meet modeling agencies, Trump "embraced me and kissed me on the lips a second time," she said. "What he did made me feel so uncomfortable that I ended up cutting my trip short, bought my own plane ticket, flew home, and never spoke to him again."

> *TRUMP RESPONSE—In October 2016, Trump told NBC News in response to Taggart's accusations: "I don't know who she is. She claims this took place in a public area. I never kissed her. I emphatically deny this ridiculous claim."*

20. Ivana Trump

The alleged "rape" claim made by Ivana that surfaced in a divorce document was obtained by author Harry Hurt.

> *TRUMP RESPONSE—Ivana issued an initial response to Hurt on April 6, 1993, stating at the end: "Any contrary conclusion would be an incorrect and most unfortunate interpretation of my statement which I do not want to be interpreted in a speculative fashion and I do not want the press or media to misconstrue any of the facts set forth above. All I wish is for this matter to be put to rest." Ivana issued a second statement about the "rape" claim during the 2016 campaign: "I have recently read some comments attributed to me from nearly 30 years ago at a time of very high tension during my divorce from Donald. The story is totally*

without merit. Donald and I are the best of friends and together have raised 3 children that we love and are very proud of."

21. Katy Tur

The NBC News star detailed an unwanted Trump kiss in her book on the 2016 campaign, *Unbelievable: My Front-Row Seat to the Craziest Campaign in American History*. The incident allegedly occurred November 10, 2015, in New Hampshire. "Before I know what's happening, his hands are on my shoulders and his lips are on my cheek. My eyes widen. My body freezes. My heart stops," she said.

> *TRUMP RESPONSE—While Trump has attacked Tur, calling her "Little Katy," "incompetent," "dishonest," and a "3rd rate reporter," he told MSNBC's Mika Brzezinski and Joe Scarborough during an interview: "But actually, Katy Tur—what happened? She was so great. I just saw her back there. I gave her a big kiss. She was fantastic."*

22. Karena Virginia

At the U.S. Open tennis event in Queens, New York, in 1998, the woman, then a twenty-seven-year-old yoga instructor, claimed Trump grabbed her arm and touched her breast. She told a news conference in 2016: "I was quite surprised when I overheard him talking to the other men about me. He said, 'Hey, look at this one; we haven't seen her before. Look at those legs,' as though I was an object rather than a person. He then walked up to me . . . and grabbed my right arm. Then his hand touched the right inside of my breast. I was in shock. I flinched. 'Don't you know who I am? Don't you know who I am?' That's what he said to me. I felt intimidated, and I felt powerless. Then my car pulled up and I got in."

> *TRUMP RESPONSE—At the time Virginia's accusations were made public, Trump spokesperson Jessica Ditto said: "Discredited political operative Gloria Allred (who represented Virginia), in another coordinated, publicity-seeking attack with the Clinton campaign, will stop at nothing to smear Mr. Trump. Give me a break. Voters are tired of these circus-like antics and reject these fictional stories and the clear efforts to benefit Hillary Clinton."*

23. *"young model hookup"*

A modeling industry source alleged witnessing Trump at a "Look of the Year" party in the early 1990s with young models. In an interview for this book, the source said Trump hooked up with at least one model from the party. "I'm confident because I heard a couple of them discussing it the next day," the source said. "These models [discussing it] ranged in age from 16 and 18." The source said there were also models at the party "as young as fourteen." The source said champagne was served at the party and cocaine entered the party from "a couple of guys. . . . The dealers would also screw some of the girls, too."

24. Summer Zervos

As of July 2019, the former *Apprentice* contestant's defamation suit against Trump was proceeding. According to media reports, including *BuzzFeed*, *Variety*, and NBC, Zervos's account was corroborated by a friend, Ann Russo, who said Zervos told her in 2010 that Trump had previously been "verbally, physically, and sexually aggressive with her" but that she had rebuffed his advances.

> *TRUMP RESPONSE—Trump repeatedly denied Zervos's accusations. Here's some of his denials she included in her court documents: (late afternoon or evening of October 14, 2016) "To be clear, I never met her at a hotel or greeted her inappropriately a decade ago. That is not who I am as a person, and it is not how I've conducted my life."; (at around 7:15 p.m. on October 14, 2016) Trump said at a rally in Charlotte, North Carolina, "These allegations are 100% false. . . . They are made up, they never happened. . . . It's not hard to find a small handful of people willing to make false smears for personal fame, who knows maybe for financial reasons [or] political purposes."; (at 3:51 a.m., October 15, 2016) Trump tweeted: "100% fabricated and made-up charges . . ."; (4:45 a.m., October 15, 2016) Trump tweeted: "the media pushing false and unsubstantiated charges, and outright lies . . ."; (8:52 a.m., October 15, 2016) Trump campaign stated: "Summer's actions today are nothing more than an attempt to regain the spotlight at Mr. Trump's expense."; (11:29 a.m., October 15, 2016) Trump tweeted: "Nothing ever happened with any of these women. Totally made up nonsense to steal the election."; (12:30 p.m., October 15, 2016) Trump said at a rally in Portsmouth, New Hampshire: "Today, the cousin of one of these people, very close to her, wrote a letter that what she said is a lie. . . . Total lies,*

and you've been seeing total lies . . . you have phony people coming up with phony allegations . . ."; (3:30 p.m., October 15, 2016) Trump said at a rally in Bangor, Maine: "False allegations and outright lies, in an effort to elect Hillary Clinton President . . . False stories, all made-up. Lies. Lies. No witnesses, no nothing. All big lies."; (October 17, 2016) Trump retweeted a statement that included a picture of Summer Zervos, stating: "This is all yet another hoax. . . . Terrible."

25. E. Jean Carroll sexual assault allegation

An excerpt from her July 2019 book, *What Do We Need Men For? A Modest Proposal,* was published in New York. The author and advice columnist revealed an allegation of sexual assault against Trump and said the incident occurred in a fitting room at the Bergdorf Goodman luxury department store on Fifth Avenue in Manhattan in late 1995 or 1996. Trump, who was married at the time to Marla Maples, allegedly asked Carroll to model lingerie he was considering purchasing. Carroll said: "The moment the dressing-room door is closed, he lunges at me, pushes me against the wall, hitting my head quite badly, and puts his mouth against my lips. . . ." She said Trump then "jams his hand under my coat dress and pulls down my tights," before an alleged act of non-consensual intercourse. After the incident, Carroll told two friends, both journalists: Lisa Birnbach and Carol Martin. They corroborated her account of the incident to the *New York Times* on June 28, 2019. In an interview for this book, Birnbach attested to Carroll's credibility and said, "I said, 'E. Jean, he raped you. If he penetrated you that was rape. Let's go to the police.' [But] she said, 'No, I'm not going to do that . . . I just want to go home.'"

> **TRUMP RESPONSE**—*"Totally lying," he told the* Hill *of Carroll's allegation of sexual assault. "I don't know anything about her. I know nothing about this woman. I know nothing about her. She is—it's just a terrible thing that people can make statements like that." He further said: "[I] never met this person in my life. She is trying to sell a new book—that should indicate her motivation. It should be sold in the fiction section. Shame on those who make up false stories of assault to try to get any publicity for themselves, or sell a book, or carry out a political agenda—like Julie Swetnick, who falsely accused Justice Brett Kavanaugh. It's just as bad for*

people to believe it, particularly when there is zero evidence."
Trump also dismissed the relevance of a candid photo that showed
him with Carroll and others. Trump also said about Carroll: "I'll
say it with great respect: Number one, she's not my type. Number
two, it never happened. It never happened, okay?" His "not my
type" comment was noted in the media and the New York Times
said the response to Carroll was similar to comments he made
about a past accuser who he inferred was not attractive enough to
gain his interest. "Believe me," he said at a campaign event in 2016
in response to a woman who accused him of sexual misconduct
on an airplane, "she would not be my first choice, that I can tell
you. You don't know. That would not be my first choice." Trump
added, "Check out her Facebook, you'll understand." Of another
past accuser he called "a liar," he had also said: "Check out her
Facebook page—you'll understand."

26. Faith Daniels kiss and cheerleader groping allegations

In July 2019, NBC News broadcast video footage shot for a November 1992 feature story on Trump for the network's talk show, *A Closer Look*. Media reports, including the *Washington Post* and *New York*, said Trump agreed to come on the show for host Faith Daniels, after he nonconsensually kissed the anchor when her husband's back was turned at a charity event. "'You kissed me on the lips in front of the paparazzi,' and I said, 'That'll cost you. I'm booking you on the show,'" Daniels said she told Trump, who responded, "Uh-huh. I know. That's great. It was so open and nice." Trump was then filmed at a party at Mar-a-Lago, which was attended by cheerleaders for the Buffalo Bills. Trump was caught groping one woman and Daniels called him on it, asking Trump how he would explain that to his then-teenage son, Donald Jr. Responded Trump, "He's fourteen, and, uh, he could really understand that one. No, that one's all right." Trump was also caught on video at the party hanging out with Jeffrey Epstein. "Look at her, back there. She's hot," Trump is heard telling Epstein about one of the women, according to the reports.

> *TRUMP RESPONSE—The* Washington Post *said the White*
> *House and an attorney for the Trump Organization declined to*
> *comment, as did Martin Weinberg, a lawyer for Epstein.*

b). other allegations of inappropriate behavior:

27. *"anonymous* Apprentice *camera operator"*

A 2016 Associated Press report by Garance Burke detailed Trump's "lewd and sexist" behavior on the set of *The Apprentice,* and specifically reported him repeatedly targeting a female camera operator as far back as 2003. According to the AP report, eight former crew members acknowledged his behavior with this woman and two said the "woman made it clear to them privately that she did not like Trump's comments." Former *Apprentice* producer Katherine Walker said: "He said something like she was cute and she had a nice ass, and it was brought to my attention by someone else that he had a crush on her. We all knew, so that's uncomfortable in and of itself," she said. In the AP report, a camera assistant, identified as Rebecca Arndt, said Trump would discuss the camera operator's blonde hair, blue eyes, and her comparison to his daughter Ivanka. The AP said it spoke twice to the camera operator's husband, who said his wife did not want to be interviewed "and denied she had been subjected to repeated, unwanted attention from Trump," according to the report. In 2018, the *New Yorker's* Patrick Radden Keefe quoted one *Apprentice* employee as saying Trump regularly made comments about the bodies of both female contestants and staffers, including, "He'd say, 'How about those boobs? Wouldn't you like to fuck her?'"

28. *"anonymous supermodel (Plaza hotel)"*

In an interview for this book, a source alleged an incident in the early 1990s in which he claimed Trump entered a suite at the Plaza hotel in New York in the belief that a supermodel was alone in her room. Instead, this man, who was in the modeling business, was with the supermodel— in bed. Trump was surprised when he entered the room but made a hasty retreat, the man said. The model and the man followed Trump downstairs but security intervened. We are withholding the name of the supermodel and the source. The incident is similar to an allegation made in court papers by Jill Harth against Trump, in which she claimed Trump entered the room of a model at Mar-a-Lago while she was sleeping. The woman woke up and forced Trump from the room.

29. *"anonymous woman (nightclub)"*

In an interview with Lucy Osborne for this book, photographer David

Webber recounted an incident in which he claimed Trump had cornered a young model ("she looked no more than sixteen") at a NYC nightclub in the 1990s. The woman, seemingly in distress, signaled for him and he said, "I cock-blocked Donald Trump basically" and freed the girl from him." Webber added: "He was a model hound—he was always chasing models. . . . But yes he (Trump) was a predator, absolutely."

30. *"anonymous woman pawed"*
In an interview with Lucy Osborne for this book, a journalist recalled once meeting Trump alone in New York where he acted like a "slimy, oily, lecherous type of person," made her feel uncomfortable, and started "pawing" her shoulder. We are withholding the name of the woman.

31. *"anonymous young girls"*
A video from a 1992 *Entertainment Tonight* Christmas special caught Trump, then forty-six, talking to an unnamed girl. He asks if she is going up the escalator. When she tells him she is, he is heard responding to someone, "I'm going to be dating her in ten years. Can you believe it?" During the 2016 campaign, the New York *Daily News* blasted this cover headline: Trump "Had Eyes for a 10-Year-Old." A similar story from a 1992 wire-story roundup in the *Chicago Tribune* was found by *Los Angeles Times* reporter Seema Mehta. It said: "Donald Trump turned up Monday for a carol sing by a youth choir outside Manhattan's Plaza Hotel. He asked two of the girls how old they were. After they replied they were 14, Trump said, 'Wow! Just think—in a couple of years I'll be dating you.'"

32. Elizabeth Beck
The lawyer—and a new mom—became a victim of Trump's outrage during a 2011 deposition in which she was representing an opposing client in a dispute over a failed real estate project in Florida. Trump lost it when she asked to take a break to pump breast milk. She told CNN's Alisyn Camerota in 2015: "He got up, his face got red, he shook his finger at me and he screamed, 'You're disgusting, you're disgusting,' and he ran out of there."

> *TRUMP RESPONSE—After the interview, Trump tweeted:* "Lawyer Elizabeth Beck did a terrible job against me, she lost (I even got legal fees). I loved beating her, she was easy."

33. Mariah Billado

Representing Vermont in the Miss Teen USA Pageant, she said Trump watched her and other young women, aged fifteen to nineteen, dressing when they were naked.

> *TRUMP RESPONSE—In October 2016, the Trump campaign said of accusations from Billado and others regarding the pageants: "These accusations have no merit and have already been disproven by many other individuals who were present. When you see questionable attacks like this magically put out there in the final months of a presidential campaign, you have to ask yourself what the political motivations are and why the media is pushing it."*

34. Lisa Boyne

Through her friend Sonja Morgan, who went on to become a cast member on *Real Housewives of New York,* the then twenty-five-year-old Boyne ended up at a dinner with Trump, John Casablancas, and other women at a Manhattan restaurant in 1996. Because of the table location, Trump insisted the women needed to walk across the table to get up. Trump "stuck his head right underneath their skirts" and commented on whether they were wearing underwear and what their genitalia looked like, she claimed during the 2016 campaign.

> *TRUMP RESPONSE—At the time the accusations were made, Trump's spokeswoman, Hope Hicks, said Trump "would never do that."*

35. Heather Braden

In an interview for this book, the model described a bizarre party she attended in Miami in the 1990s with dozens of other models and just four men—three unnamed actors and Trump. The men worked the room, she said, and selected models who were then taken into private rooms. Braden, twenty-three at the time and one of the oldest women in the room, said she turned down an invitation from Trump directly to join him privately for what she believed would be a sexual encounter. Braden first revealed details of the party to the BBC.

36. NaKina Carr

In an interview with Lucy Osborne for this book, the model said Trump came uninvited backstage to a show intent on seeing the women undressing. "I knew right then that he was the absolute creepiest kind of man," Carr said. "One, that he would do that at all, and two, in front of his pregnant wife with no shame." Among her model friends, Carr said Trump was known as the "creepy groper."

37. Tasha Dixon

Representing Arizona during the 2001 Miss USA pageant, she said Trump watched contestants while they were changing, including some who were nude. She told KCAL TV in Los Angeles that contestants were told to "fawn all over him."

> TRUMP RESPONSE—The Trump campaign, in October 2016, denied Dixon's accusations in a statement, reading: "These accusations have no merit and have already been disproven by many other individuals who were present. When you see questionable attacks like this magically put out there in the final month of a presidential campaign, you have to ask yourself what the political motivations are and why the media is pushing it."

38. Kristi Frank

Former *Apprentice* staffers claimed the season one contestant was sexually objectified by Trump. "They wanted us to be sexy," Frank was quoted by the *Hollywood Reporter*. Frank and three other women on the show were featured in a lingerie shoot for an issue of *FHM* in 2004, after each turned down $250,000 to pose nude in *Playboy*.

> TRUMP RESPONSE—Trump later told Howard Stern—according to Newsweek and Factba.se—"You know Kristi, they all got in because of the brain, but Kristi, turned out to be a, I don't know if the word 'stripper,' but something pretty close to that. Kristi has an amazing, should I say figure as opposed to body, it's a little bit more respectful? Her body is amazing."

39. Jennifer Hawkins

The former Miss Universe 2004, from Australia, was "sexually humiliated" by Trump at an event in Sydney in 2011, according to the *Huffington Post*. A video of the incident caught Trump telling the audience that Hawkins was "a beautiful girl on the outside but she's not very bright." He added: "Now this is about getting even. I was so angry at her yesterday." Trump then made a point of emphasizing that Hawkins *"came"* to the event—reportedly repeating the word several times. Trump then said: "See, they have the same filthy minds in Australia. . . . She got in that car and she got her ass over here and I love her." While Hawkins stood apparently embarrassed by his remarks, Trump is then seen grabbing her by the waist and kissing her on the cheek. She then told Trump: "Can I sit down now? You've embarrassed me—thank you very much." She later told Australian media she had a "lot of respect" for Trump.

40. Samantha Holvey

Trump sexually objectified the North Carolina contestant at the 2006 Miss USA pageant by personally inspecting her, she said, and the other women, leaving her feeling "disgusted." In an opinion essay for NBC News, Holvey wrote in part: "So many women have fought so long and hard for women to have the right to vote, and now we were using it to support a man with a long history of sexual misconduct."

> *TRUMP RESPONSE—After Holvey appeared on* Megyn Kelly Today *on NBC in December 2017, the White House said: "These false claims, totally disputed in most cases by eyewitness accounts, were addressed at length during last year's campaign, and the American people voiced their judgment by delivering a decisive victory. The timing and absurdity of these claims speaks volumes. And the publicity tour that has begun further confirms the political motives behind them."*

41. Victoria Hughes

Competing for New Mexico in the Miss Teen USA pageant in 1997, she confirmed Trump enjoyed checking out the girls in the changing room. "It was certainly the most inappropriate time to meet us all for the first time," she told *BuzzFeed News* in 2016.

> *TRUMP RESPONSE—Trump appeared to confirm this type of behavior, telling Howard Stern in 2005 that he regularly walked into contestants' dressing rooms while the women were unclothed. He said: "I'll go backstage before a show and everyone's getting dressed and ready and everything else. And you know, no men are anywhere. And I'm allowed to go in because I'm the owner of the pageant. You know, they're standing there with no clothes. And you*

see these incredible-looking women. And I sort of get away with things like that."

42. Vendela Kirsebom

The Norwegian model and *Sports Illustrated* swimsuit issue cover girl was seated next to Trump at the White House Correspondents' Association Dinner in 1993, after being invited by *Vanity Fair* editor Graydon Carter. He later wrote that the model came to his table in tears, begging him to move her. "It seems that Trump had spent his entire time with her assaying the 'tits' and legs of other female guests and asking how they measured up to those of other women, including his wife," Carter wrote. "'He is,' she told me, in words that seemed familiar, 'the most vulgar man I have ever met.'" (Rowanne Brewer similarly recalled that Trump asked her to rate Ivana and Marla.) In October 2016, Kirsebom told *the Daily Mail:* "He talked about big breasts, small breasts, how one was better than the other and the differences between them. His main focus was breasts and the sizes of women's bodies. Fat women were not real women in his opinion. He basically said if you are not attractive and beautiful, then you don't have any purpose as a woman."

43. Brook Antoinette Mahealani Lee

In 1997, during the Miss Teen USA pageant, the then Miss Universe said Trump, who was sitting in the audience, asked her about his "hot" daughter Ivanka. "That's just weird. She was sixteen," she told the *New York Times.*

44. Shawna Lee

In an interview with Lucy Osborne for this book, she recounted an incident from her participation in the "Look of the Year" contest in 1992. She was a Canadian contestant and ended up a runner-up to the winner. Lee—who was age fourteen at the time—said he was asked to attend an event on a boat and "dance" in front of Trump and John Casablancas. She said: "I felt uncomfortable. So I walked down the stairs, I didn't dance, I blew a kiss at them, spun around and walked away. . . . Some of the girls were like booty dancing, but I was like, no thank you."

45. Shayna Love

In an interview with Lucy Osborne for this book, the former Elite "New

Faces" model said she was instructed to go out to dinner with Trump when she was sixteen. She said there were other models at the dinner table—some as young as fourteen—and the only other adult besides Trump was agency owner John Casablancas. "Pretty sleazy" is how she described the experience, adding: "I did my very best to stay very far away from him [Trump]."

46. Alicia Machado
Despite fat-shaming the Venezuelan beauty pageant contestant who won the 1996 Miss Universe competition, Trump still tried to sleep with her, she claimed.

> *TRUMP RESPONSE—According to* New York *magazine, Trump also tried to disparage Machado by insinuating she was tied to a "sex tape, which doesn't exist." He also called her "disgusting" and questioned her "past," which included appearances in the Mexican edition of* Playboy, *said* New York *magazine.*

47. Ksenia Maximova
In an interview with Lucy Osborne for this book, the British-Russian model, then eighteen, worked for Trump Model Management in 2004, and was called to Trump Tower for what she thought was a business meeting—but was, in fact, a casting call of sorts to find a boyfriend for Trump's son, which she viewed as inappropriate.

48. Karen McDougal
In a 2018 report by Ronan Farrow in the *New Yorker*, Trump and his mistress, according to multiple sources, were driving in a limousine with a female friend. Trump said the friend liked "the big black dick," and according to Farrow, "began commenting on her attractiveness and breast size," adding: "The interactions angered the friend and deeply offended McDougal." Author Michael Wolff, in his 2019 book *Siege*, also quoted Trump as making a disparaging remark to a friend about sleeping with black women "to get a little chocolate in his diet." When Howard Stern once asked Trump, "Have you had a black woman in bed?" Trump responded: "Well, it depends on what your definition of black is . . . The rainbow coalition, as Rev. Jesse [Jackson] would say."

> *TRUMP RESPONSE—In a response to the* New Yorker, *"a White House spokesperson said in a statement that Trump denies having*

had an affair with McDougal: 'This is an old story that is just more fake news. The President says he never had a relationship with McDougal." Additionally, a White House spokesperson discredited Wolff's book.

49. Marlee Matlin

Trump was accused of "making sexual comments" to the Oscar-winning actress when she appeared on *Celebrity Apprentice,* according to the *Daily Beast* in October 2016. The report also said Trump allegedly wrote notes during the show tapings, including one that said: "Marlee, is she retarded??" The allegation was made by a source—"a person familiar with the notes who helped clean up after tapings," said the report. In addition, two other sources confirmed to the *Beast* that Trump called Matlin "retarded." She appeared on *Celebrity Apprentice* 4, which premiered in March 2011, and was "fired" in the season finale, finishing second to Big & Rich singer John Rich. In response, Matlin said the term used by Trump was "abhorrent"; "there are millions of deaf and hard-of-hearing people like me in the United States and around the world who face discrimination and misunderstanding like this on a daily basis. It is unacceptable." A *People* magazine report said one of the contestants that season—*Survivor* winner Richard Hatch—accused Trump of making "sexual comments" to female contestants on the show, including Matlin and actress Lisa Rinna.

> *TRUMP RESPONSE- At the time, the Trump campaign did not respond to a request for comment regarding Matlin. But the Trump campaign responded to* People *regarding Hatch: "Just take a look at Richard Hatch's record, or lack thereof."*

50. Paromita Mitra

A competitor in the 2013 Miss USA pageant from Mississippi, Mitra confirmed fellow contestant Cassandra Searles's claims of Trump's misogynistic treatment of the women.

51. Eli Nessa

In an interview with Lucy Osborne for this book, the 1991 "Look of the Year" contestant from Norway said young girls were victimized during their stay for the contest and the events that surrounded it, including parties arranged by Trump. "The whole thing wasn't right," she said. Nessa, seventeen at the time, said she was fortunate to have her agent there to protect her and that she and some of the other girls "protected each other."

52. Rhonda Noggle
Riding with Trump in his limousine with a group of other models following the launch of a competition called "American Dream Calendar Girls" in Manhattan in December 1992, Rhonda told the *Boston Globe* in 2016, she asked the driver to stop the car after Trump declared "all women are bimbos" and said most were "gold diggers." She added, "I told him I would rather be with a trash man who respected me than someone who was a rich, pompous ass. And I got out. And I took a cab ride home."

53. Nancy O'Dell
"I moved on her like a bitch." That was Trump talking to Billy Bush about Bush's then coanchor, who was married. The comment was recorded in 2005 in the infamous *Access Hollywood* tape. Added Trump: "I moved on her very heavily. In fact, I took her out furniture shopping. . . . But I couldn't get there. And she was married." Trump allegedly tried to have O'Dell fired from hosting the Miss USA pageant two years later for being pregnant. She later issued a statement saying in part: "Everyone deserves respect no matter the setting or gender."

54. Caitriona Perry
While placing a call from the Oval Office to Ireland's newly elected leader Leo Varadkar in June 2007, Trump flirted with one of the Irish reporters in attendance in what was described as a "creepy" moment in the White House. The RTE reporter was summoned over to the president's desk and told she had "a nice smile." The correspondent shared a video of the incident on Twitter and also told RTE the incident was "bizarre" after "I caught his eye and he called me over." Another journalist said, "It was utterly inappropriate in the workplace. They weren't on a date."

55. Lauren Petrella
According to a lawsuit filed against Trump by Jill Harth (which was eventually settled), twenty-two-year-old Petrella allegedly found Trump, unannounced and uninvited, in her bed at Mar-a-Lago in the predawn hours before she kicked him out of the room. She was a

contestant in the "American Dream Calendar Girls" competition and stayed at Mar-a-Lago in January 1993.

> *TRUMP RESPONSE—Asked for comment about the incident by the* Boston Globe, *Trump said, "It's total nonsense. It's not true. I never even heard of the person!"*

56. Barbara Pilling

When she was seventeen, the Canadian model was hit on by Trump at a Manhattan party, she first told the BBC and then confirmed in an interview with Lucy Osborne for this book. "I remember him talking to me for quite a while and I could see that his eyesight kept going, not to my eyes, but to my chest area and I was starting to feel uncomfortable," she said. Pilling claimed she also saw Trump "slap the bottom" of a cocktail waitress during the time he was attempting to pick her up.

57. Carrie Prejean

The Miss USA 2009 first runner-up from California said Trump inspected the women and asked some to comment on each other's looks. During the 2016 campaign, Prejean told Sean Hannity on Fox News: "I have nothing but positive things to say about Donald. . . . He helped me tremendously."

> *TRUMP RESPONSE—Trump denied the accusation to the* New York Times *and said he would "never do that. I wouldn't hurt people, that's hurtful to people." Trump also told* Extra: *"Carrie should be ashamed of herself. Certainly I would never do a thing like that . . . it would be too hurtful." He also claimed Prejean had admitted she made an erotic tape for an ex-boyfriend, which she called the "biggest mistake of my life." Trump said: "She's trying to act like she's a nun. . . ."*

58. Brande Roderick

The 2001 *Playboy* Playmate of the Year appeared on *Celebrity Apprentice* eight years later and then again in 2013. Multiple show staffers said Trump was obsessed with her and, according to the *Daily Mail*, repeatedly said he wanted her "as his wife" and talked about how badly he wanted to "f—k her." The *Daily Beast*, speaking to former staffers, said Trump made graphic comments about Roderick's "gorgeous and perfect body" and "t—s." The *Beast* quoted a show source: "He kept leering after her the whole time she was on for (that 13th) season (in 2013). She definitely became something of a sexual obsession to him, and everyone could see it. . . ." But Roderick told MSNBC: "He's never been disrespectful to me."

59. Selina Scott
In 2016, the British broadcaster wrote a first-person story for *the Daily Mail* and detailed how she rejected the advances he made while she profiled him in 1995, and said Trump "failed to seduce her and then stalked her for 20 years." She also said Trump stalked her friend Princess Diana.

60. Bridget Sullivan
A contestant in the 2000 Miss Teen USA Pageant, representing New Hampshire, she said Trump walked through the dressing room and "we were all naked," adding Trump would "hug you just a little low on your back" and give the young women "a squeeze like a creepy uncle would."

> TRUMP RESPONSE—*At the time of the accusations, Trump's campaign issued a denial, calling Sullivan's claims and others made by beauty pageant contestants "totally false."*

61. *"Swedish model, Cathleen"*
In an interview with Lucy Osborne for this book, a Swedish model for Elite—Cathleen (who asked her last name be withheld)—said she was fifteen when she attended a dinner with Trump in the mid-1980s. She claimed Trump showed up with two young models and made out with one of them in front of the others. "They offered us alcohol but I didn't drink it; others did though," she said.

62. Kari Wells
A former model and *Bravo* actress, Wells was in her early twenties when she experienced Trump's belief in sexual entitlement in December 1992. According to the *Guardian* in 2016, Wells was in Aspen, Colorado, for a fashion show with her girlfriend Kelly Ann Sabatasso, who was dating Trump at the time. Wells said, "He asked if I would like to come up to his room as Kelly was coming over and he thought that the three of us could have some fun together. He pushed his room key forward on the table for me to pick up." She quickly made an excuse, but said of the incident: "What gave him a right to ask me such a thing? Just

because I had been polite and friendly towards him, and the fact that I was a model?"

63. Stacy Wilkes
In an interview with Lucy Osborne for this book, the five-eleven, blue-eyed blonde participated in the 1991 "Look of the Year" contest when she was age sixteen. She claimed Trump and John Casablancas body-shamed her, telling her she needed to lose more weight. "I mean there was no way to be skinnier for me," she said.

64. *"seventeen-year-old contestant"*
In a lawsuit against Trump (which was settled), Jill Harth alleged "on or about November 20th, 1993, defendant Trump demanded that plaintiff provide defendant with access to a seventeen-year-old contestant from Czechoslovakia, who was a contestant in the 'Calendar Girl' competition, and whom Trump referred to with "sexual innuendo" in describing the contestant's status as a woman and "sex object" in the eyes of defendant."

> *TRUMP RESPONSE—Trump denied Harth's accusations during the 2016 campaign, according to his spokesperson at the time, Hope Hicks.*

65, 66. *"wine incidents"*
Trump boasted about inappropriate behavior involving two women—journalist Marie Brenner and Leona Helmsley, the notorious New York City real estate executive and so-called Queen of Mean. In Brenner's case, he told *New York* magazine in 1992 that he "poured a whole bottle of wine down Marie Brenner's back after she wrote a story on him that [he] hated." Brenner later told the *Daily Beast:* "It wasn't a bottle, actually—it was a glass." She also once quoted Trump as referring to her as "a disgrace to humanity" and a "vicious, horrible woman" and told a *New York Times* reporter he once "took an entire bottle of red wine and poured it into the hood (of her dress hanging over the back of her chair)." He added, "I don't take it back and I hope Leona didn't get overly wet. I hope the dress she was wearing wasn't an expensive one, though that's not likely."

> *TRUMP RESPONSE—Regarding Brenner, Trump denied making the "treat 'em like shit" comment and told* New York *magazine: "I*

didn't say that. The woman's a liar, extremely unattractive, lots of problems because of her looks."

67. Trump National Golf Club sexism allegations

A 2012 labor relations lawsuit (since settled) involved former employees of the golf club in Rancho Palos Verdes, Calif. An investigation of the lawsuit by the *Los Angeles Times* (by Matt Pearce on Sept. 29, 2016) reported alleged sexism. A former catering director, Hayley Strozier, was quoted as saying in a sworn declaration: "I had witnessed Donald Trump tell managers many times while he was visiting the club that restaurant hostesses were 'not pretty enough' and that they should be fired and replaced with more attractive women." A former restaurant manager also said in a sworn declaration that Trump once saw "a young, attractive hostess working named Nicole" and later asked her, "Do you like Jewish men?" Another former employee, a woman, said Trump's behavior toward her was "inappropriate" and said he regularly asked her, "Are you still happily married?"

> **TRUMP RESPONSE**—*At the time of the lawsuit, the Trump Organization called the allegations "meritless" and an attorney said, "We do not engage in discrimination of any kind. . . ."*

Additionally noted:

George Houraney comments (Trump, Epstein Mar-a-Lago "Calendar Girl" party)

After Jeffrey Epstein was arrested on federal sex-trafficking charges in July 2019, a Florida businessman disclosed he arranged a 1992 party at Mar-a-Lago at Trump's request that only was attended by Trump and Epstein and two dozen or so women from a "calendar girl" competition.

In an interview with the *New York Times*, George Houraney, who ran American Dream Enterprise and partnered with Trump to host events at his casinos, said: "I arranged to have some contestants fly in. At the very first party, I said, 'Who's coming tonight? I have 28 girls coming.' It was him and Epstein."

Houraney said he expected other guests to attend the party. He told the *Times*: "I said, 'Donald, this is supposed to be a party with V.I.P.s. You're telling me it's you and Epstein?'"

(Houraney had previously accused Trump of inappropriate behavior involving his ex-wife and business partner Jill Harth, who alleged Trump groped and sexually harassed her in a 1997 lawsuit. Harth withdrew the suit as part of settling a separate financial dispute with Trump but told ABC News in 2017 that she stood by her allegations.)

> *TRUMP RESPONSE—The White House did not comment on Houraney's comments to the* New York Times *about the 1992 party involving Trump, Epstein, and the "calendar girl" women. Trump, however, spoke out against Epstein in the wake of the charges filed against Epstein in New York. He told reporters in the Oval Office that he "knew him [Epstein] like everybody in Palm Beach knew him." But Trump added: "I had a falling-out with him. I haven't spoken to him in 15 years. I was not a fan of his, that I can tell you." But comments Trump made to* New York *magazine in 2002 were widely recycled in the media. Trump was quoted as saying: "I've known Jeff for 15 years. Terrific guy. He's a lot of fun to be with. It is even said that he likes beautiful women as much as I do, and many of them are on the younger side."*

II. DISPARAGING OR SEXUALLY FUELED COMMENTS DIRECTED AT SPECIFIC WOMEN

Mika Brzezinski
The MSNBC *Morning Joe* cohost has been a longtime target of Trump, eliciting these type of tweets from him: "dumb as a rock," "was bleeding badly from a face-lift," "low I.Q.," "Crazy," "crazy and very dumb," "had a mental breakdown while talking about me," "very insecure," "clown," "off the wall," "neurotic," "not very bright," "mess!," "has gone wild with hate."

Halle Berry
Trump told Howard Stern about the actress, according to *Newsweek* and the website Factba.se: "I love her upper body. . . . I think her skin is beautiful. . . . What I hate about Halle Berry is that there's always, like, drama around her. It's always like fighting automobile accidents. You know, fistfights, boyfriends, fighting ex-husbands, fighting for a child. . . . She's fine."

Beyoncé
According to the *Daily Beast,* Trump criticized the singer's Super Bowl performance: "When Beyoncé was thrusting her hips forward in a very suggestive manner, if someone else had done that, it would've been a national scandal. I thought it was ridiculous. . . . I just thought it was not appropriate. . . ."

Christine Blasey Ford
Before the midterm elections, Trump attacked the accuser of his Supreme Court nominee Brett Kavanaugh. In Cape Girardeau, Missouri, Trump told an audience "the accuser of Brett Kavanaugh" had recanted all her allegations. "It was false accusations, it was a scam, it was fake, it was all fake," he said. While Ford had not recanted her allegations, Trump was referring to another accuser but by not naming her, Trump left the impression he was talking about Ford. Trump closed out his midterm campaigning by inciting a "lock her up" chant regarding sexual harassment accusations during a rally in Indiana.

Carla Bruni
Trump blasted the Italian-French model and singer, telling Howard Stern: "[Carla] was trying to get me to leave Marla, something I had in mind anyway, and she was using every psychological trick in the book. In the end, Carla became a woman who is very difficult to even like." Trump also disparaged Bruni's bra size to Stern, saying it was "smaller than A cup—minus A." She later told the *Daily Mail:* "Trump is obviously a lunatic. . . . I'm deeply embarrassed by it all. I've only ever met him once. . . ."

Jessica Chastain
Trump told Howard Stern about the actress: "She's certainly not, she's not hot," reported the *Washington Post* in 2017.

Cher
During a 2012 interview with Greta Van Susteren on Fox News, Trump said: "Cher is somewhat of a loser. She's lonely. She's unhappy. She's very miserable. And her sound-enhanced and computer-enhanced music doesn't do it for me. I've watched her over the years. I knew her a little bit. And you know, she reminds me of Rosie [O'Donnell] with slightly more talent, not much more talent, but slightly more talent."

Hillary Clinton

According to the *New York Times*, Trump's tweet attacks on his 2016 rival included these comments: "If Hillary Clinton can't satisfy her husband what makes her think she can satisfy America?"; "Crooked"; "A PATHOLOGICAL LIAR!"; "a loose cannon"; "guilty as hell"; "ill-fit"; "Corrupt"; "stupidity"; "pathetic"; "she looked lost"; "incompetent"; "brainpower is highly overrated, decision making is so bad"; "you have failed, failed and failed"; "Crooked Hillary"; "totally Crooked"; "extraordinary bad judgment & instincts."

Gail Collins

She wrote a 2011 column for the *New York Times* titled "Donald Trump Gets Weirder." In it, she revealed that in one down period related to his business, she referred to Trump in print as a "financially embattled thousandaire." Trump's reaction? Collins wrote that he sent her a copy of the column "with my picture circled and 'The Face of a Dog!' written on it."

Ann Coulter

During the 2016 campaign, the conservative commentator went on *Good Morning Britain* to defend Trump against allegations of sexual assault. But she became critical of Trump over his campaign promise to build the border wall and called Trump out as the biggest "wimp" in presidential history. Trump hit back, calling her "very hostile" and a "wacky nut job."

Princess Diana

Three years after her tragic death, he joked to Howard Stern that he would have "nailed" the divorced wife of England's Prince Charles after making her take an HIV test. "Go back over to my Lexus because I have a new doctor. We wanna give you a little checkup," Trump joked.

Maureen Dowd

Trump has tweeted about the *New York Times* op-ed columnist, calling her "a neurotic dope" and "crazy." He's also said she "pretends she knows me well—wrong!" In a July 2017 column titled "Cruella de Trump," she wrote: "I gave Trump the benefit of doubt after his comment on Megyn Kelly about 'blood coming out of her whatever' when he claimed he meant her nose. But later, a longtime Trump associate

told me that Trump had practiced the line before he said it on CNN
and that it was meant to evoke an image of Kelly as hormonal."

Paris Hilton

Trump sexualized the heiress-turned-reality star in a 2003 interview
with Howard Stern, according to *Politico* in 2016. "I've known Paris
Hilton from the time she's twelve," which led Stern to reply, "She's hot."
Trump continued: "Her parents are friends of mine, and the first time
I saw her she walked into the room and I said, 'Who the hell is that?'"
Stern: "Did you want to bang her?" Trump replied, "She's a very . . .
Well, at twelve, I wasn't interested. I've never been into that." Trump
admitted to Stern he watched Hilton's leaked "sex tape" she made at
age nineteen, and that "Melania showed it to me." Hilton said Trump's
comments about her on Stern weren't "creepy at all." She also defended
him on the *Access Hollywood* tape, saying: "I've heard guys say some
pretty crazy things. Like worse than that . . ." A year later, Hilton walked
back her comments and said, "I always believe in helping women have
their voices heard and helping create an environment where women
feel empowered and believe in themselves." She eventually criticized
Trump for his border policy, telling *TMZ* after it was reported that
children were separated from their families: "This is inhumane. No
child should be treated this way. I'm disgusted."

Arianna Huffington

Trump tweeted about the media star and founder of the *Huffington
Post* website in 2012: "@ariannahuff is unattractive both inside and
out. I fully understand why her former husband left her for a man—he
made a good decision." Huffington was asked on CNBC about Trump's
personal attacks against her and she said: "That's his style, he always
attacks people."

Angelina Jolie

On *Larry King Live*'s CNN show in 2007, Trump took a shot at the
Hollywood star and activist while discussing her falling-out with her
father Jon Voight. Snapped Trump, "I really understand beauty. And I
will tell you, she's not—I do own Miss Universe. I do own Miss USA. I
mean I own a lot of different things. I do understand beauty, and she's
not." Trump further went off on Jolie to Howard Stern: "I don't think
she's got good skin. I don't think she's got a great face. I think her lips

are too big, to be honest with you. You know, they look like too big. She's a seven, but a seven is not a ten."

"Intern Julie"

Promoting *The Apprentice* in 2003 on Howard Stern, Trump ogled the shock jock's attractive new intern on her first day of work. "By the way, your intern is incredible, Julie. It's her first day. Get her out here, she's amazing . . . this could be a star. Come here, Julie. Look at the face. . . ."

Khloe Kardashian

"She is a fat piglet. Why did we get the ugly Kardashian?" Jason Cherkis and Sam Stein, writing for the *Huffington Post* in October 2016, quoted multiple *Celebrity Apprentice* sources as saying Trump made those disparaging comments about Khloe's weight when she appeared on the show in 2009. Before she was fired, the sources said Trump "complained to producers about Kardashian's looks and itched to have her removed," according to the *Huffington Post* report. One editor on the show said Trump asked: "What is this? We can't even get the hot one?"—referring to Khloe's sister, Kim. Another source told the *Huffington Post*: "Why don't we fire Khloe? She is a fat piglet. Why did we get the ugly Kardashian?" In response, the *Keeping Up with the Kardashians* star told Chelsea Handler: "I hated every minute of it. . . . I didn't care to do *Celebrity Apprentice.* My mom made me do it."

Kim Kardashian

The reality show queen successfully lobbied the president in the Oval Office to commute the sentence of a nonviolent female drug offender serving a life sentence. Years before, Trump told Howard Stern: "She's got a huge trunk . . . it's seriously big." And in an interview on HLN's *Showbiz Tonight* in 2013, Trump made comments about her weight when she was pregnant: "She's gotten a little bit large. I would say this: I don't think you should dress like you weigh 120 pounds."

Heidi Klum

In a 2015 interview, Trump dumped on the German model and TV personality: "Heidi Klum. Sadly, she's no longer a ten." She responded by posting a video on Twitter in which a man wearing a Trump mask ripped a number 10 off her T-shirt, revealing a 9.99 underneath."

Mila Kunis

According to the *Daily Beast,* Trump told Howard Stern about the actress: "No [she's not hot]. Not to me. She's an attractive person, but when you look at Dayana Mendoza [Miss Universe 2008], when you look at the Miss Universe people, that's why I'm so jaded."

Monica Lewinsky (and Paula Jones)

When the Clinton-Monica scandal was brewing, Trump weighed in to Neil Cavuto during an interview on Fox News on August 19, 1998. Trump said: "I don't necessarily agree with his victims, his victims are terrible. He is really a victim himself. But he put himself in that position. The whole group, Paula Jones, Lewinsky, it's just a really unattractive group. I'm not just talking about physical." Cavuto then asked, "Would it be any different if it were a supermodel crowd?" Replied Trump, "I think at least it would be more pleasant to watch."

Lindsay Lohan

In 2004, Trump was discussing the then teen star with Howard Stern, who said, "I think she's hot." Trump responded: "There's something there, right? But you have to like freckles. I've seen a, you know, close-up of her chest and a lot of freckles. . . ." Stern went on: "Can you imagine the sex with this troubled teen?" Replied Trump, "Yeah, you're probably right. She's probably deeply troubled and therefore great in bed. How come the deeply troubled women, you know, deeply, deeply troubled, they're always the best in bed?"

Meghan Markle

The American actress who married Prince Harry refused to meet Trump during his state visit to the United Kingdom in June 2019. The British *Sun* newspaper said Markle told the U.S. talk show *The Nightly Show with Larry Wilmore* in 2016: "Yes, of course Trump is divisive, think about female voters alone, right?" She added: "That is a huge number and with as misogynistic as Trump is, and so vocal about it, that is a huge chunk of it. . . ." According to the *Sun,* "Trump branded the comments made by the Duchess of Sussex as 'nasty'" and the newspaper said it had an audio recording of his comments.

> ***TRUMP RESPONSE**—Trump tried to clarify his comment in an interview with Piers Morgan, saying: "I wasn't referring to she's*

*nasty. I said she was nasty about me. And, essentially, I didn't
know she was nasty about me."*

Omarosa Manigault Newman

The former reality show star and Trump aide was fired from the White
House, resulting in a book she wrote titled *Unhinged*. According to the
New York Times, in 2018, among the hateful things Trump tweeted about
her: ". . . Wacky, Deranged . . . People in the White House hated her,
vicious, but not smart, heard really bad things. Nasty to people & would
constantly miss meetings & work, a loser, nothing but problems."

Jill McCabe

Trump called the wife of the former FBI deputy director "a loser" following her failed campaign for Virginia's state legislature in 2015.
Andrew McCabe, who was fired for allegedly lying to investigators
about his interactions with reporters, made the disclosure to *60 Minutes* in February 2019.

Bette Midler

"While @BetteMidler is an extremely unattractive woman, I refuse to
say that because I always insist on being politically correct," he tweeted
in 2012, about the singer, songwriter, and actress. Trump resumed an
attack on Midler in June 2019, blasting her in an early morning tweet,
according to the *New York Post*, as a "washed-up psycho" after she
had attributed a quote to him that had been widely debunked. Trump
added: "She got caught, just like the Fake News Media gets caught. A
sick scammer!"

Elin Nordegren

Trump told Howard Stern about Tiger Woods's ex-wife, a Swedish
model: "A solid nine . . . Well, ten is very, very sacred territory."

Rosie O'Donnell

The TV star attended Trump's nuptials to Marla, but years later trig-
gered an ongoing war with Trump when she described him as "a
snake-oil salesman" in 2006. A few months later, according to Trump
biographer David Cay Johnston, he referred to her as "a pig," "a degenerate," and "a slob" at an event. He then attacked her in his 2007 book,
Think Big: "You've got to hit a bully really hard really strongly, right
between the eyes. . . . [I] hit that horrible woman right smack in the

middle of the eyes." He also added in the book: "I love getting even when I get screwed by someone. . . . You need to screw them back fifteen times harder . . . go for the jugular, attack them in spades!" Trump further, in various interviews, called the former host of *The View* an "animal" after she took issue with his defense of troubled Miss USA Tara Conner. O'Donnell responded: "He's the moral authority. Left the first wife—had an affair. Left the second wife—had an affair. . . . But he's the moral compass for twenty-two-year-olds in America. Donald, sit and spin, my friend!" In 2006, Trump threatened to sue O'Donnell after she said he was bankrupt. But after Rosie suffered a heart attack six years later, in 2012, he tweeted: "get better fast. I'm starting to miss you."

Condoleezza Rice
The Trump campaign in 2016 reportedly considered the former secretary of state as a possible vice presidential candidate. But according to the New York *Daily News* he said in a speech: "Condoleezza Rice, she's a lovely woman, but I think she's a bitch."

Lisa Rinna
The TV personality had appeared on *Celebrity Apprentice*, but Trump said about her: "She had those big puffed-up lips, I don't know why women do that, but the lips were like, gigantic."

April Ryan
In 2018, the White House correspondent for American Urban Radio Networks was the subject of an unprompted attack by Trump. "You talk about somebody that's a loser; she doesn't know what the hell she's doing," Trump said. "She gets publicity, and then she gets a pay raise or a contract with, I think, CNN. But she's very nasty. . . ." Trump, at the time, also attacked another African American journalist, Abby Phillip of CNN: "What a stupid question. But I watch you a lot—you ask a lot of stupid questions."

Stephanie Seymour
"Awfully close" to perfect was Trump's take on the Victoria's Secret model and actress to Howard Stern, who asked: "Is there anything wrong with her?" Trump replied, "Nothing, whatsoever."

Nicole Brown Simpson
Trump made disparaging comments about the slain ex-wife of O. J.

Simpson; she was murdered with Ron Goldman on June 12, 1994. A decade later, in September 2004, he described to Howard Stern a dinner at a California restaurant. "There were six of us, and O.J. came up," he said. "And he's talking with us for about three minutes. . . . And Nicole was with her mother, I think, and she came over and she started screaming at him 'Get over to the table!' What the hell are you . . .' She was rough; okay? In all fairness . . . So he decided, obviously to kill her. . . . She was very tough. She came over and she really embarrassed him. She was screaming at him 'get over there!' She didn't care. And that was before *The Apprentice,* so she didn't give a damn about me. Now she'd be kissing my ass. Now, I'm the biggest star on television, she'll kiss my ass." Only months before the slayings, O.J. was a guest at Trump's wedding to Marla in 1993.

Anna Nicole Smith
Four days after the model and reality show star died in 2007, at age thirty-nine, Trump was on Howard Stern. "It looks like she had the lips pumped," Trump said. "For all of your many women listening, why do women have their lips pumped? It's the most disgusting thing to look at these big fat pumped-up tires."

Dr. Ginger Lea Southall
During a tour of Mar-a-Lago for an article in the *New Yorker* in 1997, writer Mark Singer said Trump introduced him to the property's resident physician, a recent chiropractic college graduate. Later, he asked Trump where she had been trained. Replied Trump: "I'm not sure. *Baywatch* Medical School? Does that sound right? I'll tell you the truth. Once I saw Dr. Ginger's photograph, I really didn't need to look at her resume or anyone else's. Are you asking, 'Did we hire her because she'd trained at Mount Sinai for fifteen years?' The answer is no. And I'll tell you why: because by the time she's spent fifteen years at Mount Sinai, we don't want to look at her."

Kristen Stewart
Trump couldn't help involving himself in the off-screen personal life of *Twilight* costars Robert Pattinson and Kristen Stewart in 2012. After the actress was caught in an affair with a film director (for which she later apologized), Trump tweeted: "Robert Pattinson should not take back Kristen. She cheated on him like a dog & will do it again—just

watch. He can do much better!" In 2017, Stewart told *Variety* about Trump: "He was mad at me a couple years ago, really obsessed with me a couple years ago, which is f—ing crazy. . . ."

Martha Stewart
Trump ended up feuding for nearly a decade with the homemaker queen after the two had a falling-out in 2005. She was given a spinoff version of *The Apprentice,* on which Trump acted as executive producer. After the spinoff was canceled after just thirteen episodes, Trump wrote in an open letter: "Putting your show on the air was a mistake for everybody—especially NBC. . . . It's about time you started taking responsibility for your failed version of *The Apprentice.* Your performance was terrible in that the show lacked mood, temperament and just about everything else a show needs for success. I knew it would fail as soon as I first saw it—and your low ratings bore me out." She responded in part: "The letter is so mean-spirited and reckless that I almost can't believe my longtime friend Donald Trump wrote it."

Charlize Theron
"To be honest, I think Ivanka is much better-looking than her," he told Howard Stern about the actress, according to the *Washington Post* in 2017.

Senator Elizabeth Warren
Trump has repeatedly gone off on the senator and 2020 presidential candidate, tweeting: "Pocahontas," "Goofy," "Very racist!," "failed Senator," "phony North American Heritage," "she doesn't have a clue," "has a career that is totally based on a lie," "a fraud!" He also tweeted: "DNA test is useless, Phony, a scam and a lie, fraud, amazing con, Pocahontas, a complete and total Fraud!"

Maxine Waters
Regarding the U.S. congresswoman, Trump tweeted about her in 2018: "the most Corrupt Member of Congress!, Crazy Crazy, ranting and raving, crazy rants, unhinged, will make America Weak Again!, an extraordinarily low IQ person."

Katarina Witt
Trump was quoted by *New York* magazine in 1992, saying about the German Olympic figure skater: "Wonderful looking while on the ice

but up close and personal, she could only be described as attractive if you like a woman with a bad complexion who is built like a linebacker."

Sally Yates

"Such a cunt." That's what Trump allegedly called his former acting attorney general, according to author Michael Wolff's *Fire and Fury*.

> **TRUMP RESPONSE:** *White House Deputy Press Secretary Hogan Gidley said: "This author is quite frankly a crackpot fake news fantasy fiction writer."*

Arianne Zucker

She played Nicole Walker on the NBC daytime soap *Days of Our Lives* from 1998 to 2018, but was caught in Trump controversy when she appeared in the infamous *Access Hollywood* tape, which was recorded in 2005. Trump was caught chatting with *Access Hollywood* host Billy Bush on and off a bus parked outside the soap opera set. At one point, Trump noticed Zucker, who was waiting to escort him onto the set where Trump was supposed to film a cameo with Zucker.

"Your girl's hot as shit, in the purple," Bush said about Zucker. Trump replied, "Whoa! Whoa!" Trump then continued to refer to Zucker: "I've got to use some TicTacs just in case I start kissing her. You know I'm automatically attracted to beautiful—I just start kissing them. It's like a magnet. Just kiss. I don't even wait." After the tape was made public, Zucker told the *Today* show: "They are offensive comments for women, period."

III. WOMEN PURSUED, FANTASIZED ABOUT, OR OBSESSED OVER

Carol Alt

Lost Tycoon author Harry Hurt included the 1982 *Sports Illustrated* swimsuit issue cover girl as one of Trump's "alleged affairs" before his split with Ivana, but Alt maintained she turned down Trump. Married at the time to hockey player Ron Greschner of the New York Rangers, she said through her manager: "Donald Trump is a fortunate man, but he's not that fortunate." Alt appeared as a contestant on *Celebrity Apprentice* in 2008, and supported him during the presidential campaign.

Kim Basinger and Madonna

Pretending to be a publicist named "John Miller," Trump told *People*

magazine writer Sue Carswell during a phone call in 1991, that while
Trump had dumped Marla at the time, the *9 1/2 Weeks* actress wanted
to date Trump. "Miller" said Madonna wanted to date Trump, too.

Christie Brinkley

The *Sports Illustrated* supermodel said Trump once offered her a ride
on his private jet to Aspen, Colorado, while she was staying at the Plaza
hotel in New York City. Dating Billy Joel at the time, she told Trump she
already had a flight arranged. "So cancel them," he responded. "I knew
he was married, and there he was asking me to go on his plane," she
later said. "He was kind of flirty about it. He was out chasing skirts."

Carla Bruni

Well before marrying former French president Nicolas Sarkozy in
2008, the singer was pursued by Trump in 1991, when she was involved
with Eric Clapton and the *Rolling Stones'* Mick Jagger. Author Harry
Hurt said Trump offered Carla and her sister a room gratis at his Plaza
hotel. Hurt said she accepted the offer but had no romantic interest in
Trump and referred to him as the "King of Tacky."

Kimberley Conrad

Trump reportedly pursued Hugh Hefner's ex and the *Playboy* "Playmate of the Year 1989" when his marriage to Marla went south in 1998,
and the New York *Daily News* said they were "very friendly," according to a "source at Trump Tower." According to the *Daily Beast*, Con-
rad told *Esquire*: "I know exactly what the Donald is about! . . . I would
really appreciate it if you could get it in somewhere that I am definitely
not in love with the Donald."

Princess Diana

She was, in Trump's words, his only regret "in the women department"
and "supermodel beautiful." Trump further said: "She had the height,
she had the beauty, she had the skin, the whole thing." He told Howard
Stern he ranked Diana as the third person on his hottest women list—
behind Melania and Ivana. Trump initially met Diana at a charity dinner in New York in 1995. According to the *Daily Mail*, that night she
was wearing diamond and pearl-drop earrings and a velvet gown "that
was alluringly low-cut." Trump reportedly offered her a complimentary
membership at Mar-a-Lago, but she declined. A year later, when she

announced her divorce from Prince Charles in July 1996, Trump sent her a huge basket of flowers on her thirty-fifth birthday, reportedly attaching a message expressing his sympathy over the split and suggesting they get together. According to the *Times* of London, BBC broadcaster Selina Scott, a friend of Diana's, said Trump gave her "the creeps" and "bombarded Diana at Kensington Palace with massive bouquets, each worth hundreds of pounds. Trump clearly saw Diana as the ultimate trophy wife. . . . It had begun to feel as if Trump was stalking her."

Alana Evans

In 2006, when Trump was with Stormy Daniels in Lake Tahoe, the couple called the porn star and friend of Daniels. Evans was in a nearby hotel but declined what she believed was an offer for a threesome.

Peggy Fleming

During the Ivana breakup in 1990, one of the women linked to Trump was the gold-medal-winning figure skater, who was forty-one, and married with two children. She was named by the New York *Daily News* as one of his possible mistresses. She later said: "The rumor of my romantic association with Donald Trump is untrue, unfounded and outrageous. . . . I've been around Donald Trump four times in my life. I wouldn't even call him a good friend."

Robin Givens

In his 2005 book *TrumpNation: The Art of Being The Donald,* biographer Timothy O'Brien reported that Trump claimed that boxer Mike Tyson once asked him, "Are you fucking my wife?" Tyson apparently produced a copy of *Vogue* magazine for Trump, showing him a photo of his then wife, actress Robin Givens, wearing a hat from the billionaire's yacht, the *Trump Princess.* Trump, according to O'Brien, told him: "Mike, it's absolute bullshit, it's false. I give you my word." Tyson shot back: "Everyone's telling me that you're fucking my wife and I think you're fucking my wife." *Lost Tycoon* author Harry Hurt added fuel to the fire when he wrote that associates of boxing promoter Don King told Tyson about an alleged sexual encounter between Trump and Givens. But Givens finally put the rumors to rest when she appeared on CNN's *Larry King Live* in 2007—years after her divorce from Tyson in 1989. Asked King: "This was at age twenty-four. One biographer of Donald Trump claimed that you had a sexual relationship with him."

"Yes," Givens responded, leading King to say: "And Donald denies that, by the way." Responded Givens: "Well, he should." When contacted for this book, Givens said she declined to comment.

Salma Hayek

During an appearance on *The Daily Show* with Trevor Noah in 2017, the actress revealed how Trump began pursuing her after he was seated behind her and a boyfriend at an event. Hayek said Trump invited them to dinner and offered to let them stay in his Atlantic City casino and took their telephone numbers—which she said was a ploy to get hers. She said: "Now [Trump] is calling and he's inviting me out and it's just me. And I said, 'What about my boyfriend? Am I crazy, are you asking me out? You know I have a boyfriend.' [And Trump said] 'He's not good enough for you. . . . You have to go out with me.'" Hayek did not go out with Trump and later said on the Spanish radio show *El Show del Mandril* that she wouldn't have dated him "even if I didn't have a boyfriend." A vindictive Trump, she said, then planted a gossip item that it was he who turned her down for a date because of her height (she's five foot two). She said he then called her and asked, "Can you believe this? Who would say this? I don't want people to think this about you."

Edith LiButti

"Donald, I'll fucking pull your balls from your legs." That was reportedly the threat made against Trump from one of his casino's highest rollers in Atlantic City to stay away from his daughter. In his book *The Making of Donald Trump,* author David Cay Johnston said Trump received that warning from Robert LiButti in the mid-1980s. At the time, mob-connected LiButti was Trump's "best customer." Johnston wrote that Trump was attracted to LiButti's daughter Edie, a stylish divorcée. When she turned thirty-five, Trump Plaza threw a lavish party for her, including a professionally made video tribute. Trump gave her a cream-colored Mercedes-Benz convertible as a birthday gift. Johnston wrote: "Furious that a married man would attempt to bed his daughter, LiButti confronted Trump, ordering to stop asking her out. 'Donald, I'll f—ing pull your balls from your legs,' he threatened. Trump backed off, and LiButti continued pouring money into Trump Plaza." LiButti died in 2014 at age eighty-two. His daughter did not respond to a request to comment for this book.

LaToya Jackson

While there was once a rumor they had dated, she had the distinction of being fired and rehired by Trump on *Celebrity Apprentice*. She's also defended Trump: "I will say that there's a lot of misconceptions about him that people don't really realize. His heart is good. He will put out a fire in two seconds. He speaks what's really on his mind, what he's thinking at the moment."

Shannon Marketic

After his split from Marla, the former Miss USA 1992 was named as one of the women Trump pursued. In an October 2016 Facebook post, she commented: "I would not be the only female not related to or employed by Mr. Trump that spent time with him but never got groped, fondled or disrespected. . . ." When contacted for this book, she declined to comment.

Michelle McLean

"Donald wastes no time in letting the media know that he is enjoying his newfound freedom," author Harry Hurt wrote of Trump's split with Marla, and the former Miss Universe 1992 was said to be one of the women Trump went after.

Georgette Mosbacher

Once wife of Secretary of Commerce Robert Mosbacher and chairman of her own cosmetics line, author Harry Hurt named her as one of Trump's "alleged affairs" during his split from Ivana. While she denied the reports ("I don't know what you're talking about," she told *People*), the socialite remained a pal and attended his wedding to Melania. She's called him a "decent man." As president, Trump made her his U.S. ambassador to Poland. In an interview with *W* magazine, she gushed: "This idea that he hates women is just . . . to have known him as long as I've known him, that's the antithesis of him. It's unfortunate. But words matter."

Catherine Oxenberg

The *Dynasty* actress was rumored to have dated Trump but she told *People*: "It's a complete joke as far as I'm concerned. I hardly know the man." Author Harry Hurt said Trump telephoned his publicist in 1988, Dan Klores, and "with a brazenly nonsensical request" told Klores "to leak to the gossip columns that Catherine Oxenberg is chasing me." Klores replied, "Donald, you're a married man with three children." But Trump replied, "Just do it." Rumors then spread that the two were dating and "several of Donald's friends later claimed to have bumped into Oxenberg while she was shopping with his credit cards," Hurt wrote.

Paulina Porizkova

"[She's] gorgeous" was Trump's reaction about the Czech-born Swedish supermodel while speaking to Howard Stern. The shock jock said they were rumored to be together but Trump shot it down, saying: "I don't know because I don't know her."

Carolyne Roehm

In 1990, the socialite and designer was married to Trump's fellow billionaire Henry Kravis. But she got caught up in his divorce to Ivana when she was named among the rumored women Trump was seeing behind his wife's back. Trump claimed she was just a good friend and Roehm denied the accusations. "It's ridiculous. I'm married to the greatest man in the world," she said.

Carolyn Sapp

Sapp reportedly caused Marla to briefly call off their engagement after Trump leered at the Miss America contestant in front of Marla, according to *People* magazine. The twenty-four-year-old from Hawaii, who went on to win the 1992 Miss America contest, was the object of Trump's interest. Trump, who had tried to ask her out a year before, was heard saying: "She's got a great body!"

Brooke Shields

Trump met the former child model and *Pretty Baby* actress at an event in 1992, and seven years later, after divorcing Marla, Trump asked her out on a date. In October 2017, she told Andy Cohen on *Watch What Happens Live:* "I was on location during a movie, and he called me right after he had gotten a divorce and said, 'I really think we should date because you're America's sweetheart and I'm America's richest man and the people would love it.'" Shields said she responded: "I have a boyfriend; he's really not gonna be happy about it." Shields, at the time, was dating Chris Henchy before their marriage and had been recently divorced from tennis player Andre Agassi.

Sharon Stone
Among the beauties linked to Trump at the time of his split with Marla Maples was the *Basic Instinct* actress. *People* magazine quoted Trump telling a friend: "I've heard Sharon Stone's name mentioned."

Emma Thompson
According to *People* magazine, the British actress revealed on a Swedish TV program that she received a surprise call from Trump when she was filming *Primary Colors* in the late 1990s, interestingly playing Hillary Clinton. Never having talked to or met him before, and divorced at the time from Kenneth Branagh, she was invited by Trump to dinner and offered free accommodations at Trump Tower. "They're really comfortable," Trump told her. She told him, "I just said, 'OK, well, um, I'll get back to you. Thank you so much for the offer.'" She never got back to him.

"potential sex partners named on Stern"
On Howard Stern's radio show in May 2000, Trump listed the following women he was interested in having sex with: Mariah Carey, Cameron Diaz, Julia Roberts, Cindy Crawford, Diane Sawyer, Gwyneth Paltrow, and Michelle Pfeiffer. Regarding Crawford, Trump said, "Her husband is a tenant of mine in one of my buildings." Stern asked if he'd sleep with his tenant's wife? "Without question," Trump replied. But there's no indication any of these women ever went out with Trump.

Additional allegation:

Nikki Haley
The former U.S. ambassador to the United Nation labeled rumors about her and Trump "disgusting" and "highly offensive" after author Michael Wolff said in his book *Fire and Fury* that the commander in chief was carrying on an extramarital affair in the White House. While he didn't cite Haley by name, an appearance on HBO's *Real Time With Bill Maher* caused speculation about the two. In his follow-up book, *Siege*, published in June 2019, Wolff explained his take on Trump-Haley, writing: "What was true here is that this was what he [Trump] had said; it was a species of his famous locker-room talk. What was far from certain was that what he had said was true, and few around him gave it much credence."

> *TRUMP RESPONSE—Trump called Wolff "a mentally deranged author" who "knowingly writes false information." The White House called his book "fiction."*

IV. TRUMP'S "LITTLE BLACK BOOK" (DATES, GIRLFRIENDS, MARRIAGES, MISTRESSES, AND ALLEGED SEXUAL ENCOUNTERS)

a). The Models:

Heidi Albertsen

The Danish model won the 1993 Elite "Look World Final," and went on to work for Victoria's Secret and Guess. She also was seen and photographed on the arm of Trump at numerous events. On June 18, 2016, she tweeted: "I'm asked many questions on my friendship" with Trump. She reportedly spent New Year's Eve 2015 with Trump and Melania at Mar-a-Lago and also was a judge for Trump's Miss Universe pageant in Thailand. In addition, she also attended charity events with Trump.

Kim Alley

In 1991, the *New York Post* heralded her as "THE NEW MARLA," and the then twenty-six-year-old Wilhelmina model gained notoriety in her Richmond, Virginia, hometown newspaper, which reported she "got a limousine joy ride and kiss on the lips from the ex-billionaire 10 days ago, then touched off a media orgy by blabbing about the details and posing in a cap with her nickname, 'Alley Cat.'"

> *TRUMP RESPONSE—Trump's secretary Norma Foerderer was quoted by the Richmond Times-Dispatch on September 29, 1991: "She's a manipulative young woman. He has not even had a date with her. This is a play to be a star."*

Candice Bergen

She was the hottest girl on the Philadelphia campus and was crowned "Miss University of Pennsylvania" in 1963. Trump, even before being a student there at the Wharton School, pursued the young blonde beauty until she finally agreed to go out on a date. Bergen recalled the date "ended early" and "there was no physical contact, *whatsoever*." Trump remembered trying to get to first base: "I did make the move. And I must say she had the good sense to say, 'Absolutely not.'"

Maureen Gallagher

A previously undisclosed relationship with Trump is reported for the first time in this book with the biracial model who worked with Elite and Wilhelmina and began appearing on covers in 1989. When she heard Trump on the *Access Hollywood* tape, she said in an interview for this book: "I was shocked. I didn't think it was the same person. If I hadn't heard his voice I wouldn't believe it."

Melissa Gallo

The brunette beauty was on Trump's arm at a screening of *Scent of a Woman* in December 1992, at the Coronet Theater in New York. Other photos show the couple that same month attending the Literacy Volunteers 100th Birthday Party for ERTE at Trump Tower in New York. At that event, they were also pictured with Tina Louise of TV's *Gilligan's Island* fame.

Allison Giannini

The then twenty-seven-year-old model—who also appeared on the soaps *The Young and the Restless* and *Days of Our Lives*—dated Trump in Aspen, Colorado, soon after he separated from Marla in 1997. In 2016, she told *Inside Edition*: "As far as treating women, he treated me just wonderfully. I really think he has a very sweet side to him that a lot of people don't know [or] see. He was very gentlemanly, opening doors, pulling out chairs for me."

Eva Herzigova

The Czech supermodel and actress dated Trump in 1992, and among the events they were photographed together was at "A Night in Casablanca Benefit Auction" that year at Casa La Femme in New York City. Author Harry Hurt cited her as one of Trump's women after his split from Marla.

Rowanne Brewer Lane

In late 1990, while he was in the middle of his separation with Ivana and on the rocks with Marla, he dated this model, who won a competition for "Best Body on the Beach" and was also a three-time winner on *Star Search* as a spokesmodel. They were first photographed together at a screening for the movie *Sea of Love* in September 1989, and apparently dated for several months into 1991, although some reports suggest they actually saw each other into 1993. She told the *New York Times* Trump once asked her, "on a scale of 1 to 10, what I thought of Marla. I thought it was very boyish of him. He asked me the same thing about Ivana. I said, obviously, she is your wife. A beautiful woman. What could you say but a 10? I am not going to judge your wife." Lane declined a request to comment for this book.

> **TRUMP RESPONSE**—*Asked about her comment by the* Times, *Trump said, "I wouldn't have asked anybody about how they rate other women."*

Marla Maples (MARRIED)

In December 2018, Marla appeared on the podcast *Journeys of Faith with Paula Faris* and said she never considered herself "the mistress" during Trump's marriage to Ivana. "I mean that's the truth. . . . When Donald and I came together I really felt that—I do believe there was divinity in it . . . two people that came together that truly loved each other in a period of time . . . wanted him to see how loved he could be for his soul, not for his money." In 2000, Marla told Christian interviewer Dan Steadman how she felt when her marriage to Trump ended. "I mean, I walked away from it because it was the emptiest, darkest place to be," she said. Steadman, who shared the conversation with the *Huffington Post* in 2016, also quoted Marla as saying: "I felt my energy was weakening and weakening more every day. And that's why it was a really tough choice to leave. But I prayed about it for many years. And, finally, after the birth of my daughter [Tiffany in 1993], I had the courage to really make the steps. And ever since then, my life has been blessed in many, many ways. I mean, I still pray for him [Trump] every day." In June 2019, *Vanity Fair* revealed details from Trump's prenuptial agreement with Marla, disclosing he had agreed to pay her $2 million if they separated within five years. She and Trump ended up separating after only four years. Maples declined repeated requests to comment for this book through an associate.

Kelly Ann Sabatasso

In Aspen, Colorado, in 1992, the model was photographed with Trump and the *Guardian* reported they dated.

Irene Saez

The 1981 Miss Universe from Venezuela was dating Trump in 1997 after his split from Marla. After being caught at Trump Tower, she told a reporter she and Trump were "just good friends."

Ingrid Seynhaeve

As a judge at the Elite "Look of the Year" contest in 1991, Trump first laid eyes on the Belgian model when she was eighteen. She ended up winning the competition. After Trump's separation from Marla six years later, he dated the Scandinavian stunner and she also signed with his modeling agency. Called one of the "10 hottest women Trump ever dated," Seynhaeve was photographed with Trump at the Victoria's Secrets Angels party at the Laura Belle club in New York in April 1997, while he stood next to Jeffrey Epstein.

Anna Nicole Smith

"Me and The Donald would make quite a team . . . you were supposed to be President and I was going to be your First Lady. . . . Okay, I wouldn't be First Lady, but I could always be your Monica Lewinsky!" That's what Smith wrote in 2005, according to a friend, when she penned a gossip column for a celebrity magazine. The tragic former Guess model, *Playboy* cover girl, and reality TV star briefly dated Trump when she was twenty-five in 1992, two years before she married octogenarian millionaire J. Howard Marshall. Trump told Howard Stern: "When she came to New York, I saw Anna Nicole Smith the first day or week she was in New York. She was six feet tall, she had the best body, she had the best face. She had the best hair I've ever seen. . . . Now, when she opened her mouth, it was different. Let's face it." According to the book *Scandal: A Manual,* by New York *Daily News* gossip columnists George Rush and Joanna Malloy, Trump said back in the 1990s: "Anna likes me a lot." Rush asked, "Have you two ever hooked up?" to which Trump responded, "Listen, you can just quote 'a friend of Donald' as saying, 'Anna likes Donald very, very much.'" When asked for a comment for this book, a former close associate said: "Anna stayed at his hotel and may have joked around with him, but that's all."

Ivana (Zelníčková) Trump (MARRIED)

She came from the most humblest of roots to become the first Mrs. Trump. In her book *Ivana Trump: A Very Unauthorized Biography,* journalist Norma King noted that while she became a ski champion in her native Czechoslovakia, and a top swimmer, for a period of time young Ivana worked inside a shoe factory at the direction of her father, hammering heels onto brogans. During their marriage, Trump was quoted by the *New York Post* as saying about Ivana: "Her level of arrogance has grown steadily worse in recent years. The bottom line is, I don't want to create another Leona Helmsley." Ivana did not respond to our request for comment.

Melania (Knauss) Trump (MARRIED)

Former roommate Victoria Silvstedt said Melania idolized screen legend Sophia Loren, while another former roommate, Matthew Atanian, told *GQ* that Melania "had some trust issues with him [Trump] at the beginning." Melania was interviewed by ABC's *Good Morning America* about accusations made by women against her husband. She said: "The stories are all totally false. . . . They are lies. . . . And as I've said before, the accusations should be handled in a court of law. Because to accuse somebody without evidence, it's very hurtful and very unfair. But honestly—do we need to talk about that? The American people want to hear about the issues."

Jennifer Yon

According to a *People* magazine cover story on Trump's split with Marla in 1997, the twenty-one-year-old Hawaiian Tropic beauty contestant was linked to Trump, which he denied.

Kara Young

The biracial model was a mainstay in Trump's life between Marla and Melania. During the 2016 election, she told the *New York Times* Trump had a propensity for stereotypes but said she never heard him making any disparaging comments. Said Young: "We went to the U.S. Open once and a lot of black people came because it was Venus and Serena [Williams]. He was impressed that a lot of black people came to the U.S. Open because they were playing," she said, adding: "I didn't hide my race from Donald Trump. He knew. He would say, 'You're like Derek Jeter.' And I would say, 'Exactly.'"

Frederique Van de Wal

The Victoria's Secret model from the Netherlands was among those named as spending time with Trump after his split from Marla. She also had been with Trump Models.

> **TRUMP RESPONSE**—*Trump once boasted to Howard Stern about Frederique: "Had her."*

b). The "Penthouse Pets":

"Sandi Korn"

While Trump was divorcing Ivana, he reportedly had a one-night stand with the busty *Penthouse* Pet in early 1991. She was quoted by the *New York Post*'s Richard Johnson in 2015, as saying: "Donald Trump was amazing in bed," and said he had his secretary track her down after spotting her in a magazine spread. "Omigosh, he was great," she added. During the date, the two went for pizza and a walk around the city before ending up back at her apartment. He gave her a copy of his book *The Art of the Deal,* and also advised her to change her name. "I've been Sandra Taylor ever since," she said, adding that he gave her this sage advice: "If you bet big, you win big. If you bet small, you win small."

Victoria Zdrok

A published interview with the Ukrainian model and 2004 *Penthouse* "Pet of the Year" infuriated Trump after she claimed "he was very racist" and allegedly admitted to her that dating Kara Young was "bad for his reputation" because "she was half-black." In an interview with journalist Chaunce Hayden, she also said: "He loves to talk about how women are chasing him all the time, which doesn't make a girl feel special on a date. The other thing he talks about is what a great lover he is. He said to me, 'Once you made love to me, you'll never be able to make love to anybody else.'"

> **TRUMP RESPONSE**—*Trump told* Steppin' Out *editor Hayden: "She looks like a fucking third-rate hooker. Gimme a break. I never took her out. She's full of shit. Chaunce, look, I have a good taste in women. Take a look at her picture. It's all bullshit. I never took her out."*

c). The "Playboy Playmates":

Kylie Bax

The supermodel from New Zealand was the *Playboy* Playmate in March

2001, but dated Trump six years earlier during a separation from Marla. She was also a *Sports Illustrated* swimsuit issue star. The two have maintained a friendship over the years and she even endorsed him for president. In an interview, Bax said: "I know a lot of things are said about him, but to me he's a great, great guy," adding he's the "perfect, perfect gentleman."

Arlene Baxter
A previously undisclosed relationship from the 1990s was with the former Elite model. She was once identified as a "luscious, and voluptuous blonde knockout" and native Californian. Baxter had major campaigns, including Victoria's Secret, and was *Playboy* Playmate of the month in December 1993. In an interview for this book, a longtime friend, another former model, Stephanie Norwood, confirmed Baxter's relationship with Trump. "In looks, she was a combination of Marla and Ivana," Norwood said. "It was a long time ago. Now, if you look at Arlene's Facebook page, you can tell she's clearly not a Trump fan."

Barbara Moore
Possibly the first publicly known *Playboy* playmate to have had an affair with Trump, she met him three months after being named "Miss December" 1992—at Trump Castle Hotel & Casino in March 1993. She confirmed the affair in an interview for this book.

> *TRUMP RESPONSE—The White House didn't respond to the accusations made by Moore when the* Daily Mail *first reported her story in April 2018.*

Elke Jeinsen
Playboy's "Miss May" 1993 confirmed an account by Barbara Moore of being present that year when Moore and Trump allegedly engaged in sex at his Trump Tower apartment. "We were talking, laughing, drinking, sitting on his bed and then he started to undress Barbara and make out with her," the German model told the *Daily Mail* of her strange date with Trump. Jeinsen said Trump had invited the two blonde models back to his home. After a private meal and champagne, Trump invited the two women into his bedroom. Jeinsen said she did not have sexual contact with Trump.

Karen McDougal
After going public with her "hush money" scandal, the December 1997

Playboy Playmate of the Year told the *New Yorker*'s Ronan Farrow in February 2018: "But now I pray to live right, and make right with the wrongs I have done." Asked about other high-profile men caught in #MeToo, she told Farrow: "I know it's a different circumstance, but I just think I feel braver. . . . Every girl who speaks is paving the way for another." While her affair overlapped for a period of time with Stormy Daniels's affair with Trump, McDougal said she had Trump's direct phone number. "I have his direct phone number. I have quite a few of the direct phone numbers. I also had his bodyguard Keith [Schiller's] phone number," she said. (Daniels said she reached Trump by calling the bodyguard. "I never had Donald's cell phone number," Daniels said. "I always used Keith's.") McDougal also told Trump her mother disapproved of him and he replied, "What, that old hag?" McDougal told him, said the *New Yorker*, "that Trump and her mother were close in age."

> **TRUMP RESPONSE**—*The White House has denied the affair with McDougal. "This is an old story that is just more fake news. The President says he never had a relationship with McDougal,"* the White House told the New Yorker. *Schiller, meanwhile, did not respond to a request for comment from the* New Yorker.

d). The "Porn Stars":

"Stormy Daniels" (Stephanie Clifford)

The inevitable comparison between Stormy Daniels and Monica Lewinsky came on March 13, 2018, in a piece by Jett Heer for the *New Republic*. He wrote: "Whereas Lewinsky was the victim of bipartisan attacks, Daniels is being celebrated by the left and largely ignored by the right. Most attempts to stigmatize Daniels for her work as a porn star have come from marginal Twitter trolls. . . . This remarkable difference can be largely attributed to the success of feminist activists who, in intervening decades, fought against the shaming of women over consensual sex. As a result of social change, Daniels has emerged as a potent adversary to President Donald Trump, whereas Lewinsky was forced to flee the spotlight."

> **TRUMP RESPONSE**—*When the* Wall Street Journal *first reported the affair and "hush money" accusations involving Stormy Daniels, Trump campaign spokeswoman Hope Hicks, on*

*November 4, 2016, said it was "absolutely, unequivocally" false
that Trump and Daniels had a relationship. On January 12, 2018,
Michael Cohen told the* Journal: *"President Trump once again
vehemently denies any such occurrence as has Ms. Daniels. This
is now the second time that you are raising outlandish allegations
against my client. You have attempted to perpetuate this false
narrative for over a year; a narrative that has been consistently
denied by all parties since at least 2011." On March 7, 2018, White
House press secretary Sarah Sanders said of the "hush money"
payment to Stormy Daniels, "I've had conversations with the
president about this. There was no knowledge of any payment from
the president, and he has denied all these allegations." The first
time Trump acknowledged any relationship to the "hush money"
case came during an interview on Fox & Friends on April 26, 2018,
in which Trump said Michael Cohen "would represent me like
with this crazy Stormy Daniels deal, he represented me." On May
3, 2018, Trump tweeted: "Money from the campaign, or campaign
contributions, played no roll [sic] in this transaction. He also called
Daniels's claims of an affair "false and extortionist." On August
23, 2018, during another* Fox & Friends *interview, Trump for
the first time said the payment funds came from him personally,
and not from campaign funds, but he only found out about the
payments "later on." Cohen had previously denied any affair
between Trump and Daniels. Trump lawyer Rudy Giuliani, on June
7, 2018, said Daniels did not deserve "respect" due to her sex work.
In July 2019, unsealed court documents showed Trump was on the
phone with Michael Cohen at least five times around the time Cohen
was negotiating the $130,000 "hush money" payment to Daniels.
One was a three-way call on Oct. 8, 2016, involving Trump, Cohen
and Hope Hicks that the FBI cited in justifying a raid on Cohen in a
warrant application. Trump told DailyMail.com he didn't remember
why he was on the three-way call. "I don't really know," Trump said.
"I'd have to look into it. That's a long time ago."*

"three anonymous porn stars"
In an interview for this book, Alana Evans alleged that she was told
Trump had sexual encounters with three other porn stars over the
years besides Stormy Daniels.

e). The "Other Women":

Lucy Klebanow
In a first-person piece penned for *Salon* in 2016, she told of their date in the early 1970s when she was about twenty-three and he was in his late twenties. She wrote: "He was nice looking, not handsome, but nice. Preppy. Normal. Not a conversationalist, but neither was I. I didn't think he was very bright."

Celina Midelfart
The blonde Norwegian cosmetics heiress earned degrees from the London School of Economics and New York University's Stern School of Business. She dated Trump for seven months after his divorce from Marla.

Kim Richards
A reality star of *The Real Housewives of Beverly Hills,* she admitted in 2017 to Andy Cohen that she and Trump had a dinner date back in 2005, after the host said, "I heard a rumor that you once dated Donald Trump." She answered, "Yes, I had a dinner with him. I had a dinner with Donald." Cast member Lisa Vanderpump chimed in, "Sex or not? Did you see him naked?" Kim replied, "I don't want to get into it! I don't want to talk about the president."

Gabriela Sabatini
The South American beauty was one of the top-ranked tennis stars in the world when Trump met her at an event in 1989. At the time, he was in the middle of a love triangle with Marla and Ivana but was on the rocks with Marla for a brief period. For a month, that July, Trump carried on an affair with the Argentine sports star before returning to his full-time mistress and divorcing Ivana, both *Newsweek* and the London *Sun* reported.

Jackie Siegel
Star of *Queen of Versailles* and wife of real estate mogul David Siegel, Jackie admitted seeing Trump in the 1990s. She told the *Huffington Post* in 2013: "We just went on a couple dates. Like, he invited us to Mar-a-Lago and to go to his parties and things like that. He's a really great person. So much charisma. I'm so glad that we're still friends."

Jan Stephenson
The Australian golf pinup could have been the first Mrs. Trump if she gave up the sport for him. She didn't. Some forty years later, she was

quoted by the *Daily Mail* as saying: "I do wonder what my life would've been or what could've happened if I did stay around." Stephenson declined comment for this book.

f). Other allegations:

"3 more women, including possible pregnancy claim"
In July 2018, Stormy Daniels's lawyer at the time, Michael Avenatti, said he was representing three other women who allegedly had relationships with Trump and were paid "hush money" before the 2016 election. Making his comments at a community forum in West Hollywood, California, he said one of the women might be pregnant. He repeated the allegations on cable news. Avenatti did not respond to requests for comment for this book.

> **TRUMP RESPONSE**—*Trump slammed him as "a third-rate lawyer" and "a total low-life!"*

"4 women"
Los Angeles lawyer Lisa Bloom reportedly represented four women considering making accusations against Trump in 2016, according to a story by John Solomon and Alison Spann in the *Hill* in 2017. Two of these women declined to go public, the report said. One of the women "ultimately declined to come forward after being offered as much as $750,000," said the report. Bloom declined to comment for this book.

"5 additional hush money conspiracies"
In March 2019, *Raw Story* reported an allegation made by former Trump Organization executive vice president Barbara Res. Appearing on MSNBC's *The Beat with Ari Melber*, Res speculated that Allen Weisselberg, the company's longtime chief financial officer, "knows of at least five additional hush money conspiracies." "How many?" Melber asked, according to the *Raw Story* report. "Just instinctively, lots," Res replied. Melber continued: "More than five?" Res said: "Probably." Res added to Melber, according to a *Mother Jones* report, "Trump would do that kind of thing and Allen would be the guy that would draw up the check."

"5 women in Russia"
In November 2017, Trump's longtime bodyguard Keith Schiller testified in front of congressional investigators that someone offered to

send five women to Trump's hotel room during a 2013 trip to Moscow for the annual Miss Universe pageant. During the closed-door session with members of the House Intelligence Committee, which was investigating Russia's efforts to interfere with the 2016 election, Schiller said he quickly rejected the offer. NBC News quoted a source as saying that Schiller discussed the conversation with Trump as they walked back to his hotel and the two men laughed about it. Schiller testified that he stood outside Trump's hotel room for a time and then went to bed.

"100 Women"

Steve Bannon, Trump's former White House chief strategist, hinted previously unknown women were hushed up during the 2016 campaign. Bannon, referring to Trump's relationship with his longtime attorney Marc Kasowitz, told Michael Wolff for his *Fire and Fury*: "Look, Kasowitz has known him for twenty-five years. Kasowitz has gotten him out of all kinds of jams. Kasowitz on the campaign—what did we have, a hundred women? Kasowitz took care of all of them."

"alleged abortions"

In an interview with MSNBC's Chris Hayes, Trump biographer David Cay Johnston said: "There are women whose names I know who are not willing to come forward because it would be difficult." In an interview for this book, Johnston said he stood by his statement and further said: "It's also entirely logical by the way for a guy who runs around as much as he does. And none of these women have seen a reason they want to come forward. I talked about it because I was hoping this might prompt some of these women to come forward and talk. Now, if you're a woman and you do that, you'll immediately be slut-shamed. And I understand that, and if you don't want to come forward, don't come forward. But if you want to, I was hoping that it might break somebody loose." Johnston further said in an interview for this book: "The [abortions] ones that I know about are from within this century and from the year I was covering him intensely, around 1990. And I think it's reasonable therefore to assume that there are others—that he's paid off a lot of women." Johnston said it's possible someone else could have paid for the alleged abortions. "Donald often used 'beards' in the physical sense—Marla often had a guy escort her to events so they [Donald and Marla] could sit by each other," he said. "This goes on all the time among people who have this kind of money and the power relationships. So if Donald needed to pay somebody off, he could have used intermediaries." During a podcast, former New York *Daily News* gossip columnist A. J. Benza said he was aware of an alleged abortion involving Trump. In an interview for this book, he stood by the allegation. (The woman allegedly involved did not respond to a request for comment.) In May 2019, Howard Stern, promoting his book *Howard Stern Comes Again,* said "Pro-Life" Trump probably financed a few abortions. Stern told ABC's *Good Morning America* coanchor George Stephanopoulos: "I don't believe his stance on abortion . . . the Donald I know I think he'd probably get a few people abortions. . . ." In addition, the *Wall Street Journal* reported that Shera Bechard, a *Playboy* Playmate, received a $1.6 million "hush money" agreement from GOP donor Elliott Broidy. Their consensual relationship resulted in a pregnancy and abortion. Trump's fixer Michael Cohen facilitated Broidy's settlement, which led to media speculation (including both *New York* magazine and *Mother Jones*) that married Broidy was actually covering up for Trump and paid the "hush money" as a favor for the president. However, the *Huffington Post* reported that contrary to speculation, two sources said Bechard had no contact with Trump. And when contacted for this book, a source close to Bechard denied she had any involvement with Trump.

> *TRUMP RESPONSE—In 2016, Trump was asked by the* New
> York Times's *Maureen Dowd if he was ever involved with anyone
> who underwent a procedure to terminate a pregnancy and his
> response was: "Such an interesting question. So what's your next
> question?"*

"alleged love child"

During a hearing in front of the House Oversight and Reform Committee in February 2019, Michael Cohen shot down the rumor. Representative Jackie Speier questioned: "Is there a *love child*?" He responded: "There is not, to the best of my knowledge." A year earlier, some media identified the woman connected to the rumor but we are withholding her name. One site, heavy.com, wrote media "have suggested Trump had an inappropriate relationship and perhaps a child with [—— ——]" but that has not been confirmed only alleged." The woman's husband, who had been a driver for Trump, filed a lawsuit against the Trump Organization, accusing Trump of failing to compensate him for about 3,300 hours of overtime pay he had worked over the previous six years. The Trump Organization responded that he "was at all times paid generously and in accordance with the law." As of August 2018, Reuters reported the lawsuit was moved to private arbitration.

"Mueller Report"

A footnote contained in Special Counsel Robert Mueller's long-awaited report into Russian interference in the 2016 election, released to the public in April 2019, referenced the unverified "Steele dossier" about alleged "compromising tapes" purportedly showing Trump with women tied to the 2013 Miss Universe pageant in Moscow. According to the report, cited by the *Daily Mail,* Trump's personal lawyer Michael Cohen received a text on October 30, 2016, from a Giorgi Rtskhiladze, a Russian businessman, stating: "Stopped flow of tapes from Russia but not sure if there's anything else. Just so you know . . ." Cohen then told Trump about the texts but, said the report, "Rtskhiladze said he was told the tapes were fake, but he did not communicate that to Cohen." Following the release of the Mueller report, the *New York Times* on April 20, 2019, wrote: "Other dossier assertions remain neither proven nor disproved, notably its claim about Mr. Trump's alleged dalliance with prostitutes."

g). Also noted:

"elevator tape"

Regarding rumors of a purported "elevator tape" that allegedly shows some sort of altercation between Trump and Melania, Michael Cohen testified in front of Congress that the tape didn't exist. He said, "Mr. Trump would never," but added he heard people tried to purchase it in a "catch and kill" operation. According to the *Daily Beast,* Beverly Hills lawyer Melissa Dagodag, in 2016, allegedly reached out to *TMZ* after the release of the *Access Hollywood* tape, claiming to represent a client who possessed "another bombshell tape of Trump in an elevator in Trump Tower." *TMZ* was reportedly given approval from its parent company, Time Warner, to spend a "fuck load of money" to buy the tape, said the *Beast.* But a meeting to view the tape never happened after Dagodag's source allegedly said they were no longer interested in making a deal. When asked to comment for this book, she emailed: "Trust me, I am a mere peripheral element without any substantive information." In his 2019 book *Siege*, Michael Wolff said of the purported tape: "Inside the White House, the view was that if the video did exist, the incident had happened in Los Angeles, probably in 2014 after a meeting with lawyers that had been arranged precisely to negotiate a revision of their marital agreement."

V. EVEN MORE CRINGE-WORTHY COMMENTS

"They'll walk up, and they'll flip their top, and they'll flip their panties. . . . [I've] been with women who had extraordinarily bad breast jobs and 'pancake tits.'"
—Trump to Howard Stern, 2008

"There is nothing in the world like first-rate pussy."
—Trump to *Maximum Golf* magazine writer Michael Corcoran in 2000; the writer told the *Daily Beast* his editors changed the word "pussy" to "talent" in the story.

"What is it at thirty-five? It's called check-out time."
—Trump to Howard Stern, discussing when to leave a woman when they get to a certain age

"Women are very special. I think it's a very special time, a lot of things are coming out and I think that's a good thing for our society and think it's very, very good for women and I'm very happy a lot of these things are coming out. I'm very happy it's being exposed."
—Trump speaking to reporters, 2017, following allegations of sexual misconduct against Senator Al Franken (D-Minn.), Representative John Conyers Jr. (D-Mich.), and senatorial hopeful Roy Moore (R-Ala.)

"I am no fan of Bill Cosby but never-the-less some free advice—if you are innocent, do not remain silent. You look guilty as hell."
—Trump tweet, 2014

"I've known Harvey Weinstein for a long time. I'm not at all surprised to see it."
—Trump to reporters, 2018

*"I've never had any trouble in bed, but if I'd had affairs
with half the starlets and female athletes the newspapers
linked me with, I'd have no time to breathe."*
—TRUMP: *SURVIVING AT THE TOP*, 1990

*"I was seated next to a lady of great social pedigree and wealth.
Her husband was sitting on the other side of the table, and
we were having a very nice but extremely straight conversation.
All of a sudden, I felt her hand on my knee, then my leg.
She started petting me in all different ways. . . . This is not
infrequent, it happens all the time."*
—TRUMP: *THE ART OF THE COMEBACK*, 1997

*"If I told the real stories of my experiences with women, often seemingly very happily married and important women, this book would be
a guaranteed bestseller (which it will be anyway!). I'd love to tell all,
using names and places but I just don't think it's right."*
—TRUMP: *THE ART OF THE COMEBACK*, 1997

VI: NOTED PUBLISHED REPORTS:

"Donald Trump—The Howard Stern Interviews 1993–2015," Factba.se.

"The Other Woman in the Stormy Daniels-Trump Saga: 'He Knows What He's Done,'" by Aurora Snow, *Daily Beast*, April 14, 2018.

"The Trump Allegations," by Lucia Graves and Sam Morris, *Guardian*, November 29, 2017.

"List of Trump's accusers and their allegations," ABC News, February 22, 2018.

"The 22 women who have accused Trump of sexual misconduct," by Eliza Relman, *Business Insider*, December 21, 2017.

"The lawsuit accusing Trump of raping a 13-year-old girl, explained," by Emily Crockett, *Vox*, November 5, 2016.

"The 19 Women Who Accused President Trump of Sexual Misconduct," by Matt Ford, *Atlantic*, December 7, 2017.

"Trump's Pee-Tape Alibi Is Falling Apart," by Bess Levin, *Vanity Fair*, April 23, 2018.

"From Angelina Jolie to Kim K, how Donald Trump rates women in new Howard Stern tapes," by Emily Heil, *Washington Post*, September 25, 2017.

"Trump Denied Dating Model, Called Her a 'F**king Third-Rate Hooker," by Lloyd Grove and Tim Teeman, *Daily Beast*, May 16, 2016.

"Former Playmate reveals she had sex with Donald Trump in front of her friend . . . ," by Ryan Parry, *Daily Mail*, April 16, 2018.

"Crossing the Line: How Donald Trump Behaved with Women in Private," by Michael Barbaro and Megan Twohey, *New York Times*, May 14, 2016.

"Trump on Anna Nicole Smith After Her Death: She Was Great Until She Opened Her Mouth," by Andrew Kaczynski, *BuzzFeed*, March 31, 2016.

"Donald Trump vs. Madonna: Everything We Know," by Brittany Spanos, *Rolling Stone*, January 27, 2017.

"In R-rated anti-Trump rant, Madonna muses about 'blowing up White House,'" by Eric Levenson, CNN, January 21, 2017.

"'Madonna is disgusting' says Donald Trump," by Helena Horton, *Telegraph*, January 27, 2017.

"Here's a Theory About That $1.6 Million Payout from a GOP Official to a Playboy Model," by Paul Campos, *New York*, May 8, 2018.

"A Tale of Two Women, and Two Eras—Monica Lewinsky & Stormy Daniels," by Jeet Heer, *New Republic*, March 13, 2018.

"Donald Trump Can't Stop Discovery in 'Apprentice' Alum's Defamation Lawsuit," by Eriq Gardner, *Hollywood Reporter*, May 17, 2018.

"Donald Trump Once Boasted He Could Have 'Nailed' Princess Diana—but Only if She Passed an HIV Test," by Tierney McAfee, *People*, May 18, 2018.

"After the Gold Rush," by Marie Brenner, *Vanity Fair*, September 1, 1990.

"The Real Story Behind Donald Trump's Infamous 'Best Sex I've Ever Had' Headline (Guest Column)," by Jill Brooke, *Hollywood Reporter*, April 12, 2018.

"Here's a Weird Fucking Story About Donald Trump and Mike Tyson," by Ashley Feinberg, *Deadspin*, October 5, 2016.

"Mike Tyson: Donald Trump Banged My Wife!," by Tyler Johnson, *Hollywood Gossip*, October 6, 2016.

"Lawsuit Charges Donald Trump with Raping a 13-Year-Old Girl," by David Mikkelson, *Snopes*, November 4, 2016.

"Voicemails Reveal Donald Trump's Cozy Relationship with the Liberal Media," by Ashley Feinberg and Andy Cush, *Gawker,* March 4, 2016.

"Watch: Donald Trump Blames Mike Tyson's Victim for Rape," by Jonathan Vankin, *Heavy*, November 4, 2017.

"TMZ Goes MAGA: How Harvey Levin's Gossip Empire Became Trump's Best Friend," by Lachlan Cartwright, *Daily Beast*, May 28, 2018.

"How much more humiliation can Melania Trump take?," by Robin Abcarian, *Los Angeles Times*, February 20, 2018.

"Do Trump's alleged affairs even matter?," by Callum Borchers, *Washington Post*, February 17, 2018.

"Opinion: Melania Knew," by Charles M. Blow, *New York Times*, March 11, 2018.

"The many terrible things Trump says about women in Wolff's explosive new book," by Ana Valens, *Daily Dot*, January 4, 2018.

"Former Donald Trump Executive: 'He's a Supreme Sexist,'" by Olivia Nuzzi, *Daily Beast*, October 11, 2016.

"Christie Brinkley claims Donald Trump hit on her while he was married to Ivana," by Taryn Ryder, *Yahoo! Entertainment*, February 6, 2018.

"Stormy Daniels Says Michael Cohen Told Melania Daniels Was a Liar," by Kate Briquelet, *Daily Beast*, June 6, 2018.

"Exclusive: Trump's 13-year-old 'rape victim' dramatically drops her case . . . ," by Ryan Parry, *Daily Mail*, November 4, 2016.

"Giuliani says people in the porn business are not credible, Trump has appeared in three softcore porn videos," by Christopher Massie, CNN, June 7, 2018.

"The 472 People, Places and Things Donald Trump Has Insulted on Twitter: A Complete List," by Jasmine C. Lee and Kevin Quealy, *New York Times*, June 10, 2018.

"Donald Trump, a Playboy Model, and a System for Concealing Infidelity," by Ronan Farrow, *New Yorker*, February 16, 2018.

"The comb-over creep who hates women—and I should know . . . ," by Selina Scott, *Daily Mail*, January 31, 2016.

"How Did Trump and Clinton Pal Jeffrey Epstein Escape #MeToo?," by Katie Briquelet, *Daily Beast*, June 22, 2018.

"Trump was taped talking of paying for *Playboy* model's story," by Eric Tucker and Jennifer Peltz, Associated Press, July 21, 2018.

"Avenatti says there are other Trump-Cohen 'tapes' and he knows 'substance of some,'" by Joy Lin, ABC News, July 22, 2018.

"'I'm not going to be punching bag anymore': Inside Michael Cohen's break with Trump," by Philip Rucker, Carol D. Leonnig, Tom Hamburger, and Ashley Parker, *Washington Post*, July 25, 2018.

"Republican's Mistress: Cohen Was Recruited to Solve Problem," by Gideon Resnick, *Daily Beast*, July 31, 2018.

"Playboy Model demands $1.4M in breach-of-contract suit against Trump donor . . . ," by Chris Spargo, *Daily Mail*, August 1, 2018.

"Elliott Broidy's Mistress: I Was Pregnant When My Lawyer 'Recruited' Michael Cohen . . . ," by Gideon Resnick, *Daily Beast*, July 31, 2018.

"Melania broke up with Trump once when she caught him with an ex," by Sam Brodsky, *Metro*, April 6, 2018.

"A Chronological List of Trump's 8 Known Mistresses," by Zachary Shucklin, *Advocate*, May 24, 2018.

"Mystery woman in Trump military academy photo unveiled," by Allan Dodds Frank and Abigail Pesta, New York *Daily News*, November 2, 2016.

APPENDIX 311

"The coverup uncovered: How Team Trump tried to bury or confuse the Stormy Daniels story," by Philip Bump, *Washington Post*, October 2, 2018.

"The Shy Pornographer: Show World's Owner May Be Times Square's Last Man Standing," by Van Smith, *New York Press*, April 7, 1999.

"What Happened to the 19 Women Who Accused Trump of Sexual Misconduct," by Margaret Hartmann, *New York* magazine, December 12, 2017.

"The Four People Who Know What Stormy Daniels Has on Trump," by Kate Briquelet, *Daily Beast*, March 9, 2018.

"Linda Stasi: Are Donald and Melania the Cruelest First Couple ever?," by Linda Stasi, New York *Daily News*, November 18, 2018.

"Mob Linked to Adult Entertainment Thefts," by John Markoff, *New York Times*, October 17, 1998.

"Gotti Ordered Hit on Porn Czar Rival," by Philip Messing, *New York Post*, September 22, 1986.

"The Trump Files: His Football Team Treated Its Cheerleaders 'Like Hookers,'" by Max J. Rosenthal, *Mother Jones*, July 5, 2016.

"Donald Trump's mother asked: 'What kind of son have I created?'" by Caroline Mortimer, *Independent*, November 4, 2017.

"Donald Trump's Immigrant Mother," by Mary Pilon, *New Yorker*, June 24, 2016.

"Donald Trump's Mommy Issues," by Peter Lovenheim, *Politico Magazine*, May 13, 2018.

"Candice Bergen once went on a date with Donald Trump. How did it go? 'I was home very early,'" by Libby Hill, *Los Angeles Times*, September 14, 2017.

"Trump flaunts Wharton degree, but his college years remain a mystery," by Dan Spinelli, *Daily Pennsylvanian*, August 19, 2015.

"Model claims she saw Trump cheat on pregnant Marla Maples," by Chris Perez, *New York Post*, May 7, 2018.

"Keith Schiller, Trump's Ex-Bodyguard, Says He Turned Down Offer of Women in Moscow," by Adam Goldman and Nicholas Fandos, *New York Times*, November 10, 2017.

"President Trump and accusations of sexual misconduct: The complete list," by Meg Kelly, *Washington Post*, November 22, 2017.

"New Jersey's Most Notorious Gamblers: Robert LiButti," NJ Online Gambling website, undated.

"Inside Donald Trump's One-Stop Parties: Attendees Recall Cocaine and Very Young Models," Michael Gross, *Daily Beast*, October 24, 2016.

"Donald Trump Used Model Parties to Seal Deals, Industry Sources Say," by Michael Gross, *Daily Beast*, July 19, 2016.

"My Bizarre Dinner Party with Donald Trump, Roy Cohn and Estee Lauder," by Peter Manso, *Politico*, May 27, 2016.

"Model Citizen?" by Michael Gross, *Chicago Tribune*, July 7, 1993.

"Trump invokes one of the worst American massacres to mock Elizabeth Warren," by Tim Elfrink, *Washington Post*, January 14, 2019.

"Alexandria Ocasio-Cortez: Hypocritical Republicans Forgive Trump's Sexual Assault, But Outraged by Tlaib's Swearing," by Ramsey Touchberry, *Newsweek*, January 5, 2019.

"Donald Trump Gets Weirder," by Gail Collins, *New York Times*, April 1, 2011.

"Exclusive: Prominent lawyer sought donor cash for two Trump accusers," by John Solomon and Alison Spann, *Hill*, December 15, 2017.

"Secrets of Trump's 3 Marriages," *In Touch*, July 7, 2017.

"The mystery that is Melania Trump," by Ken Otterbourg, *Washington Post Magazine*, August 18, 2016.

"Meet Celina Midelfart, the Glamorous Norwegian Businesswoman Donald Trump Allegedly Dumped for Melania," by Gabriella Paiella, *New York*, May 3, 2016.

"Opinions/Trump's resume is rife with mob connections," by David Von Drehle, *Washington Post*, August 10, 2018.

"Marla Maples Finds Her Groove," by Judith Newman, *New York Times*, November 14, 2012.

"A History of Sex and Abuse in the Trump Administration," by Tim Dickinson, *Rolling Stone*, February 23, 2018.

"I like being sexually assaulted, says Trump advocate Ann Coulter," *Sunday Times*, November 4, 2018.

"Trump hits back at 'very hostile' Ann Coulter after 'wimp' jab," by Mark Moore, *New York Post*, January 28, 2019.

"'I don't envy them': Hope Hicks and other White House women struggle to defend Trump in the #MeToo era," by David Nakamura, *Washington Post*, March 2, 2018.

"Stormy Daniels' Friend Turned Down Threesome with Donald Trump: He's No Brad Pitt," by Diane Herbst, *People*, February 14, 2018.

"Two new books recall the day Trump and his team watched the infamous 'Access Hollywood' tape," by Brian Niemietz, New York *Daily News*, January 29, 2019.

"All the Women Donald Trump Claims He Dated but Really Didn't," by Olivia Nuzzi, *Daily Beast*, April 12, 2016.

"Donald Trump Sued Everyone but His Hairdresser," by Olivia Nuzzi, *Daily Beast*, July 6, 2015.

"The Playboy President: Trump and Hugh Hefner Bonded for Decades Over Their Love of Licentiousness, but the Relationship Soured," by Tom Porter, *Newsweek*, September 28, 2017.

"Every time Donald and Melania Trump have faked holding hands with each other," by Greg Evans, *Independent*, August 23, 2018.

"Every Embarrassing Story Michael Cohen Tried to Squash," by Margaret Hartmann and Matt Stieb, *New York*, February 27, 2019.

"House Democrats want Jeffrey Epstein sex case reopened," by Julie K. Brown, *Miami Herald*, March 1, 2019.

"Ex-Trump Org VP speculates CFO Weisselberg probably knows of more Trump hush money payoffs," by Bob Brigham, *Raw Story*, March 1, 2019.

"A Timeline of Donald Trump's Inappropriate History with Women," by Marissa G. Muller, *Glamour*, October 13, 2016.

"Exclusive: The private Donald—Lounging on the bed in his robe . . . The extraordinary trove of hundreds of Trump family photos found in a Thrift Shop showing his softer side," by Robert E. Hartlein, *Daily Mail*, November 8, 2016.

"'Apprentice' Contestant Says Donald Trump Sexually Assaulted Her at the Beverly Hills Hotel," *Hollywood Reporter*, October 14, 2016.

"Reams of Paper Reportedly Missing from Donald and Ivana Trump's Divorce Documents," by Timothy Bertrand, *Reverb Press*, September 18, 2016.

"Exclusive: Court docs from Ivana Trump's prenuptial challenge reveal Donald's 'cruel and inhuman' treatment, but little else as lots of pages were suspiciously concealed," by Barbara Ross and Stephen Rex Brown, New York *Daily News*, September 17, 2016.

"Judge tosses Stormy Daniels' lawsuit against Trump over hush money agreement," by Sara Sidner and Kate Sullivan, CNN, March 7, 2019.

"A Florida Massage Parlor Owner Has Been Selling Chinese Execs Access to Trump at Mar-a-Lago," by David Corn, Dan Friedman, and Daniel Schulman, *Mother Jones,* March 9, 2019.

"President Trump Hits Back Hard at TV Pundit Ann Coulter: 'Wacky Nut Job,'" by Bruce Haring, *Deadline*, March 9, 2019.

"Stormy Daniels' Explosive Full Interview on Donald Trump Affair: 'I Can Describe His Junk Perfectly,'" *In Touch*, May 4, 2018.

"The Wild Tahoe Weekend Where Trump Allegedly Hosted Karen McDougal, Met Stormy Daniels," *Inside Edition*, March 23, 2018.

"'The Apprentice' cast, crew say Donald Trump demeaned women with sexist talk," Associated Press, October 3, 2016.

"Donald Trump responds to Melania's newly-surfaced racy photo shoot," *New York Post*, August 1, 2016.

"Trump admits sexual assault allegations against him have affected his defense of Kavanaugh," by Li Zhou, *Vox*, September 26, 2018.

"Jenna Jameson Weighs In on Stormy Daniels, Shares Her Own Trump Story," by Tim Kenneally, *Wrap*, January 17, 2018.

"President Trump in Woodward book: 'You've got to deny' accusations by women," by Christal Hayes, *USA Today*, September 11, 2018.

"Court docs from Donald and Ivana Trump's divorce proceedings to remain sealed, judge rules," by Barbara Ross, New York *Daily News*, September 22, 2016.

"Marla Maples 'bedded Michael Bolton' while with Donald Trump, reveals FBI probe of publicist . . . ," by Chris Spargo, *Daily Mail*, March 26, 2019.

"Porn Star Stormy Daniels is taking a victory lap after Michael Cohen's guilty plea . . . ," by Kate Taylor, *Business Insider*, August 25, 2018.

"The Heart of the Deal: The Love Story of Marla Maples and Donald Trump," by Maureen Orth, *Vanity Fair*, November 1, 1990.

"Video shows Donald Trump humiliate Jennifer Hawkins during speech in Sydney," by Fiona Byrne and Maria Bervanakis, *News AU*, October 29, 2016.

"Paris Hilton Apologizes for Donald Trump Sexual Assault Comments," by Joyce Chen, *Rolling Stone*, August 17, 2017.

"Trump Admits He Found 12-Year-Old Paris Hilton Attractive," by Alana Horowitz Satlin, *Huffington Post*, September 30, 2016.

"Trump and the Testosterone Takeover of 2016," by Danielle Kurtzleben, NPR, October 1, 2016.

"Trump, the Divorce Case: The Accusations Are Flying," by Nick Ravo, *New York Times*, February 13, 1990.

"Trumps Settle, The Donald Claims Victory," by Paula Span, *Washington Post*, March 21, 1991.

"With 'Dynasty' Dead, Just Tune to the Trumps," by Cheryl Lavin, *Chicago Tribune*, February 18, 1990.

"The Hunt for 'Every Trump Reporter's White Whale': The Elevator Tape," by Maxwell Strachan, *Huffington Post*, July 12, 2018.

"Do Trump & Kristin Davis Know Each Other? Mueller May Subpoena The 'Manhattan Madam,'" by Lani Seelinger, *Bustle*, July 22, 2018.

"MSNBC Host Asks Trump If His Use of 'Pu**y' Was 'Presidential,'" TPM, February 9, 2016.

"Hush-Money Probe Gathered Evidence from Trump's Inner Circle," by Nicole Hong, Rebecca Ballhaus, and Rebecca Davis O'Brien, *Wall Street Journal,* April 10, 2019.

"President Trump is a 'self-admitted sexual predator,' says 'Me Too' founder Tarana Burke," by Max Zahn and Andy Serwer, *Yahoo Finance,* February 28, 2019.

"Meet the Trumpettes: Inside the World of Donald Trump's Most Adoring Fans," by Sam Dangremond, *Town & Country,* January 22, 2018.

"Ihan Omar says death threats have increased since Trump tweet," by Chris Perez, *New York Post*, April 15, 2019.

"Men Who Don't Wear Wedding Bands—and Why," by Abby Ellin, *New York Times*, May 7, 2016.

"The First Porn President," by Caitlin Flanagan, *Atlantic*, May 3, 2018.

"Robin Givens Recalls Mike Tyson Abuse in the Wake of #MeToo," by Jessica McKinney, *Vibe*, December 22, 2018.

"When Donald Trump Said He'd Marry Obama, Called Kim Kardashian a 'Fat Ass,' and Ripped Beyonce," by Marlow Stern, *Daily Beast*, August 6, 2015.

"Mila Kunis Lashes Out Against Donald Trump's Anti-Refugee Rhetoric," by Maria Efrem, *Forward*, July 6, 2016.

"Mila Kunis Loves Abortion but Hates President Trump," by Christina Vazquez, *Life News,* August 1, 2018.

"The Night Donald Trump Partied with a Porn Star," by Daniel Maurer, *Bedford and Bowery,* January 20, 2017.

"Trump Made a Cameo in a *Playboy* Soft-core Porn Video," by Chas Danner, *New York*, October 1, 2016.

"Why Can't the President Watch Porn in the White House?" by Ryan Bort, *Rolling Stone,* June 7, 2018.

"Russia businessman says he told Michael Cohen about 'compromising tapes' of Trump during Miss Universe in Moscow . . . ," by Geoff Earle, *Daily Mail*, April 18, 2019.

"Donald Trump tried to get Salma Hayek to cheat on her boyfriend with him," by Megan C. Hills, *Marie Claire*, December 13, 2018.

"With 'Dynasty' Dead, Just Tune to the Trumps," by Cheryl Lavin, *Chicago Tribune*, February 18, 1990.

"Donald Trump's Craziest Interview Ever: 'Any Girl You Have, I Can Take from You,'" by Marlow Stern, *Daily Beast,* August 2, 2015.

"'Donald Trump 'partied at the Playboy Mansion with playmate Holly Madison,'" by Nick Allen, *Telegraph*, May 17, 2016.

"Donald Trump: The Poor Man's Hugh Hefner," by Erin Gloria Ryan, *Daily Beast,* September 28, 2017.

"The coverup uncovered: How Trump Team tried to bury or confuse the Stormy Daniels story," by Philip Bump, *Washington Post*, October 2, 2018.

"The Fading Neon of Times Square's Sex Shops. Elusive, Undisputed King of Midtown Pornography May Be Forced out of Business," by Dan Barry, *New York Times*, October 28, 1995.

"Michael Cohen's Last Days of Freedom," by Jeffrey Toobin, *New Yorker*, April 29, 2019.

"Trump calls Kamala Harris 'very nasty' after she grills Bill Barr . . . ," by David Martosko, *Daily Beast,* May 2, 2019.

"One Night with Stormy Daniels, the Hero America Needs," by Denver Hicks, *Rolling Stone,* March 9, 2018.

"As Cohen heads to prison, Trump is ensnared in more questions about possible illegal behavior," by Philip Bump, *Washington Post*, May 6, 2019.

"Trump's Hush Money Payments Were Likely a Criminal Offense," by Alex Tausanovitch, Center for American Progress, December 19, 2018.

"My Night with Stormy Daniels," by Amanda Whiting, *Washingtonian*, July 10, 2018.

"Noel Cintron: 5 Fast Facts You Need to Know," by Ellyn Santiago, heavy.com, July 9, 2018.

"Lawsuit seeks records of Trump's Beverly Hills bungalow stays," by Frances Stead Sellers, *Washington Post*, June 19, 2018.

"Donald Trump just called Stormy Daniels 'horseface.' Don't act surprised," by Chris Cillizza, CNN, October 16, 2018.

"My awful date with Donald Trump: The real story of a nightmare evening with a callow but cash-less heir," by Lucy Klebanow, *Salon*, March 24, 2016.

"When Kiwi model Kylie Bax met Donald Trump and Bill Clinton," by Nikki Preston, *NZ Herald*, September 11, 2016.

"Here's the advice Donald Trump gave Bill Cosby about sexual assault allegations," by Peter Holley, *Washington Post*, October 13, 2016.

"Michael Wolff's Siege shows Trump as even worse than you thought," by Stuart McGurk, *British GQ,* May 29, 2019.

"Michael Wolff blames Trump-Haley affair rumor on 'locker room' talk," by Daniel Chaitin, *Washington Examiner*, May 30, 2019.

"Taylor Swift Slams Donald Trump for Hypocrisy in LGBTQ Policies," by Elura Nanos, Law & Crime/a Dan Abrams Production, June 1, 2019.

"What did Meghan Markle say about Donald Trump, what was his response and how did he find out?" by Jon Rogers, London *Sun,* June 1, 2019.

"'Horndog' Trump bragged about sleeping with black women . . . ," by Daniel Bates, *Daily Mail*, June 3, 2019.

"'Marla Was Under Duress': Revealed in His Marla Maples Prenup, Donald Trump's Draconian Art of the Marriage Deal," by Gabriel Sherman, *Vanity Fair,* June 4, 2019.

"Trump blasts 'washed up psycho' Bette Midler for tweeting fake quote," by Ben Feuerherd, *New York Post*, June 5, 2019.

"Split-Screen View of Trump Trip: Respectability vs. Score-Settling," by Maggie Haberman and Mark Landler, *New York Times*, June 6, 2019.

"Trump calls Nancy Pelosi 'nasty, vindictive, horrible person,' after prison remark," by Sean Rossman, *USA Today*, June 7, 2019.

"Trump Responds to Adult Actress Jessica Drake's Accusations: 'Oh, I'm Sure She's Never Been Grabbed Before,'" by Leah Rodriguez, *New York*, October 24, 2016.

"A Timeline of Donald Trump's Inappropriate History with Women," by Marissa G. Muller, *Glamour*, June 22, 2019.

"Trump wanted to fire women who weren't pretty enough, say employees at his California golf club," by Matt Pearce, *Los Angeles Times*, September 29, 2016.

"Palm Beach trial could reveal details of billionaire's alleged abuse of teen girls," by Marc Fisher, *Washington Post*, December 3, 2018.

"Everything We know About the Sex Crimes Case Against Jeffrey Epstein," by Chas Danner and Matt Stieb, *New York*, July 8, 2019.

"Why the Trump White House Is Caught Up in the Jeffrey Epstein Scandal," by Vivian Wang, *New York Times*, July 7, 2019.

"Hideous Men/ Donald Trump assaulted me in a Bergdorf Goodman dressing room 23 years ago. But he's not alone on the list of awful men in my life," by E. Jean Carroll, *New York*, June 21, 2019.

"Why Now? What Made a Trump Accuser Confront Her Silence," by Jessica Bennett, Megan Twohey, and Alexandra Alter, *New York Times*, June 28, 2019.

"Exclusive: Trump vehemently denies E. Jean Carroll allegation, says 'she's not my type,'" by Jordan Fabian and Saagar Enjeti, *Hill*, June 24, 2019.

"'Terrific Guy' to 'Not a Fan': Friendship with Investor Became Liability to Trump," by Annie Karni and Maggie Haberman, *New York Times*, July 10, 2019.

"Behind the scenes the night Trump partied at Mar-a-Lago with Jeffrey Epstein and NFL cheerleaders" by Rosalind S. Helderman and Beth Reinhard, *Washington Post*, July 17, 2019.

"NBC Obtained Trump-Epstein Footage After Trump Kissed an Anchor Without Consent" by Matt Stieb, *New York*, July 17, 2019.

"New Video Shows Trump and Jeffrey Epstein Ogling Women at Mar-a-Lago" by Madeleine Aggeler, *New York*, July 17, 2019.

VII: Comment request to White House

From July 1, 2019 to July 10, 2019, the authors made repeated requests to the White House seeking a response from President Trump to the allegations made in this book.

We also requested an interview with President Trump or one of his surrogates.

A nineteen-page memo to the White House outlined the allegations involving John Tino, Karen Johnson, and thirty-five other specific claims of inappropriate behavior against Trump regarding women.

The memo was emailed to both White House press secretary Stephanie Grisham and Deputy Press Secretary Hogan Gidley.

The memo was also sent by FedEx to both Grisham and Gidley at the White House.

The authors also left voice mail messages for Grisham and Gidley, repeating our request for comment. In one short call, Gidley said he would look at the memo.

But as this book went to the printer, there was no response from the White House on the allegations made in this book.

NOTES

We conducted more than one hundred interviews for this book, both with people who have been on the record about their experiences with Trump, and with people who had never spoken publicly before. We named as many as we could, but some asked to remain anonymous. At the same time, we also relied heavily on the extensive body of work that has already been published about the president, particularly on news archives—especially those of the New York Daily News, the New York Post, the New York Times, the Washington Post, and the Wall Street Journal. We are indebted to the reporters who have covered Trump so closely. In an effort to be transparent and to credit those whose work we relied upon, we list our sources in the chapter-by-chapter section below; the list is not always exhaustive. If a source is used repeatedly in proximity to the first citation, we don't list it multiple times. If something was widely reported, such as quotes from a press conference, we did not include it in our list, nor do we include citations when the source of something is made clear in the text.

We also turned to the many books that have been published about the President. Many are cited specifically in the chapter notes, but others were not, including:

Michael Wolff, *Fire and Fury* (New York: Henry Holt, 2018).

David Cay Johnston, *The Making of Donald Trump* (New York: Melville House, 2017).

Nina Burleigh, *Golden Handcuffs: The Secret History of Trump's Women* (New York: Gallery Books, 2018).

Nicholas von Hoffman, *Citizen Cohn: The Life and Times of Roy Cohn* (New York: Doubleday, 1988).

Michael Gross, *Model: The Ugly Business of Beautiful Women* (New York: William Morrow, 1995).

A.J. Benza, *Fame: Ain't It a Bitch: Confessions of a Reformed Gossip Columnist* (New York: Hyperion, 2001).

Josh Alan Friedman, *Tales of Times Square* (New York: Delacorte Press, 1986).

Bill Landis and Michelle Clifford, *Sleazoid Express: A mind-twisting tour through the grindhouse cinema of Times Square!* (New York: Fireside, 2002).

Seka with Kerry Zukus, *Inside Seka: The Platinum Princess of Porn* (Albany, GA: BearManor Media, 2013).

Donna Hogan, *Train Wreck: The Life and Death of Anna Nicole Smith* (Beverly Hills, CA: Phoenix Books, 2007).

Insider Guide: The Beverly Hills Hotel and Bungalows, Dorchester Collection.

NOTE FROM BARRY LEVINE

References to Douglas Fairbanks, Humphrey Bogart, Elizabeth Taylor, Howard Hughes, John Lennon: From *Insider Guide/The Beverly Hills Hotel and Bungalows,* Dorchester Collection. (The promotional booklet is not dated.)

"started to trace his finger": Stormy Daniels with Kevin Carr O'Leary, *Full Disclosure* (New York: St. Martin's Press, 2018), p. 146.

"Did he actually": CNN transcript of Anderson Cooper's interview with Karen McDougal, March 22, 2018.

"He did. He did": Ibid.

"immediately started kissing": Summer Zervos court documents.

"grabbed her shoulder": Ibid.

"he paced around": Ibid.

"a dozen young American women": Frances Stead Sellers, "It was a Trump favorite. Now lawyers want the famously discreet Beverly Hills Hotel to share its secrets," *Washington Post*, June 18, 2018.

"defined an airbrushed": Carrie Pitzulo, "When Ruth Bader Ginsburg Thanked Hugh Hefner," *Politico Magazine*, September 28, 2017.

"Donald has been living": David Cay Johnston interview, January 10, 2019.

"Trump came swooping in": Daniels, *Full Disclosure*, p. 115.

Reference to photo showing Trump, Melania, and Dominique Swain from Getty Images caption, February 29, 2004.

stashed his mistress: Maureen Orth, "The Heart of the Deal: The Love Story of Marla Maples and Donald Trump," *Vanity Fair*, November 1, 1990.

"I remember it was a beautiful day": Bonnie Robinson interview, February 21, 2019.

"To put it mildly": Ibid.

"It suddenly became focused": Orth, *Vanity Fair*.

"When they stopped": Russell Turiak interview, November 20, 2018.

"When the Trumps escort": Harry Hurt III, *Lost Tycoon: The Many Lives of Donald J. Trump* (Brattleboro, VT: Echo Point Books & Media, 1993, 2016), p. 243.

"in embarrassment": Ibid.

INTRODUCTION

Access Hollywood **tape:** The existence of the tape was made public on October 7, 2016, when the *Washington Post* published an article about it. It had been recorded in September 2005.

47 percent of whom voted for him: That figure comes from the Pew Research Center's "An examination of the 2016 electorate, based on validated voters," published August 9, 2018.

Jonathan Chait wrote in New York: *"Donald Trump's Locker Room Is the Entire World," New York*, October 13, 2016.

CHAPTER ONE: ACCESSORIES MAKE THE MAN

"I think we said 'hi'": Interview with Fran D'Agati Dunn conducted October 11, 2018.

"It's truly not talked about": This and all following Peter Brant quotes are taken from a transcript of an interview the *Washington Post* conducted with him for *Trump Revealed*: https://www.washingtonpost.com/wp-stat/graphics/politics/trump-archive/docs/peter-brant.pdf.

children are starting to distance themselves: This and all following quotes from Dr. Sue Kolod come from an interview conducted with her on February 25, 2019.

"We rarely saw Mrs. Trump": Michael Kruse, "The Mystery of Mary Trump," *Politico Magazine*, November/December, 2017.

"His father would be around and watch him play": Ibid.

"That's the way it was": Ibid.

"My father was the power and the breadwinner": Donald Trump, *The Art of the Deal* (New York: Ballantine Books, 1987), loc. 830.

If something got interrupted: Michael Barbaro and Megan Twohey, "Crossing the Line: How Donald Trump Behaved with Women in Private," *New York Times*, May 14, 2016.

"My father came home": Gwenda Blair, *The Trumps: Three Generations of Builders and a Presidential Candidate* (New York: Simon & Schuster, 2015), p. 227.

"He was a tough, hard-driving guy": This and following Tony Schwartz quotes are taken from an interview with PBS's *Frontline* conducted July 12, 2016. https://www.pbs.org/wgbh/frontline/interview/tony-schwartz/.

throwing rocks at the baby next door: Peter Schwartzman and Michael E. Miller, "Confident. Incorrigible. Bully: Little Donny was a lot like candidate Donald Trump," *Washington Post*, June 22, 2016.

"Even in elementary school": Trump, *The Art of the Deal*, loc. 856.

"I used to fight back all the time": Marie Brenner, "Trumping the Town," *New York*, November 17, 1980.

"When somebody tries to push me around": From *Playboy,* as reported in Harry Hurt III, *The Lost Tycoon* (Brattleboro, VT: Echo Point Books & Media, 2016), loc. 195.

Attachment theory: Peter Lovenheim, *Politico Magazine,* May 13, 2018, https://www.politico.com/magazine/story/2018/05/13/trump-mothers-day-218363.

"The most important influence on me": Trump, *The Art of the Deal,* loc. 786.

"Drive and ambition,": Ibid., loc. 836.

"He doesn't really have anything to say about her": This and other quotes come from an interview conducted with Dr. Justin Frank on March 1, 2019.

"A very severe response": Peter Schwartzman and Michael E. Miller, "Confident. Incorrigible. Bully: Little Donny was a lot like candidate Donald Trump," *Washington Post*, June 22, 2016.

"If you stepped out of line": Trump, *The Art of the Deal,* loc. 870.

Trump loved that about Dobias: Michael Gross, *The More Things Change* (New York: Cliff Street Books, 2001), p. 33. The book had previously been published under the title *My Generation: Fifty Years of Sex, Drugs, Rock, Revolution, Glamour, Greed, Valor, Faith, and Silicon Chips.*

"The worst I ever heard": Unless otherwise noted, quotes from Sandy McIntosh are taken from an interview conducted with him in February 2019.

he didn't spare them the same rough treatment: Scott Melker's Facebook post about Don Jr. is public and can be found here: https://www.facebook.com/scottmelker.

"Donald, within the rules": George White quotes come from an interview conducted with him in February 2019.

"Either Donald was the most seductive man in the world": *Le Parrain de Manhattan,* directed by Frédéric Mitterrand, Morgane Productions, Boulougne-Billancourt, France, 2018.

King of Miami Beach: Hurt, *The Lost Tycoon,* loc. 1084.

"He was very respectful": Ernie Kirk quotes come from an interview conducted with him in February 2019.

"Our whole idea of what sex was": Quotes in this and the following paragraph are taken from an interview Sandy McIntosh gave PBS's *Frontline*, September 27, 2016: https://www.pbs.org/wgbh/frontline/article/the-frontline-interview-sandy-mcintosh/.

"It was a young woman who was really beautiful": Audio recording of interview with Howard Stern available here: https://soundcloud.com/user-735086019/100j.

She agreed, she says, because she was bored: Ale Russian, "Candice Bergen Says Her Date with Donald Trump When She Was 18 Was 'Really a Dud,'" *People*, May 10, 2018.

"I don't think anybody had more sex than I did": Gross, *The More Things Change,* p. 80.

"dark, dingy little apartment": Description of Trump's apartment comes in his book *The Art of the Deal,* loc. 1091.

He picked her up in a white Cadillac: Lucy Klebanow wrote about her date with Donald Trump in *Slate.* Lucy Klebanow, "My Awful Date with Donald Trump: The real story of a nightmare evening with a callow but cash-less heir," *Slate,* January 1, 2017.

one of the first things he did: The accounts of Trump joining Le Club and of his first meeting with Roy Cohn were drawn from *The Art of the Deal* as well as from the meticulously reported book by *Washington Post* reporters Michael Kranish and Marc Fisher, *Trump Revealed: An American Journey of Ambition, Ego, Money, and Power* (New York: Scribner, 2016).

"You had drugs, women, and booze all over the fuckin' place": Gross, *The More Things Change,* p. 193.

"My view is tell them to go to hell": Trump, *The Art of the Deal,* loc. 1144.

"Roy was a confident narcissist": This and other David Marcus quotes come from interviews conducted on October 19, 2018 and December 7, 2018.

"Donald is my best friend": Marie Brenner, "How Donald Trump and Roy Cohn's Ruthless Symbiosis Changed America," *Vanity Fair,* August 2017.

"Tough as he was": Trump, *The Art of the Deal,* loc. 1162.

They turned out to be knockoffs: Jonathan Mahler and Matt Flegenheimer, "What Donald Trump Learned from Joseph McCarthy's Right-Hand Man," *New York Times,* June 20, 2016.

"Donald pisses ice water": Brenner, "How Donald Trump and Roy Cohn's Ruthless Symbiosis Changed America."

Peter Manso quotes come from an interview conducted with him on January 21, 2019.

CHAPTER TWO: ALMOST ORDINARY

"You can have a thousand mistresses if you want": Hurt, *The Lost Tycoon,* loc. 1086.

Golf's first sex symbol: Leigh Mackay, "Celebrity Golfer: Jan Stephenson," Golf Content Network, August 18, 2014.

"We kind of started seeing each other": Tim Southwell, "The Remarkable Story of Golf Disrupter Jan Stephenson," Golf Punk, November 7, 2018.

"Donald was good looking, charming": Cindy Tran, "I actually said 'thanks, but no thanks': How Australian pin-up athlete Jan Stephenson chose golf over Donald Trump—who even filled a plane with roses to tempt her on a dinner date in Paris while she was playing at a US tournament," *Mail Online,* April 3, 2016.

"My friends really wanted to go out": Ivana's account of meeting Trump comes from Ivana Trump, *Raising Trump* (New York: Gallery Books, 2017), loc. 448.

"At least one young woman is said to have paraded": Craig Claiborne, "Yes, Some People Actually go to Maxwell's Plum for the Food," *New York Times,* July 30, 1970.

"He was seeing Ivana and I at the same time": Luke Kerr-Dineen, "Why an LPGA sex symbol turned down Donald Trump, and what she thinks about him now," *USA Today,* November 2, 2016.

"I'd given up so much": Southwell, Golf Punk.

"So I drove out to the plane": Ibid.

"Modeling is a job": "The Two Faces of Ivana—Model and Sportswoman," *Montreal Gazette,* December 31, 1975.

"I happened to notice a tall blond man": Trump, *Raising Trump,* loc. 508.

"I disappeared": Michael D'Antonio, *The Truth About Trump* (New York: Thomas Dunne Books, 2015), loc. 2388.

"She was an accomplished skier at the time": Kerr-Dineen, "Why an LPGA sex symbol turned down Donald Trump, and what she thinks about him now."

Trump gives his account of meeting first wife Ivana in Trump, *The Art of the Deal,* loc. 297.

"From the start, Ivana was different": Donald Trump, *Surviving at the Top* (New York: Random House, 1990), p. 53.

"If you don't marry me": Trump, *Raising Trump,* loc. 535. The rest of her account of the couple's Aspen trip and Trump's proposal is taken from the same source.

Trump's family and friends: Brennan, "Trumping the Town."

"a really brutal father": Ivana described her lunch with the Trump family at Tavern on the Green in an interview with ABC's Amy Robach in October 2017: https://abcnews.go.com/US/ivana-trump-opens-surprising-facts-life-donald-trump/story?id=50330454.

"He booked the church": Trump, *Raising Trump,* loc. 645. The rest of her account of her wedding comes from the same source. Ivana's account of the couple's early marriage and birth of Don Jr. is taken from the same source.

"Which is probably a good thing": Gross, *The More Things Change,* p. 193.

"Donald was perceived as a brash young kid": Michael Gross, *House of Outrageous Fortune* (New York: Atria Books, 2014), p. 84.

"They were attractive": Liz Smith, *Natural Blonde* (New York: Hyperion, 2000), p. 317.

"Donald became bigger and bigger": Ibid.

"Donald calls me his twin as a woman": Michael Shnayerson, "Inside Ivana's Role in Donald Trump's Empire," *Vanity Fair,* January 1988.

"She saw herself as his helpmate": Michael Gross, "Ivana's New Life," *New York,* October 15, 1990.

"They really complemented each other": Nikki Haskell interview with PBS's *Frontline,* September 27, 2016, https://www.pbs.org/wgbh/frontline/article/the-frontline-interview-nikki-haskell/.

"Donald stood on the side": Smith, *Natural Blonde,* p. 318.

"Surrounded as she is": Shnayerson, "Inside Ivana's Role in Donald Trump's Empire."

"I always stand by the man": Bill Bell, "They met, they saw and they conquered: Donald and Ivana Trump seemed to have it all," New York *Daily News,* February 11, 1990.

"She was second in her life to him": Gross, "Ivana's New Life."

"If Donald were married to a lady who didn't work": Otto Friedrich, "Flashy Symbol of an Acquisitive Age: Donald Trump," *Time,* January 16, 1989.

"I think that was the single greatest cause": Trump's interview with Nancy Collins can be seen here: https://abcnews.go.com/Politics/donald-trump-1994-putting-wife-work-dangerous-thing/story?id=39537935.

Ivana reportedly cried to her friends: Marie Brenner, "After the Gold Rush," *Vanity Fair,* September 1990.

"Edwardian paternalism": "All the Dresses She Can Buy," *New York Times,* March 29, 1988.

"There's not a lot of disagreement": The Trumps' interview with Oprah aired on April 25, 1988, and can be seen here: http://www.oprah.com/own-oprahshow/donald-trump-ultimately-ivana-does-exactly-as-i-tell-her-to-do.

Plastic breasts: Hurt, *The Lost Tycoon,* loc. 493.

"Donald began calling Ivana": Brenner, "After the Gold Rush."

cash bonus: Ibid.

"He put her there, but he couldn't stand it": Gross, "Ivana's New Life."

"You don't stand between the sun king and the sun": Interview conducted with Gross on January 12, 2019.

CHAPTER THREE: GIRLS ON FILM

"I'm very rich": Trump's interview with Ashley Banfield of ABC's *Good Morning America* aired on March 17, 2011, and can be seen here: https://abcnews.go.com/Politics/donald-trump-president-trump-weighs-sheen-palin-obama/story?id=13154163.

she heard someone shout: NaKina Carr spoke with Lucy Osborne in an interview for this book on January 10, 2019.

"Trump would be at every model party": David Webber spoke with Lucy Osborne in an interview for this book on January 8, 2019.

"I would compare him to the spectrum of model fuckers": Gross, author interview.

"It was an agency dinner": Cathleen, the Swedish model, spoke to Lucy Osborne for this book on January 30, 2019.

"There's a lot of pressure": Interviews with Samantha Panagrosso conducted on November 22, 2018, and on December 26, 2018.

was not yet eighteen: Barbara Pilling spoke to Lucy Osborne for this book on January 8 and January 12, 2019.

models were sometimes encouraged: Shayna Love spoke to Lucy Osborne for this book on January 11, 2019.

was representing Norway: Eli Nessa spoke to Lucy Osborne for this book on January 7, 2019.

remembers Trump coming backstage: Stacy Wilkes spoke to Lucy Osborne for this book on January 7, 2019.

She also attended an event: Shawna Lee spoke to Lucy Osborne for this book on January 9, 2019.

The two were in bed together: The supermodel's companion spoke with us on January 31 and February 1, 2019.

Trump sometimes hunted: Heather Braden spoke with us on March 15, 2019.

the "dates" were standard: Maureen Gallagher spoke to us on March 28, 2019.

"Terrific guy": Landon Thomas Jr., "Jeffrey Epstein: International Moneyman of Mystery," *New York,* October 28, 2002.

filed a civil lawsuit: The legal documents pertaining to the Katie Johnson lawsuit can be found here: https://www.courtlistener.com/docket/4154484/katie-johnson-v-donald-j-trump/.

"It didn't smell right": John Connolly spoke with us on December 13, 2018.

Trump campaign dismissed: Alexandra Berzon, Joe Palazzolo, and Charles Passy, "Video Puts Spotlight on Donald Trump's History of Lewd Comments," *Wall Street Journal,* October 9, 2016.

"One-stop date shopping": Michael Gross, "Inside Donald Trump's One-Stop Parties: Attendees Recall Cocaine and Very Young Models," *Daily Beast,* April 13, 2017.

There was a certain point: Gross, author interview.

Indeed a date farm: Gross, author interview.

Now Trump had the girls: Ksenia Maximova spoke with Lucy Osborne for this book on January 22, 2019.

"You're not allowed to have a working visa": Pilling, Osborne interview.

unofficial boycott of Trump models: Edward Helmore: "'The Trump Name Is Becoming Toxic': Model Agency Faces Rumoured Boycott," *Guardian,* February 13, 2017.

CHAPTER FOUR: HEAD HUNTING

"suddenly turned on me and started groping me": Interview with Jessica Leeds conducted on October 15, 2018.

article disclosing the existence: David A. Farenthold: "Trump Recorded Having Extremely Lewd Conversation About Women in 2005," *Washington Post,* October 8, 2016.

first cluster of Trump's alleged gropings: Kristin Anderson's story was reported by Karen Tumulty: "Woman says Trump reached under her skirt and groped her in early 1990s," *Washington Post,* October 14, 2016.

"Is it just for the night": The lawsuit Jill Harth filed against Donald Trump can be seen here: https://www.scribd.com/doc/300193678/1997-Jill-Harth-Lawsuit.

"It was a shock": Jill Harth, August 12, 2016, interview with WNYC, which can be found here: https://www.wnyc.org/story/jill-harth-accuses-donald-trump-of-sex-assault/.

She was worried he would rape her: Nicholas Kristof, "Donald Trump, Groper in Chief," *New York Times,* October 7, 2016. This is the column referred to farther down in the chapter.

"Donald gets what he wants": WNYC, August 12, 2016.

"He constantly called me": Lucia Graves, "Jill Harth Speaks Out about Alleged Groping by Donald Trump," *Guardian,* July 20, 2016.

"I am surprised at how good looking": E. Jean Carroll, "Hideous Men: Donald Trump assaulted me in a Bergdorf Goodman dressing room 23 years ago. But he's not alone on the list of awful men in my life," *New York,* June 21, 2019.

"She's not my type": Jordan Fabian and Saagar Enjeti, "EXCLUSIVE: Trump vehemently denies E. Jean Carroll allegation, says 'she's not my type,'" *Hill,* June 24, 2019.

"He was a douchebag": Lisa Boyne's description of her night with Trump comes from an interview conducted on January 19, 2019.

"made their living room": Brian Sloan, "Raoul's, a Discreet Celebrity Hangout in Soho, Turns 40," *New York Times,* December 16, 2015.

"He took my hand": Molly Redden, "Donald Trump 'grabbed me and went for the lips' says new accuser," *Guardian,* October 16, 2016.

Virginia was waiting for a car: Karena Virginia's statement can be found here: https://www.gloriaallred.com/Gloria-s-Videos-and-Statements/10-20-16-Statement-of-Karena-Virginia.pdf; video of the press conference can be seen here: https://www.youtube.com/watch?v=liub4yvhJ1g.

One of those incidents: Karen Johnson told us about her New Year's Eve encounter with Donald Trump in an interviews conducted on February 7 and 18, 2019.

"The next thing you know": McGillivray's December 12, 2017, interview with NBC's Megyn Kelly can be seen here: https://www.today.com/video/woman-tells-megyn-kelly-that-trump-groped-her-i-was-sick-to-my-stomach-1114705475561.

"I stand there, I'm stunned": Richard Bilton, "Trump: Is the President a Sex Pest?" BBC, Panorama, July 11, 2018.

she decided to introduce herself: Rachel Crooks recounted her story in an interview on December 2, 2018.

"He walked me to the elevator": "Exclusive: 'Married Trump Kissed Me at His Offices,'" *Grazia*, October 10, 2016.

"It didn't really bother me": Murphy spoke to Erin Burnett on the CNN show *Out Front* on October 14, 2016.

he planted one: Juliet Huddy's appearance on compoundmedia.com's *Morning!!! With Bill Shulz* in which she spoke about being kissed by Trump was reported by Emily Smith, "Ex-Fox News Anchor Claims Trump Tried to Kiss Her," *New York Post*, December 8, 2017.

Stoynoff wrote about her encounter with Trump: Natasha Stoynoff, "Physically Attacked by Donald Trump—a PEOPLE Writer's own Harrowing Story," *People*, October 12, 2016.

Ninni Laaksonen: Harriet Alexander, "Former Miss Finland becomes 12th woman to accuse Trump of sexual assault," *Telegraph*, October 27, 2016.

He kissed her multiple times: Video of the October 14, 2016, press conference with Summer Zervos can be seen here: https://youtu.be/PGorCg2_LZw.

Alva Johnson lawsuit: Beth Reinhard and Alice Crites, "Former campaign staffer alleges in lawsuit that Trump kissed her without her consent. The White House denies the charge," *Washington Post*, February 25, 2019, and Ronan Farrow, "A Lawsuit by a Campaign Worker Is the Latest Challenge to Trump's Nondisclosure Agreements," *New Yorker*, February 25, 2019.

"Like you're some kind of stuffed animal": Tumulty, "Woman says Trump reached under her skirt and groped her in early 1990s."

"I really felt like I must be putting out this vibe": Author interview.

When Karena Virginia talks about being groped: Jia Tolentino, "Karena Virginia Told Her Story About Trump in 2016. It's Been a Long Two Years," *New Yorker*, November 5, 2018.

She worried about how she dressed: Christina Wilkie, "Woman Alleges Donald Trump Groped Her at 1998 Tennis Tournament," *Huffington Post*, October 20, 2016.

"I feared that because I had been a dancer": Author interview.

"I spout off about a lot of these men": Author interview.

"To me, this is a feature of his narcissism": Author interview.

"They aren't real people": Author interview.

CHAPTER FIVE: ICARUS FALLS

"Cindy Adams had asked me": Trump, *Raising Trump*, loc. 1837.

Maples herself said: Maples talked about when she met Trump on ABC's *The View* on March 11, 2016.

They met at a tennis match: Dareh Gregorian, "It's no Peach of a Deal—Marla Settles with Donald for Mere $2M," *New York Post,* June 9, 1999.

Introduced to Trump in 1985: D'Antonio, *The Truth About Trump,* loc. 3374.

Maples hung around: Chuck Jones spoke with us on January 24 and January 26, 2019.

"By '88 I knew I truly loved this guy": Maples interview with Michael Gross, "30th Anniversary Issue/Marla Maples: Tabloid Life," *New York,* April 6, 1988.

Trump also enlisted Alan Lapidus: Banks Tarver, *The Trump Dynasty,* A&E, 2019.

"Donald used a lot of us that way": Ibid.

"We wound up comping all of her service": Ibid.

"Beautiful wife, beautiful girlfriend": The transcript of Nancy Collins's 1994 *Primetime* interview was republished by the *Hollywood Reporter* on October 13, 2016.

Indeed, a month later: The *New York Post*'s blind item has been widely reported, including by Mary H. J. Farrell, "The Trumps Head for Divorce Court," *People,* February 26, 1990.

tried to blackmail Trump: David Cay Johnston spoke with us on January 10, 2019.

"It wasn't a very well-kept secret": Tarver, *The Trump Dynasty.*

"never seemed to touch each other": Brenner, "After the Gold Rush."

"He seemed to be tired": Ibid.

"I really wasn't aware of growing apart": Ivana Trump's interview with Barbara Walters was reported by Gabrielle Bluestone, "Remember When Donald Trump's Wife and Donald Trump's Mistress Got in a Public Brawl in Aspen?" *Gawker,* January 25, 2016.

enough misgivings of her own: Raoul Felder spoke to us on March 29, 2019.

"Donald was not really very discreet about it": Maureen Orth, "The Heart of the Deal: The Love Story of Marla Maples and Donald Trump," *Vanity Fair,* November 1990.

it became clear that the two were together: Hurt, *The Lost Tycoon,* loc. 1017.

"You're going to hate me": Ibid., loc. 713.

His personal stake: Russ Buettner and Charles V. Bagli, "How Donald Trump Bankrupted His Atlantic City Casinos, but Still Earned Millions," *New York Times,* June 11, 2016.

He agreed to pose for group photos: Hurt, *The Lost Tycoon,* loc. 1038.

"He was talking about Marla": Bluestone, "Remember When Donald Trump's Wife and Donald Trump's Mistress Got in a Public Brawl in Aspen?"

"When we saw each other in Colorado": Gross, "30th Anniversary Issue/Marla Maples: Tabloid Life."

"Ivana and I were standing near the restaurant": Collins, *Primetime.*

"She was talking and he was trying to shush her": Cheryl Lavin, "With 'Dynasty' Dead, Just Tune to the Trumps," *Chicago Tribune,* February 18, 1990.

"Trump, who was sitting within earshot": Farrell, "The Trumps Head for Divorce Court."

"Putting on a brave front": Trump, *Raising Trump,* loc. 1852.

"any man enjoys flirtations": Glenn Plaskin, "The 1990 *Playboy* Interview with Donald Trump," *Playboy,* March 1, 1990.

"Donald didn't love her anymore,": Smith, *Natural Blonde,* p. 321.

The soap opera made headlines: Hurt, *Lost Tycoon,* loc. 4431.

"the most extraordinary thing I ever witnessed": Maureen Orth, "The Heart of the Deal: The Love Story of Marla Maples and Donald Trump."

"He's getting a kick out of it": John Taylor, "Trump: The Soap—Stay Tuned," *New York,* March 5, 1990.

Maples finally emerged: Marla Maples appeared on *Primetime Live* on April 19, 1990.

Donald insisted that he had been totally faithful: Hurt, *Lost Tycoon,* loc. 4767.

"Donald, during the divorce, was brutal": From Ivana Trump's October 10, 2017 interview with ABC News's Amy Robach.

a sworn deposition: The account of Donald's alleged rape of Ivana comes from Hurt, *Lost Tycoon,* loc. 929.

"She said at one point": Lucy Osborne spoke with the unnamed journalist for this book on January 31, 2019.

"There is enormous sympathy for her": Farrell, "The Trumps Head for Divorce Court."

"Ivana is now a media goddess": Taylor, "Trump: The Soap."

"If you don't stop what you're doing": Hurt, *Lost Tycoon,* loc. 4569.

"What kind of son have I created?": Brenner, "After the Gold Rush."

"Whatever the media says now is irrelevant": Hurt, *Lost Tycoon,* loc. 4566.

"I think that was the turning point": Barbara Res spoke to the *Washington Post* for *Trump Revealed.* The transcript of her interview can be found here: https://www.washingtonpost.com/wp-stat/graphics/politics/trump-archive/docs/barbara-res-with-drew-harwell.pdf.

"He used to be deferential to women": Barbara Res, "Trump hired me as a powerful woman. I saw how sexism became his trademark," *Guardian,* April 27, 2016.

CHAPTER SIX: LUST AND MARRIAGE

"It was a wrong time for me to have a relationship": The episode of *Intimate Portrait* about Marla Maples was detailed by Brandy Zadrozny, "Donald Trump Made Out with Marla Maples as She Delivered his Child," *Daily Beast,* September 5, 2016.

"primed to be the next Mrs. Trump": Orth, "The Heart of the Deal."

Trump would often pop over: Author interview.

"I'm a great star maker": Collins, *Primetime.*

"Once we started going out in public": Gross, "Marla Maples: Tabloid Life."

"They might love each other": Edward Klein, "Trump Family Values," *Vanity Fair,* March 1994.

"She was very emotional": Chuck Jones interview.

"There are women who have had abortions": David Cay Johnston interview.

"ever involved with anyone who had an abortion": Maureen Dowd, "Trump Does It His Way," *New York Times,* April 2, 2016.

Trump asked the Elite agency: Hurt, *Lost Tycoon,* loc. 6067.

"I came out and he said, 'Wow'": Michael Barbaro and Megan Twohey, "Crossing the Line: How Donald Trump Behaved with Women in Private," *New York Times,* May 14, 2016.

Wayne Grover spoke with us on April 22, 2019.

***New York Post* reported that Trump:** The *New York Post* headline was reported by Sue Carswell, "Trump Says Goodbye Marla, Hello Carla," *People,* July 8, 1991.

Bruni repeatedly denied any involvement: Hurt, *Lost Tycoon,* loc. 6637.

Sue Carswell, a young reporter from *People*: Kranish and Fisher, *Trump Revealed,* loc. 2110.

he phoned in to *Live with Regis and Kathie Lee*: Hurt, *Lost Tycoon,* loc. 6643.

$3.4 billion in debt: Russ Buettner and Charles V. Bagli, "Donald Trump's Business Decisions in '80s Nearly Led Him to Ruin," *New York Times,* October 3, 2016.

"He said he borrowed it": Kranish and Fisher, *Trump Revealed,* p. 203.

When journalist David Cay Johnston: Author interview.

at the Miss America Pageant in Atlantic City: Karen S. Schneider, "Off-Again Romance," *People,* October 7, 1991.

the *Deseret News* reported: "Marla Hooks Up with Bolton," *Deseret News,* October 2, 1991.

"She was very hurt": Klein, "Trump Family Values."

Maples hadn't trapped him: Ibid.

"Excuse me, what happened?": Melina Delkic, "When Trump Found Out Marla was Pregnant with Tiffany, He Said, 'Oh, Great,'" *Newsweek,* September 26, 2017.

"You have to remember": Barbara Moore spoke with us on November 20, 2018.

"There was a photo of him": Wayne Grover spoke with us on April 22, 2019.

"Aiko, who calls herself a nurturer": Klein, "Trump Family Values."

"I was very nervous, because she was in a lot of pain": Linda Stasi, "The stork visits Donald & Marla: Inside their hospital room after Trump becomes a father to daughter Tiffany in 1993," New York *Daily News,* October 14, 1993.

"Arthur Caliandro and I prayed together": Klein, "Trump Family Values."

"Mom, I'm going to have to make a decision": Ibid.

Marla lamented to Caliandro: Hurt, *Lost Tycoon,* loc. 6554.

At the same time, neither parent was thrilled: Author interview with Wayne Grover.

"This was the big battle all along": Klein, "Trump Family Values."

After five years: Karen S. Schneider, "The Donald Ducks Out," *People,* May 19, 1997.

Legal experts cast doubts: Klein, "Trump Family Values."

united in matrimony: Description of Trump and Maples's wedding from Georgia Dullea, "VOWS; It's a wedding blitz for Trump and Maples," *New York Times,* December 21, 1993.

Velvet rope: Schneider, "The Donald Ducks Out."

"I was bored when she was walking down the aisle": Timothy O'Brien, *Trump Nation: The Art of Being the Donald* (New York: Grand Central, 2005), p. 7.

staff said there were often models: Lawrence Leamer, "It Was Camelot on Steroids," *Vanity Fair,* February 2019.

"She was bickering with him in public": Author interview with Maureen Gallagher.

she was discovered by police: The account of Maples and Wagner getting caught on the beach can be found in Leamer, "It Was Camelot on Steroids."

"He was never a playboy": Mary Miller spoke with us on February 1, 2, and 3, 2019.

Trump put Wagner up: Leamer, "It Was Camelot on Steroids."

Marla learned about it the next day: Robert Slater gave his account of how Maples learned Trump was leaving her in a speech at the Library of Congress that he gave in 2005. The video can be seen here: https://www.buzzfeednews.com/article/andrewkaczynski/trump-biographer-trump-had-me-remove-unflattering-divorce-de.

"Marla's a good girl": Gross, *The More Things Change,* p. 340.

"He basically didn't want to get married": Schneider, "The Donald Ducks Out."

"After giving Donald two years": Gregorian, "It's No Peach of a Deal—Marla Settles with Donald for Mere $2M."

"Donald was never the man I wanted to marry": The *Daily Telegraph* article was re-reported by Bill Hoffman, "Marla to Ivana: Sorry—Regrets Swiping Her 'Ego-Driven' Hubby," *New York Post,* October 19, 1999.

CHAPTER SEVEN: SWAGGER, STRUT

"I think the only difference": Maureen Dowd, "Liberties; Living la Vida Trumpa," *New York Times,* November 17, 1999.

"It's a very, very great entertainment format": Associated Press, October 23, 1996.

In fact, the ratings were sinking: Kranish and Fisher, *Trump Revealed,* loc. 2876.

The pageant was a "sick puppy": Trump's comments on the Howard Stern show about Miss Universe were reported by Tessa Stuart, "A Timeline of Donald Trump's Creepiness While He Owned Miss Universe," *Rolling Stone,* October 12, 2016.

"I made the bikinis smaller and the heels higher": Ibid.

"I was about to cry in that moment": Barbaro and Twohey, "Crossing the Line: How Donald Trump Behaved with Women in Private."

"This is somebody who likes to eat": Michael Barbaro and Megan Twohey, "Shamed and Angry: Alicia Machado, a Miss Universe Mocked by Donald Trump," *New York Times,* September 27, 2016.

Machado pushed back: Trump and Machado's joint CBS interview can be seen here: https://www.youtube.com/watch?v=56lW8MJjHeQ.

When asked years later: Machado's interview with Telemundo was reported on by Cristina Maza, "Trump Tried to Have Sex with Teenage Beauty Queen Alicia Machado While He Fat-Shamed her, Former Miss Universe Claimed," *Newsweek,* April 9, 2018.

"He'd come to our pageants": Matt Viser, "The Pageant of Donald Trump's Dreams," *Boston Globe,* April 16, 2016.

"He talked about the food": Michael LaForgia, "How Trump Bought a Mansion, Bucked Palm Beach and Made the Sunshine State His Second Home," *Tampa Bay Times,* September 21, 2016.

"I'll go backstage before a show": Andrew Kaczynski, Chris Massie, and Nate McDermott, "Donald Trump to Howard Stern: It's okay to call my daughter a 'piece of ass,'" CNN, October 9, 2016.

"The curtain opened and there was Donald Trump": Victoria Hughes spoke with Lucy Osborne on February 9, 2019.

"I remember putting on my dress really quick": Kendall Taggart, Jessica Garrison, and Jessica Testa, "Teen Beauty Queens Say Trump Walked In on Them Changing," *BuzzFeed,* October 12, 2016.

"Don't you think my daughter's hot?": Barbaro and Twohey, "Crossing the Line: How Donald Trump Behaved with Women in Private."

"He was always very flirtatious and very touchy": Victoria Hughes Osborne interview.

"He kissed me directly on the lips": Barbaro and Twohey, "Crossing the Line: How Donald Trump Behaved with Women in Private."

"He just came strolling right in": Tasha Dixon's October 11, 2016, interview with CBS can be seen here: https://losangeles.cbslocal.com/2016/10/11/former-beauty-queen-she-other-contestants-were-forced-to-greet-trump-even-when-not-fully-dressed/.

"He would step in front of each girl": Scott Zamost, "Ex-contestant: Trump inspected each woman before pageant," CNN, October 14, 2016.

"He basically told us": George Wayne spoke to us on January 22, 2019.

"It's just kind of common knowledge": Lisa Respers France, "Pageant Choreographer Quoted as Saying Trump Picks Finalists," CNN, September 2, 2009.

Miss Universe Organization said in a statement: Ibid.

TMZ later obtained audio: Marlow Stern, "The Trump Rule: Leaked Audio of Trump Ogling Miss USA Beauty Queens," *Daily Beast,* October 2, 2016.

during their dress rehearsal: Carrie Prejean, *Still Standing* (New York: Simon & Schuster, 2009), p. 68.

he treated her and her fellow Miss USA contestants "like cattle": Stuart, "A Timeline of Donald Trump's Creepiness While He Owned Miss Universe."

"We called it the Trump card": Jeffrey Toobin, "Trump's Miss Universe Gambit," *New Yorker,* February 19. 2018.

how the process unfolded: Michael Isikoff and David Corn, *Russian Roulette: The Inside Story of Putin's War on America and the Election of Donald Trump* (New York: Twelve, 2018), p. 12.

"It could be a conflict of interest": Kaczynski, Massie, and McDermott, "Donald Trump to Howard Stern: It's okay to call my daughter a 'piece of ass.'"

"one of the most beautiful women I have ever seen:" Bill Carter, "Trump Redevelops His Own Series," *New York Times,* August 31, 2005.

"He came in to The Apprentice": Katherine Walker spoke with us on March 14, 2019.

"All the women on *The Apprentice* flirted": Donald Trump, *How to Get Rich* (New York: Ballantine Books, 2004), p. 223.

"It must be a pretty picture": "Some of Donald Trump's Most Insulting Comments About Women," Associated Press, October 8, 2016.

"He turns to me directly": Author interview with Walker.

"It makes me a little sick": Garance Burke, "'Apprentice' Cast and Crew Say Trump Was Lewd and Sexist," Associated Press, October 3, 2016.

"There were times when I heard him say": Author interview with Walker.

"Donald would take the occasion": Randall Pinkett spoke with us on February 19, 2019.

had a similar impression: Surla Yalamanchili wrote about his experience with Trump in "My Night at the Playboy Mansion with Donald Trump," *Politico,* April 15, 2016.

Trump wanted the women to wear shorter skirts: Gene Folkes spoke with us on February 11, 2019.

"You'd fuck her": Burke, "'Apprentice' Cast and Crew Say Trump Was Lewd and Sexist."

"He was extremely supportive": Ibid.

"playful banter": Ibid.

"You look at how much he respects": Ibid.

"Is it possible for some men like him": Author interview with Walker.

"Because our allegiance to our country": Nolan D. McCaskill, "Former 'Apprentice' contestants to America: Don't hire Trump," *Politico*, April 15, 2016.

CHAPTER EIGHT: THE NUPTIALS WILL NOT BE TELEVISED

"It's rough, it's dirty, it's in your face": Mervyn Rothstein, "Theater; In Three Revivals, the Goose Stepping Is Louder," *New York Times*, March 8, 1988.

"I went crazy": Melania and Donald Trump spoke to Larry King on CNN's *Larry King Live* on May 17, 2005.

She was impressed when he gave her all his numbers: Alex Kuczynski, "Melania Trump's American Dream," *Harper's Bazaar*, January 6, 2016.

Melania and Donald met much earlier: Burleigh laid out the case for the earlier meeting on KrassenCast on March 5, 2019.

Melania was already in the picture: Author interview with Miller.

Gallagher said she found the titan genuine: Author interview with Gallagher.

"He and I—what's the word?—we crossed over": A. J. Benza spoke with us on January 22, 2019.

"He was known as a ladies' man": Melania Trump speaking to Barbara Walters, "Meet the Trumps," ABC, *20/20*, November 20, 2015.

"A lot of people want to say that being monogamous": Donald Trump, *The America We Deserve* (New York: St. Martin's Press, 2000) loc. 42.

"I think the mistake some people make": Ken Otterbourg, "The Mystery That Is Melania Trump," *Washington Post*, August 18, 2016.

"How do the breasts look?": Trump's comments on Howard Stern have been widely reported, including by Marc Fisher, "More Trump tapes surface with crude sex remarks," *Washington Post*, October 8, 2016.

"She ran into Donald just at the right time": Richard Johnson, "How Trump 'Iced' the Deal—$2 Mil Sparkler for his Yugo Girl," *New York Post*, April 30, 2004.

"He's a very successful businessman": Joyce Wadler, "PUBLIC LIVES; A Model as First Lady? Think Traditional," *New York Times*, December 1, 1999.

"Do you think my wife is with me": Author interview with Gene Folkes.

"If I weren't beautiful": Paul B. Brown, "No, Seriously. Save the Bananas," *New York Times*, August 13, 2005.

"Of all three women": Kranish and Fisher, *Trump Revealed*, loc. 4654.

her former roommate said: Julia Ioffe, "Melania Trump on Her Rise, Her Family Secrets, and Her True Political Views: 'Nobody Will Ever Know,'" *GQ*, April 27, 2016.

reportedly because she wanted nothing to do: Richard Johnson, "Trump Nixes Knauss—Donald-Dumped Supermodel Is 'Heartbroken,'" *New York Post,* January 11, 2000.

"the Portrait": Kranish and Fisher, *Trump Revealed,* loc. 4627.

Trump reminded Stern: Andrew Kaczynski, "Trump Isn't Into Anal, Melania Never Poops, And Other Things He Told Howard Stern," *BuzzFeed,* February 16, 2016.

separate bathrooms are the key: Julie Mazziotta and Charlotte Triggs, "Here's the Kind of First Lady Melania Trump Will Be, in Her Own Words," *People,* November 9, 2016.

The ring was worth: Alex Williams and Eric Dash, "At Celebrity Nuptials to Die for, Vendors Give Themselves Away," *New York Times,* January 13, 2005.

"She's shown she can be": Otterbourg, "The Mystery That Is Melania Trump."

Melania nixed the idea: Jennifer Fermino, "Trump Rings up Number 3; Weds Melania in Celeb-Filled Seaside $how," *New York Post,* January 23, 2005.

"We had a little smile": Karen S. Schneider, "A Magical Merger," *People,* February 7, 2005.

As party favors: Author interview with John Connolly.

"I've seen beautiful women": Chris Tognotti, "Trump Gave Melania One Week to Lose the Baby Weight, Months Before His Reported Stormy Daniels Affair," Bustle, January 20, 2018.

get her antepartum body back: Evgenia Peretz, "Inside the Trump Marriage: Melania's Burden," *Vanity Fair,* May 2017.

"I think it's very sexy for a woman": Helin Jung, "A Definitive Timeline of Donald and Melania Trump's Relationship," *Cosmopolitan,* January 27, 2017.

"We talked for a couple hours": Ronan Farrow, "Donald Trump, a Playboy Model, and a System for Concealing Infidelity," *New Yorker,* February 16, 2018.

at least five times a month: McDougal's March 22, 2018, interview with Anderson Cooper can be seen here: https://edition.cnn.com/videos/us/2018/03/23/karen-mcdougal-full-interview-ac.cnn.

CHAPTER NINE: YOU GET WHAT YOU PAY FOR

GQ reconstruction: Ben Schreckinger, "When Trump Met Stormy Daniels: The Strange Story of Four Wild Days in Tahoe," *GQ,* March 22, 2018.

"I want to come talk to you": "Stormy Daniels' Explosive Full Interview on Donald Trump Affair: "I Can Describe His Junk Perfectly," *In Touch,* May 4, 2018.

black silk pajamas: The account Daniels gave TheDirty.com can be found here: https://thedirty.com/donald-trump/exclusive-what-stormy-daniels-told-thedirty-com-about-her-affair-with-president-donald-trump/#post-2235519.

showed her a magazine: Daniels's March 25, 2018, interview with Anderson

Cooper can be seen here: https://www.cbsnews.com/news/stormy-daniels-describes-her-alleged-affair-with-donald-trump-60-minutes-interview/.

showed her a picture of Melania: Daniels, *Full Disclosure*, p. 121.

"Come on, Alana": Alana Evans spoke with us on March 13, 2019.

"He grabbed me in more of a forceful way": Bilton, "Trump: Is the President a Sex Pest?"

"Well, picture this": Author interview with Alana Evans.

When she said no, he said, "Come on": Daniels, *Full Disclosure*, p. 137.

She avoided sex with him: Daniels, *Full Disclosure*, p. 146.

"Clearly his type is fake blondes": Author interview with Alana Evans.

didn't just hear about: John Tino spoke with us on Sept. 21, 2018; Sept. 22, 2018; Oct. 2, 2018; Oct. 4, 2018; Oct. 5, 2018; Oct. 7, 2018; Oct. 10, 2018; Oct. 13, 2018; Oct. 14, 2018; Oct. 15, 2018; Oct. 16, 2018; Oct. 17, 2018; Oct. 21, 2018; Oct. 24, 2018; Oct. 25, 2018; Oct. 26, 2018; Oct. 27, 2018; Oct. 28, 2018; Oct. 29, 2018; Oct. 30, 2018; Oct. 31, 2018; Nov. 3, 2018; Nov. 10, 2018; Nov. 13, 2018; Nov. 18, 2018; Nov. 28, 2018; Dec. 1, 2018; Dec. 5, 2018; Dec. 6, 2018; Dec. 10, 2018; Dec. 23, 2018; Jan. 2, 2019; Jan. 7, 2019; Jan. 8, 2019; Jan. 9, 2019; Jan. 11, 2019; Jan. 18, 2019; Jan. 20, 2019; Jan. 24, 2019; Feb. 13, 2019; Feb. 22, 2019; March 27, 2019; March 28, 2019; March 30, 2019; March 31, 2019; April 1, 2019; April 6, 2019; April 7, 2019; April 9, 2019; April 24, 2019; and May 8, 2019.

"See if you can find": source interview.

"I've been coughing up": John Tino interview (series of interviews dating from September 21, 2018 to May 8, 2019).

"It's my dying wish": Ibid.

"The stuff he got nailed on": source interview.

John Tino's criminal record: (Record 1) Offense date: 2004, Conviction date: 2005, Offense name: fraudulent use of auto teller (misdemeanor); not specified (felony); larceny 4th deg. (misdemeanor); credit card theft (misdemeanor); $500 revoked on credit card (felony); (Record 2) Offense date: 2004, Conviction date: 2005, Offense name: forgery 3rd deg. (misdemeanor); larceny 3rd deg. (felony), probation maximum duration 5 years; forgery 3rd deg. (misdemeanor); (Record 3) Offense date: 2003, Conviction date: 2005, Offense name: forgery 3rd deg. (misdemeanor); larceny 3rd deg. (felony); (Record 4) Offense date: 2003, Conviction date: 2005, Offense name: larceny 3rd deg. (felony), probation maximum duration 5 years; (Record 5) Offense date: 1990, Conviction date: unspecified, Offense name: federal, Case type: unspecified.

"I remember 'Blue Eyes'": source interview.

"I don't remember what happened to them": Ibid.

"Now almost 96": Email, April 9, 2019.

"Concrete trucks": *archive.org.*

"That's ours": Ibid.

"But Trump was not clean as a whistle": David Cay Johnston, "Just What Were Donald Trump's Ties to the Mob?" *Politico Magazine*, May 22, 2016.

"Several prominent New York City": Johnston interview.

"some of [Roy] Cohn's Mafia clients": Jeff Stein, "Donald Trump's Mafia Connections: Decades Later, Is He Still Linked to The Mob?" *Newsweek*, January 10, 2019.

"provided women for": bitterqueen.typepad.com.

Exterior photos of the Times Square building housing the Doll Theater: 1.bp. blogspot.com and photobucket.

"flourished in the 1970s and 1980s": cinematreasures.org.

"It's nighttime on Times Square": vanishingnewyork.blogspot.com, March 23, 2011.

"was basically a mellow, secure place": Ibid.

"dime-a-dance": Ibid.

"the building was disfigured": Vitali Ogorodnikov, "Foundations Are Excavated For Retail Project At 719 Seventh Avenue, Times Square," newyorkyimby. com, January 4, 2016.

"about 50 patrons": "Pipe Bombs Shake 2 Sex-Film Houses; 50 Patrons Routed," *New York Times*, January 10, 1973.

"I didn't want to know": source interview.

old fleabag hotel: The Fulton Hotel, 264 West 46th Street and Eighth Avenue, Manhattan, has since been demolished.

"was definitely in on the sex parties": Raven De La Croix interviews, October 18–21, 2018.

"ran these (sex dens) for men with deep pockets": Ibid.

"People did those things": Samantha Fox interview.

"I'm told a lot of companies": Seka with Kerry Zukus, *Inside Seka: The Platinum Princess of Porn* (Albany, GA: BearManor Media, 2013), p. 142.

"A whore does it for money": Josh Alan Friedman, *Tales of Times Square* (New York: Delacorte Press, 1986), p. 113.

"I had media calls": Josh Alan Friedman interview, October 9, 2018.

"A double dose of Quaaludes": Friedman, *Tales of Times Square*, p. 121.

"But she was hot": Friedman interview.

"Yes [he]": Ibid.

"Much of Times Square": Ibid.

"Listen, by 1977": Ibid.

"(She) did what I asked her to do": Shaun Costello interview, October 10, 2018. (Costello produced and directed more than seventy adult feature films in the 1970s and early 1980s.)

"Once you had a name": Ibid.

"But she didn't stick around long": Ibid.

"I've known Donald Trump since high school": Ibid.

"So, you watching any porn": Transcript of Howard Stern and Robin Quivers interview with Trump, factba.se.com, February 6, 2013.

"I've never been totally into it": Ibid.

"was well known and had connections": Costello interview.

"I was raised in a sexual atmosphere": Bonnie Sherr Klein, *Not a Love Story: A Film About Pornography*, 1981 documentary. (Klein, the filmmaker, declined comment.)

"It was easy from the beginning": Ibid.

"I'm not raunchy": Ibid.

"The average white businessman": Ibid.

"rose with stem": theclassicporn.com.

"I tried to convince her": Tino interview.

"She was just the same": Jordi Lippe-McGraw spoke with us on January 15, 2019.

"I saw his Converse": Daniels, *Full Disclosure*, p. 220.

news of McDougal's arrangement: Joe Palazzolo, Michael Rothfeld, and Lukas I. Alpert, "Shielded Donald Trump from Playboy Model's Affair Allegation," *Wall Street Journal*, November 4, 2016.

News of that hush money payment: Michael Rothfeld and Joe Palazzolo, "Trump Lawyer Arranged $130,000 Payment for Adult-Film Star's Silence," *Wall Street Journal*, January 12, 2018.

An investigation by the *Wall Street Journal*: Joe Palazzolo, Nicole Hong, Michael Rothfeld, Rebecca Davis O'Brien, and Rebecca Ballhaus, "Donald Trump Played Central Role in Hush Payoffs to Stormy Daniels and Karen McDougal," *Wall Street Journal*, November 9, 2018.

"Where's my Roy Cohn?": Michael S. Schmidt, "Obstruction Inquiry Shows Trump's Struggle to Keep Grip on Russia Investigation," *New York Times*, January 4, 2018.

"Michael Cohen in a weird way": Author interview with Marcus.

She was "blindsided": Katie Rogers and Maggie Haberman, "Melania Trump, Out of Sight Since Report of Husband's Infidelity, to Attend State of the Union," *New York Times*, January 29, 2018.

"not a concern and focus": Melania Trump's October 5, 2018, interview with ABC's Tom Llamas can be seen here: https://abcnews.go.com/Politics/transcript-abc-news-chief-national-affairs-correspondent-tom/story?id=58469532.

Laurence Leamer told CNN: Kate Bennett, "Melania Trump's Mar-a-Lago: Reserved and Restful," CNN, June 12, 2019.

"They were holding hands": Liz McNeil and Sam Gillette, "Inside Mar-a-Lago: Trump Teaming Up with Melania, Yelling at Chefs & More 'Winter White House' Details," *People,* February 20, 2019.

CHAPTER TEN: DEVINE TOOL

reminded him of his father: Robert Costa and Jenna Johnson, "Evangelical leader Jerry Falwell Jr. endorses Trump," *Washington Post,* January 26, 2016.

he had "heard": Sarah Posner, "How Donald Trump Divided and Conquered Evangelicals," *Rolling Stone,* July 21, 2016.

"I can tell you with confidence": Napp Nazworth, "Paula White on Donald Trump's Christian Faith," *Christian Post,* July 8, 2016.

"I don't believe it, I know it": Paula White spoke with us on April 14, 2019.

name his favorite passage: Stoyan Zaimov, "Donald Trump Declines to Name His Favorite Bible Verse: 'That's Very Personal,'" *Christian Post,* August 27, 2015.

"Because of the judges": Monique El-Faizy, "With his judicial appointments, Trump is courting his base where it counts," France 24, January 9, 2018.

propensity of evangelical women: Heather Quintero spoke with us on April 8, 2019.

loss of Protestant privilege: Bill Leonard spoke with us on April 15, 2019.

"He has really bent": Ashley Easter spoke with us on April 15, 2019.

"I liked his frankness": Deb G. spoke with us on April 10, 2019.

the man she sees depicted in the press: Author interview with Paula White.

CHAPTER ELEVEN: POWER PLAYS

"This photo is what patriarchy looks like": Rhiannon Lucy Coslett, "This Photo Sums Up Trump's Assault on Women's Rights," *Guardian,* January 24, 2017.

associated with an increase in abortions: Eran Bendavid, Patrick Avila, and Grant Miller, "United States aid policy and induced abortion in sub-Saharan Africa," World Health Organization, September 27, 2011.

leads to lack of access to birth control: Nita Lowey and Jean Shaheen, "Trump Pushes an Anti-Abortion Agenda Abroad While Paying Lip Service to Women's Empowerment," NBC, February 7, 2019.

The strange thing about this: "How the Trump administration is remaking federal policy on women's reproductive health," Associated Press, May 30, 2018.

As of May 2019: The Guttmacher Institute keeps abreast of abortion laws here: https://www.guttmacher.org/state-policy/explore/abortion-policy-absence-roe.

directed to a "life affirming" pregnancy resource center: Jeremy W. Peters, "Under Trump, an Office Meant to Help Refugees Enters the Abortion Wars," *New York Times,* April 5, 2018.

when it comes to abortion rights: Ibid.

"Their rhetoric is one thing": Shilpa Phadke spoke to us on May 20, 2019.

"I think he has shown": Charlotte Bunch spoke to us on May 20, 2019.

enforcing white Christian hetero patriarchy: Soraya Chemaly spoke with us on May 23, 2019.

A study conducted across ninety-seven countries: The International Center for Research on Women published the study here: https://www.icrw.org/wp-content/uploads/2018/11/ICRW_UAPQ3_PolicyBrief_v7_WebReady-Enabling-Womens-Economic-Empowerment.pdf.

"Look at that face!": Paul Solotaroff, "Trump Seriously: On the Trail with the GOP's Tough Guy," *Rolling Stone,* September 9, 2015.

"He totally denies it": Michael D. Shear and Alan Blinder, "Trump Defends Roy Moore, Citing Candidate's Denial of Sexual Misconduct," *New York Times,* November 21, 2017.

his ex-wife said he had been emotionally and physically abusive: Elise Viebeck, "Second White House official departs amid abuse allegations, which he denies," *Washington Post,* February 9, 2018.

"We have literally gone back to the 70s": Maya Oppenheim, "Trump administration 'rolling back women's rights by 50 years' by changing definitions of domestic violence and sexual assault," *Independent,* January 24, 2019.

Older white women have grown more convinced: "What group of people is most hostile to #MeToo?" *Economist,* January 12, 2019.

no agency in which Trump appointees reached gender parity: Annie Lowrey and Steven Johnson, "The Very Male Trump Administration," *Atlantic,* March 28, 2018.

CHAPTER TWELVE: SHE CHANGE

"The forces he has unleashed": Author interview with Bunch.

Trump would be a factor in their 2018 voting: "Most say Trump is a factor in their congressional vote," Pew Research Center, November 1, 2018.

the impact these women were having was apparent: Emily Wax-Thibodeaux, "Where Women Call the Shots," *Washington Post,* May 17, 2019.

"The silver lining": Author interview with Crooks.

"We thought now no one is going to come": Debbie Walsh spoke with us on January 18, 2019.

"They've never knocked on a door": Melanie Ramil spoke with us on May 17, 2019.

Solidarity Sundays: Kate Schatz spoke with us on March 21, 2019.

"The week after the election": Amy Bettys spoke with us on April 27, 2019.

team of women produced: Sharyn Rothstein and Kate Pine spoke with us in January 2019.

obtain information: Mariann Wang spoke with us on April 30, 2019.

AFTERWORD

"I'm fine with women": Mitchell Sunderland, "Stormy Daniels Is Not Here to Be Your Headline," *Penthouse*, May/June 2018.

"The women I see on the road": Daniels, *Full Disclosure*, p. 5.

"a huge mushroom head": Ibid., p. 129.

Kentucky Derby: The 145th running of the race ended in controversy when the favorite, Maximum Security, appeared to have won but twenty minutes after the race ended, and after an objection had been lodged, the race stewards at Churchill Downs disqualified the horse for impeding the path of at least one other horse. A 65-1 odds long shot, Country House, was then named the winner.

"for the principal purpose of influencing the election": William K. Rashbaum, Maggie Haberman, Ben Protess, and Jim Rutenberg, "Michael Cohen Says He Arranged Payments to Women at Trump's Direction," *New York Times*, August 21, 2018.

In a brief phone call: January 10, 2019.

"He [Trump] asked me to pay off an adult film star": Caitlin Yilek, "Michael Cohen apologizes to Melania Trump for lying about Stormy Daniels: 'She did not deserve that,'" *Washington Examiner*, February 27, 2019.

"a mushroom lineup": Ryan Reed, "Stormy Daniels Identifies Trump's Penis from Mushroom Lineup on 'Kimmel,'" *Rolling Stone*, October 3, 2018.

So it didn't bother you: Jordan Fabian, "Trump Calls Stormy Daniels 'Horseface,'" *Hill*, October 16, 2018.

Stormy had tweeted: Alexandra Hutzler, "Stormy Daniels Suggests 'Tiny' Donald Trump Has 'Penchant for Bestiality,'" *Newsweek*, October 16, 2018.

Karen apologized to Melania: Christal Hayes, "Karen McDougal to Melania: I'm sorry for sleeping with Donald Trump," *USA Today*, March 23, 2018. McDougal told Anderson Cooper on CNN: "What can you say except I'm sorry? I'm sorry. I wouldn't want it done to me."

"The only one I know of is that lying bitch Jessica Drake": While Stormy Daniels has questioned Drake's accusations against Trump, Drake interestingly told ABC's *Good Morning America* that Daniels was telling the truth about the 2011 parking lot incident in which Daniels was threatened by a man and warned about going public about her alleged affair with Trump. "She actually told me about the threat twice," Drake said.

"feeling Stormy Daniels's breasts against your cheek": Amanda Whiting, "My Night with Stormy Daniels," *Washingtonian*, July 10, 2018.

As I drove back to my hotel: Denver Nicks, "One Night with Stormy Daniels, the Hero America Needs," *Rolling Stone*, March 9, 2018.

INDEX